Edited by James P. Mackey & Enda McDonagh

Religion and Politics in Ireland
at the turn of the millennium

ESSAYS IN HONOUR OF
GARRET FITZGERALD
ON THE OCCASION OF HIS SEVENTY-FIFTH BIRTHDAY

the columba press

First published in 2003 by
the columba press
55A Spruce Avenue, Stillorgan Industrial Park,
Blackrock, Co Dublin

Cover by Bill Bolger
Origination by The Columba Press
Printed in Ireland by ColourBooks Ltd, Dublin

ISBN 1 85607 381 5

Contents

Introduction

This collection of essays is offered to Garret FitzGerald to commemorate his seventy-fifth birthday, which coincided roughly with the turn of the millennium. A *festschrift* then, but a *festschrift* with a difference, this difference: whereas most collections for such occasions consist in gatherings of pieces with little more than a broad belonging to some broad discipline to unite them, and little more *raison d'être* as publications than that of colleagues wanting to offer them as publicly as possible to one who made a professional career in that discipline, the present collection was conceived from the outset as a coherent and comprehensive treatment of a distinctive topic, a topic that was considered both important and of considerable general interest in its own right. The contributors were then chosen and invited on the basis of their proven expertise in the subjects of the essays, which are then sub-divisions of the main topic and emerge as chapters in a cohesive monograph on the topic named in the title. It should follow that the *festkind* would be more honoured rather than less, by being offered a volume that deserved publication in its own right. We, both editors and contributors, believe that this volume will prove to be a valuable addition to modern Irish intellectual history; but that, of course, is for readers and reviewers to decide.

The topic, *Religion and Politics in Ireland at the turn of the millennium*, may need some initial comment, if only to restrict expectations of the ensuing content. The religion in question refers mostly, though not entirely, to the current Roman Catholic version of Christianity; the politics refers mostly, although once again not entirely, to the Republic of Ireland. And in both cases most of the attention is paid to the institutions of church and state, and related personnel – on the political side, the government, its departments and agencies, the oireachtas and associated personnel; on the religious side, the actions and reactions of the hierarchy, and largely those of clergy and religious. On the religious side, if one were to go on the declared priorities of Vatican II, one might expect that it is the Roman Catholic laity rather than clergy and religious who would have been most numerous and effective in forging the most creative relationships with such 'temporal' affairs as the social engineering in which governments engage through their laws, policies and programmes. But as things turned out, this was just another aspect of Vatican II's attempted *aggiornamento* that never actually took off, in Ireland in any case. This was no doubt partly due to the fact that the lay Catholic's education in religion was generally confined to religious instruction at secondary if not, in the case of many people, primary level.

With the exception of Trinity College, Irish universities failed to provide in the case of religion that critical and creative study which is designed to advance human affairs in every other sector of human life, social and individual, and for which third level education is uniquely responsible – and up to a few decades ago Trinity's chairs of Divinity and Hebrew trained mostly candidates for the ministry of the Church of Ireland. There was also the odd spectacle of the department of scholastic philosophy at the Queen's University, Belfast; there were certain features of the department of philosophy at UCD; and there was Alfred O'Rahilly's ill-fated attempt to introduce what certainly seemed like a predominantly catechetical type of theology to UCC. The departments at Queen's and at UCD, for long largely staffed or led by Catholic clergy (it was said that the grey eminence, Archbishop McQuaid, regarded the department at UCD as the remnant of the Catholic University, to which he had the right of nomination), were seen by their critics as little more than departments of Catholic apologetics, and their more acerbic critics accused them of prostituting philosophy itself to that process. Such criticism of such departments was for the most part unjust. At the very least they provided an alternative system of philosophising to that progeny of Hume and British empiricism, the analytic philosophy which dominated philosophy departments in much of the English-speaking world for most of the last century, without doubt the most jejune and inept system of philosophy ever to have emerged in the long and proud history of that discipline. This was particularly important in Queen's as it was an integral part of the British university system. Yet some of the criticism did stick, and with some evidence to support it. But in any case it was the failure of Irish universities to deal critically and creatively with religion in its own right, as it is their duty to deal with all dimensions of human existence, that deprived Ireland of a laity educated in the critique of religion to an extent and a degree requisite for the advance of any of the other affairs that concern their social and political existence.

That is not to say that the clerical and religious constituency also failed to provide a substantial body of critical and creative thought on the religious as well as the political side of the equation. The picture to be painted here cannot be cast in the unrelieved contrasts of black and white: a totally conservative and reactionary church facing a gradually liberalising state. And when regrets are expressed at the absence of a laity trained to the proper extent and level in the critical and creative understanding of their faith, on the grounds that such a lay body would provide the most naturally experienced group to bring about the most promising encounters of religion and politics, it must not be forgotten – and it is certainly not forgotten in this volume – that many lay people in public life, and not just those fine journalists who covered Vatican II, made their own arrangements for their religious education, and that to a very high standard of critical intelligence indeed. Amongst these Garret FitzGerald must certainly be numbered. In short, then, on any balanced account of the matter, Ireland in church and state, and relative to the size of both, produced a reasonable number of clergy, religious and laity who exhibited the education, intelligence and, when necessary, the courage to engage publicly in that hard thinking debate about matters religious and political and the interaction of the two, that is so essential for the health of both internal and external affairs in any democracy.

A final thought must be added on this particular issue: the turn of the millennium has already seen the beginning of the end of this relative dearth of lay persons highly educated in their religion. More lay theologians are appearing on the Irish scene, and these inevitably bring more hope than do 'laicised' theologians to the encounter of religion and politics. For the latter have been trained in seminary theology, a different animal from university theology, even where some of the seminaries have university status. For it is the business of seminaries to train ministers for current church preaching and practice, and they are under the strict control of sometimes very conservative and intrusive hierarchies. So that it is difficult – though by no means impossible, as some 'laicised' Irish theologians have shown – for a 'laicised' theologian to bring himself to that balance of critical intellectual loyalty, to that mean between too servile an obedience and too adolescent a fit of wholesale rejection, which should be the natural outcome of exposure to any discipline in any true university. The increase of programmes in theology and religious studies in Irish third level institutions, adding to Trinity's opening of its theological and biblical studies to the normal constituency of any department in the Faculty of Arts, is unreservedly welcome. Although just as unreservedly regrettable is the continuing opposition in some of the main colleges of the original National University to a full and proper entry to the curriculum of theology and religious studies; and not least because such opposition seems to be led by academics who either still fear the 'belt of the crozier' (some perhaps smarting from such a 'belt' received earlier in other contexts) at a time when the Irish hierarchy hardly dares to appear outside of its bunker, or who are intellectually suffocated by some version of the empiricist dogma, or the pie-in-the-sky hope, expressed well over a century ago by Marx, that religion, being a then necessary fantasy of the adolescence of the human race, will surely soon now fade away, or by the even more naïve view that it is the encounter of religions that is the cause of the wars that still threaten the well-being and, increasingly, the very future of humankind. Quite to the contrary, the foundations of a much more creative and constructive encounter of religion and politics are being laid in Ireland, and not least in the increase of lay exposure to the higher study of religion; and these may well prove, in Ireland as elsewhere in the West, to be the foundations also of a much more hopeful encounter between the still largely Christianised West and the great Muslim cultures, an encounter currently bedevilled by a volatile mixture of cynical political opportunism and well-nigh invincible ignorance.

But back to Garret FitzGerald and the relevance of all this to the status of a *festschrift*. Since this is a second *festschrift* for the man, it needs a more select cause of celebration than a first one might require. And so the topic of the book, in addition to its own inherent interest and indeed importance, was chosen to coincide with a selected area of his interests and achievements during his long and distinguished career as a professional politician and statesman, the area of the interaction of religion and politics in Ireland. The following may serve as a brief set of indications of that interest and of these achievements:

Garret FitzGerald's involvement in matters of state, which themselves saw some inevitable encounter of religion and politics – the so-called liberal agenda of the late decades of the twentieth century, for instance, centring on such issues as health and welfare, contraception, divorce, abortion; or the interaction between political and religious traditions in Ireland, North and South – does not of itself point to the present collection with its essential and substantial theological content, as the most obvious choice for a second *festschrift*. Many politicians who held office or shadow office experienced such involvement; but few if any others in this company tackled these encounters as well equipped with the kind of studied (in this case theological) understanding of the religion side of the equation, as did Garret FitzGerald. His father had known Jacques Maritain and other prominent Catholic intellectuals of the 1930s. As a student at UCD he received a second-class honours diploma in theology (a voluntary night course) without, he says, attending any lectures. In 1977 he spoke to the annual conference of the Irish Theological Association which was discussing liberation theology in an Irish context, and he was a frequent attender at its subsequent conferences. His wife Joan, who had if anything a more persistent interest in theology, took him with her to a 'Living Theology' week in England in 1980. As a result of that experience she prompted *The Furrow* to start its own theology courses at which both were frequent attenders.

In consequence, his notable political contributions, in particular both to the promotion of the liberal agenda and to the still on-going process of healing the divided religio-political divisions of Ireland, North and South, were not only practical, but intellectual also, as the chapter on state and church in his recent book *Reflections on the Irish State*, for instance, amply illustrates. On the other hand, his contribution to the study of theology in Ireland was as practical as it was intellectual: in March of 1987, in his final days as Taoiseach, he cleared the way for grants from public moneys for the study of theology at third level in the Republic. It is because Garret FitzGerald exhibited in his life and work the high requisite level of education and intelligence with respect to both sides of the equation in the encounter of religion and politics in Ireland at the turn of the millennium, that a cohesive collection of essays on that topic, resulting in a publication which must be both important and of wide interest in its own right, may also properly be presented to him as a *festschrift*.

The volume itself consists of four chapters in the first part, each containing a general overview, respectively, of the internal politics of the Roman Catholic Church which did, and still does so much to determine all of the following relationships, of relationships between the state and the Roman Catholic Church in what is now the Republic of Ireland during the last century of the second millennium, of relationships between other Christian churches and the same state, and, finally, of relationships between the Christian churches and the entity that is Northern Ireland. In the second part the analysis of the relationship between religion and politics is broken down in order to take closer account of the finer detail that emerges in the more specific areas of interest to both, namely: the area of family law and morality (marriage, separation, divorce, abortion, contraception); the area of education; the area of the health services, including the specific area of the (absence in Ireland of) law and morality of bio-medical practice or bio-technology; the area of the just society, of economic policy and practice, of concern for the foreigners both in our midst and in need in their own countries; the area of the media and the three-way interactions with politics and religion. From this combination of general overview and closer focus on detail, it is hoped to gain a better view of both wood and trees; a clearer comprehension and a truer assessment of religion and politics in Ireland at the turn of the millennium, warts and all, and perhaps some inklings of how things might improve as the new millennium proceeds. The collection concludes with Garret FitzGerald's own critical overview and assessment of all that has been written on this topic in this volume in his honour.

JPM
February 2003

CHAPTER ONE

The internal politics and policies of the Roman Catholic Church at the turn of the millenium

James P Mackey

The manner in which a Christian church, any Christian church, relates to the broader society, to any particular society, will depend as much on its prevalent vision of itself – of its structures, its rituals, its credo, its ethos, its mission and purpose – as on any other set of factors one might imagine. That probably goes without saying. But what probably does not go quite so well without saying is this: that the prevalent vision in question is most evident at any point of time in the current form of the foundation myth of the society in question, and thereafter on current understandings of related elements within that myth, such as government, credo, ethos and ritual.

Two points perhaps in passing:

First, myth is used here, if that is still possible, in a non-pejorative sense, to refer to a story which presents not only the facts of what a founder said and did and the forms in which the founder then embodied the formative vision, but the changed forms in which changed time and circumstance demand that the vision be re-embodied, if it is to remain both efficacious and true to the founder. Second, and consequently, foundation myths change with change of time and place and culture. This change or, rather, series of changes, can be ascertained in the case of any church or nation state or other form of society that preserves some memory of the history of its foundation myth; and it can be accepted on grounds of its very necessity for continuing fidelity to the founder – that is, of course, where there are foundation myths and founders to be seen. In the case of Christianity both have been visible from the beginning.

The fulcrum of the Christian foundation myth, on which all its other features must be balanced, is expressed in one of its earliest forms at the outset of the gospel according to John: 'And the Word (through which the world is created and which therefore enlightens everyone in that world) became flesh and dwelt amongst us, full of grace and truth … and from his fullness we have all received … For grace and truth came through Jesus Christ.' (Jn 1: 2, 9, 14, 16, 17) Fast-forward now to the form which that foundation myth has taken late in the twentieth century, and in particular to those parts of it which envisage how the fullness of grace and of truth that came with Jesus of Nazareth is made available to be received by all of us down to the present day; and take the account of this from the Second Vatican Council, for Roman Catholics the most authoritative account available in and for our time.

This twentieth-century Roman Catholic version of the Christian foundation myth, long centuries in the making, focuses upon a priestly caste which is said to be distinct in essence, and not just in degree, from what is more generally known as 'the priesthood of the people', that is to say, of the laity, 'the faithful'. Priesthood properly so called is a cultic, indeed hierarchical priesthood – the bishop rather than the ordinary parish priest enjoys the 'fullness' of this priesthood. And its distinctive essence results from the conferring upon its members of a 'sacred power', the nature and effects of which are illustrated in the assertion that it enables the men who receive it – women need not apply – to do two things: to 'bring about the eucharistic sacrifice' and to rule the 'priestly people'. A sacred power, then, which when conferred on certain men sets them apart as a distinct clerical caste, whose role it is to rule the rest of the followers of Jesus and to provide these with eucharist. (See Vatican II's *Dogmatic Constitution on the Church*, nos 10, 18, 21, 28; the *Decree on Bishops*, no 15; and the *Decree on Priests*, nos 2, 3)

Now the eucharist is the principal sacrament instituted by the founder of Christianity. To it the six other sacraments are ordered, in the manner in which the preparatory or partial is ordered to the complete. And as the sacraments, as any Roman Catholic textbook of theology will say, are the primary instruments or channels of the fullness of grace which came with Christ, then it must follow that the eucharist is given us as the ordained or ordinary instrument or channel by which the fullness of grace is made available to human kind. Another way of saying the same thing: the eucharist symbolises, and by symbolising makes present … the eucharist represents and therefore makes present, for a symbol participates in the reality it symbolises … the Christ with whom the fullness of divine grace came, and still comes, to sanctify and save human kind. (*Decree on Priests*, no 5)

So, then, the sacred power to bring about the eucharist, conferred on some and by these passed on to others, results in the selection of those thereby ordained to make the fullness of divine grace available to human kind. But the same sacred power, in the current Roman Catholic version of the Christian foundation myth, it has already been indicated, enabled this same hierarchical group which is empowered to bring about the eucharist, also to rule the laity. And in this latter respect, if one studies the detail of the myth, the sacred power turns out to be both a power of jurisdiction, that is to say, a power to promulgate and enforce laws, and a power to teach, a *magisterium* as it is called in Latin. This means, to make a long story short, that the fullness of truth which came with Jesus the Christ, though presented from the outset to all who would hear and heed, is entrusted especially to those ordained by Jesus himself to the fullness of priesthood, that is to say, to the apostles whose successors would be bishops under the leadership of Peter, first Bishop of Rome, and his successors, the popes. These further related elements of the Roman Catholic foundation myth cannot be afforded more space here, though they do make plain why this is a Roman Catholic foundation myth. All that it is necessary to note for present purposes is this: that the same hierarchical group which can make available the fullness of grace in the eucharist, is also the privileged custodian of the fullness of truth, final court of appeal for or against anyone else who would claim to be expressing any part of that truth, and so, when acting as a group under the reigning pope, this hierarchical group is to be considered the privileged repository of the fullness of truth entrusted to it by Jesus, with the ruling authority to teach that truth to the faithful of every age. (*Dogmatic Constitution on Divine Revelation*, esp no 10)

Two points perhaps about this grace and this truth, before considering further this particular version of the Christian foundation myth: First, the connection between grace and truth. Briefly, in the textbooks of the time leading up to Vatican II Roman Catholic theology defined grace as a supernatural entity infused by God into the soul in order to enable the recipients to lead good lives in imitation of Christ, and in general to save and sanctify them. The life of grace was correspondingly deemed a supernatural life, that is to say, a life over and above that natural life that we live and experience from cradle to grave. Hence of course we could not know about it as we know our natural lives, through exercise of our natural faculties of experience and knowledge; we need to be told about it. Thence the necessity of having the fullness of truth transmitted together with the fullness of grace.

Second, then, the extent of the claim that is made concerning the proprietorship of the fullness of grace and truth. This contemporary Roman Catholic foundation myth does not claim this church to be the sole proprietor of divine grace and truth. In the *Decree on Ecumenism* from Vatican II it is allowed that 'truly Christian endowments from our common heritage ... are to be found amongst our separated brethren' (no 4), and it goes on to enumerate the elements of grace and truth that are to be found in other Christian churches and 'ecclesial communities'. Indeed almost all of the fullness of grace and truth are said to be found in those Eastern churches closest in structure and theology to the Roman Catholic Church. Further, this foundation myth of course allows that God dispenses grace and revelation outside of Christianity altogether, in other religions and most particularly in Judaism, and even through the natural world and its history.

But the official and prevailing Roman Catholic view of all of this is best summed up in a part or kind of Roman Catholic theology which can best be described as a theology of franchise. God has given to the Roman Catholic Church, and entrusted in particular to its clerical hierarchy, the one and only franchise to the fullness of grace and truth that came in Jesus the Christ. And if there is evidence – and there is – that recognisable elements of this grace and truth were and still are available to peoples before Christianity came or comes to them, the purpose of such distribution of these elements is the dual purpose of helping to bring people to God in the absence of Christianity in their places and times, and to prepare them for the coming of Christianity; a distribution of sample goods, as it were, before the sole franchise has come to your area, in preparation for its extension to your area, a *preparatio evangelica*. On the other hand, in the case of these Christian churches and 'ecclesial communities', other than the Roman Catholic Church, the image is of groups who have broken away from the sole franchise, the one and only authorised holder of the fullness of grace and truth. These groups have taken some of the goods away with them and are still trading in these. All of which is to be welcomed, not only because God is thereby active through all these groups, churches and religions for human healing and eternal blessedness, but because friendly dialogue is thereby facilitated which can bring all back, or in, to the fullness of grace and truth, or as the *Decree on Ecumenism* puts it, back or in under the rule of 'the apostolic college alone, of which Peter is the head, (to which) we believe Our Lord entrusted all the blessings of the New Covenant, in order to establish on earth the one Body of Christ into which all those should be fully incorporated who already belong in any way to God's people'. (no 3; see also the *Declaration on the Relations of the Church with non-Christian Religions*)

What is to be said about this current version of the Roman Catholic foundation myth, and of current understandings of elements within it such as the theologies of grace and of (the revelation of) truth? Well, that depends largely upon one point in particular: whether or not it considers itself to be the one and only true foundation myth. For if it does, it is already engaged in the propagation of falsehood. For one thing, the foundation myth(s) of the New Testament, which most Christians take to be authoritative, differ quite radically from our current Roman Catholic foundation myth in some of its definitive elements. For example, the church(es) of the New Testament times, let us say the first two or three generations of Jesus' followers, knew nothing of a priesthood different in essence from some general priesthood of all the faithful and in consequence, in the earliest centuries of Christian history, neither was such a priesthood thought necessary in order to 'bring about the eucharist'. In fact, the one New Testament document which has a good deal to say about priesthood argues quite strenuously that a cultic priesthood acting as intermediary between the rest of us and God, bringing our gifts and prayers and returning with God's grace, was abolished by Jesus who gave his life to blaze the trail that showed all of us our direct access to the throne of grace.[1] Jesus did not ordain anyone to priesthood in the proper and essentially distinct sense, nor any group to whom could then be confined the process of making really present in the eucharist the risen Jesus, the life-giving Spirit, as Paul called him (1 Cor 15:45) and with that presence the fullness of grace which the creative Word focused through his flesh in this world. Nor is there any New Testament evidence to suggest in the least adequate degree that Jesus confined to such a priestly caste a proprietory possession of and power over the fullness of truth which was focused in this world through Jesus' 'perishable' humanity (see Paul again, 1 Cor 15:50; Rom 1:3-4, for the meaning of being 'flesh', hence of 'becoming flesh'). The principal incarnation text in the New Testament, the opening of the fourth gospel, is the very text which proclaims that the life which the creator Word continually pours out to the world, then seen through the image of light, enlightens everyone in all the world and at all times, only the darkness within the world and in human hearts could not comprehend it.

All of this does not mean that the current Roman Catholic foundation myth is a falsehood through and through. But neither does it mean that no false or discordant notes have crept into it over the long course of its composition. Myths are visions of reality fashioned from the very praxis by which we come to know it, and to know its prospects and ours within it, visions which then influence our further and future praxis. The issue of the truth of a myth is therefore neither as simple nor as straightforward as that of so-called assertions of fact. The truth of myth has much more to do with the most adequate perception of and prescription for emergent well-being, for the salving and saving of humanity and its world in the course of their co-creative praxis, than with any simple correlation of image or idea with bare and value-free fact. Furthermore, since myth, like language, is always communal or public and never purely private, its content emerges and can be judged from everything from the structures of the carrying community to that community's ritual, ethos and, of course, verbal or other artistic formulations of the practical vision by which it lives. Any community's myth is perceptible from its institutional shape and its characteristic behaviour patterns, both moral and ritual, as much as it is from its verbal and artistic productions. Further still, since we live in a continuously co-created, hence evolving world, the categories of social structures, ritual, mores, philosophy and art change from time to time and from place to place. So the myth will change with these category changes in order to remain true – well, that is to say, if it wishes to remain true – to an original vision-in-praxis.

To make a long story short once again, when expanding in or into societies that had cultic priesthoods, it was wise of Christians to select, educate and 'ordain' particular people to preside over the local Christian communities in the celebration of the eucharist, and eventually even to call these priests. But it would then be necessary, in fidelity to the vision seen in the life, death and raising of Jesus, to show that this select and especially trained group was simply serving the whole people in their bringing about eucharist, in the eucharistic offering of their lives in imitation of Christ to their neighbours and thereby to God, in this way healing the alienation, the discord and the divisions between each other and God, brought about by their wrong-doing – in short, inviting the real presence of the life-giving Spirit, the risen Jesus, to the point where they become the body of Christ in the world. The best way to improve a society, if that is what as a follower of Jesus you are bold enough to think you can do, is to adopt the categories in which that society operates, and infuse these with the vision of Jesus from within. This is what Jesus would have wanted his followers to do – as we often say of those who have gone before us but whose presence and influence upon us we want to acknowledge – though he did not himself ordain priests, nor did his followers for some considerable time after his death.

This particular part of a foundation myth, the part which brought a specialised priesthood into it, was then true even when people, in times with far less knowledge of their past, or indeed very much of a sense of history, told it as a story of what Jesus did. But it would only be and remain true to Jesus and to what he did, as long as this special priesthood was understood, not as a cultic priesthood which stood as intermediary between a priestly people and God, but as a function or office that convened the priestly people for their priestly eucharistic function and led them in the exercise of that function. Just as Jesus himself was a priest, not of the essentially distinctive cultic kind – that was confined to members of a particular Jewish family to which he did not belong – but of the general priesthood-of-the-laity kind, offering his life to God for others. For this reason also, then, the myth was only true to the point at which it understood Christian priesthood as a priesthood of all the faithful, exercised as explained just now, in all of those gathered together bringing about the eucharist. 'Where two or three are gathered in my name, there am I in their midst.' Real presence? Of course, and never more so than when they break to each other the bread, staff and symbol of life, and pour out the wine in willingness to pour out their very lives for others, all the while in memory of Jesus' own action and words and as a means, the prime means, of having his Spirit mould them into his body in the world.

Later followers were wise also to construe the leadership, the government of an expanding community, along the lines of the government structures of the Roman Empire, the natural aid and space for that expansion. That this is what Jesus would have wanted is expressed this time by cobbling together some words of Jesus on Peter's leadership of the twelve (a group incidentally that did not have any successors as such, and could scarcely have had after the break with Judaism, which neither Jesus nor his early followers intended or foresaw) with a legend about Peter's (and Paul's) death in Rome. And the real rationale for this move is the same as in the previous example of priesthood: in respect of government also one can best improve the human condition, infuse it with the Spirit of Jesus, by imitating its structures, thereby providing a powerful example of how such structures can embody a spirit of service to all, rather than a spirit of the power of lording-it-over, of command and corresponding obedience.

It was also wise of later followers, in the course of these early centuries, to express the fullness of truth that came in Jesus the Christ in terms of the linguistic, imaginative and conceptual currency of the times and places to which Christianity expanded. This early cultural currency was summed up and critically developed by the Platonised Stoicism of the time and the succeeding Neo-Platonism. The former, a Platonised Stoicism which held a dominant position in the empire at the time of the origins of Christianity, described what it also called the Word as the continuous creator of the world, ever working within it, and particularly within and through those sparks from its own fire, the creative minds and consciences of human beings, who were thereby invited to co-create the world with it, co-creating simultaneously under the instress, inspiration and illustrations of the Word working constantly within them and their world the ever developing visions, ideals, principles, guidelines, rules, norms even, necessary for the task; and, yes, acting destructively sometimes instead, causing offence, in the sense of an offensive against other co-creators and especially against the Supreme Co-Creator working for and within all; then having to suffer the damage done to themselves in the process, as well as re-doubling their creativity in order, at whatever additional expense to themselves, to repair the damage done to others to whom they should have continued to break the bread of life and life more abundant, in the first place. (Real redemption from evil and its effects is always a new or re-creation.) By adopting and adapting to what they had to tell about Jesus this dominant, profoundly religious morality of their time, these early Christians gave to succeeding centuries a model of developing morals, known as the natural law model – the very model which was so misleadingly misapplied in the case of contraception by the papal encyclical of 1968, *Humanae Vitae*.

The latter, the Neo-Platonists, then placed this Creator Word – the one through whom, the opening of John's gospel proclaims, God created the world – they placed this Word (or *Nous*, mind) in a trinitarian theology of which one called Soul or Spirit formed the third member. These three *hypostaseis* of the one Being of God (Greek-speaking Christians borrowed that term also from these non-Christian Neo-Platonic trinitarian theologies, whereas Latin-speaking Christians used of the Three what was potentially a much more misleading term, *personae*, persons), were revealed and therefore known from the overflow of that creative and infinite Goodness which characterises the One true God. That one Being was thereby known, according to these Neo-Platonists, to be a primordial Source of all (Father) and also and simultaneously a Mind (Word) and Soul (Spirit). By this further adoption and adaptation these early Christians illustrated the similarity of their foundation myths to those of other religions – later Platonists called Plato a divine man who had a human mother but no human father, and commented on his extant dialogues as inspired writings – and incidentally endorsed the view of the opening of John's gospel, to the effect that the Creator Word enlightens everyone who comes into the world. They illustrated the deep similarity in what 'pagan' and Christian theologians believe is to be known about God, and what is to be done about morals in order to have a continuing destiny with God; a destiny which one could then hope, with Socrates and Plato and every other human being, might involve such *homoiosis theou* in Plato's own phrase for our human calling, such likeness to God as to entail a future with God and others across even that dissolution of our present bodily form, that death with which a spacetime continuum now necessarily marks our finiteness. (Jesus' Sermon on the Mount refers to the same human calling in his words: 'Be perfect as your heavenly Father is perfect.')

In this evolution of the Roman Catholic foundation myth, is there any unavoidable and invasive falsehood to the founder and the faith that formed round his life, death and destiny? No, there is not. But did falsifications creep in nevertheless and have these accumulated in the current version of the myth? Undoubtedly, yes; and it is increasingly obvious that these falsifications are at the root of the self-destructive decline of the Roman Catholic Church, even in such traditionally staunch Roman Catholic populations as that of the Republic of Ireland, and not least in the manner in which the Roman Catholic version of the Christian religion has interacted with civic and political society in that country. It is difficult to set out in the context of a short essay any well-argued account of these intrusive falsifications, their origins, nature, number and unfortunate practical consequences. So let the following be a brief suggestive account, offered for the sake of a more extensive argument, one that has actually been going on since before Vatican II, but in scattered efforts over various areas of modern Roman Catholic theology, so that it all still badly needs to be pulled together and critically considered as a whole, if Roman Catholic theologians are to render to their church the full and thorough service demanded of them by their very vocation.

Observe first the fairly obvious fact that, together with the clear advantages of formulating your faith in general and your foundation myth in particular – its constitutive elements of creed, cult, code and constitutional structures – in the corresponding cultural categories of those with whom you wish to share it, there goes the danger of importing into that faith some elements of these cultures which are simply not adaptable to the faith of the founder. When this danger is not averted, you end up losing sight of some of the very elements in the lived vision of Jesus which would actually improve the lives of those you wish to enrich, and you yourselves become impoverished in precise proportion to your failure to offer such improvement to others. A net loss to you, no gain to them, and the ground gone from under you on which you presumed to preach to others in the first place.

Examples? Look no further than the list of features of the Roman Catholic foundation myth already so briefly set out above. Take priesthood first. The current official form of the Roman Catholic foundation myth persists in interpreting its priesthood in such a way as to suggest the re-instalment of a cultic priesthood, comprised of intermediaries between God's people and the unconditionally gracious God. By doing so, it goes back on the first entailment of what Christians call the incarnation, namely, that God's grace is poured in and through the ordinary human being; that neither the fullness of grace itself nor the means of its pouring out is first confined to any particular group of people, male or female. So if in the matter of access to the throne of grace the Roman Catholic Church thinks it has something to say to Judaism, for example, then we find ourselves in the ironic, but potentially salutary position of having to note that it is in Judaism today that we find a people, Jesus' people, relating to the God Jesus called Father, without any go-between priesthood. This state of affairs may have come about more by historical accident than design – the ancient destruction of their temple with the ensuing redundancy of its priesthood – but only an extreme unbeliever would deny that history at times might coincide with providence and, in this instance, bring his own people back to their original calling as the people of God, as Jesus tried to do. In this instance at least, Judaism today has a lesson for Catholics from Jesus the Jew, rather than the other way round.

Something very similar must be said about the leadership structures necessary for the Christian church(es), as for any other community, and developed by the Christian community in the world at first on the model of government in the Roman Empire. The personnel involved in this leadership soon came to be identical with those who had taken over presidency of the eucharistic ritual. Now this very coincidence of personnel should have copper-fastened the process by which the newly forming government in the church gave an example of self-sacrificing service of their fellows to all who would lead in all human societies, thereby weaning these also away from their tendency to lord it over their fellows and make the latter feel their power. The constitutive spirit of eucharist, the life-giving Spirit that enables each and all to take life and all the supports of life as gift from God and in overflow of thanksgiving (eucharist in Greek) to break and pour one's life out to enrich the lives of all, that spirit should have acted for this dual leadership to corroborate the words of Jesus who specifically defined their governmental style by insisting that their leadership should take the form of service to all (in the language and culture of Jesus' time the word used referred to slavery), adding specifically that these governmental leaders should not lord it over the rest, not make the rest feel their power.

Yet here also in this twinned factor of the Roman Catholic version of the foundation myth of the Christian religion (constitutional structure twinned with the structures of the cult), it was the spirit of Roman *imperium* that slowly influenced and re-informed the Christian structures of leadership modelled upon them. To that extent the flow of influence was reversed, and the real presence of the life-giving Spirit of service in the world, as well as in the sacrificial sacrament, was robbed of its efficacy, if not ousted altogether.

The long process by which the spirit of lording-it-over-others weakened and on occasion even replaced the spirit of loving service cannot be chronicled here. It probably reached its theoretical apogee in medieval times when Boniface VIII formulated the foundations for claims that popes should anoint emperors, and could depose them. But it is seen in practice to this day (still?) in the imagery of members of the Roman Catholic hierarchy adopting the feudal titles of lordship and expecting people to kneel before their sacred persons and kiss their hands, as serfs would in feudal times who depended for their means of livelihood on their lords temporal. It is not that these titles or rituals in themselves do the damage: in themselves, like the robes the hierarchs wear, these need represent no more that a piece of pageantry, part entertainment and part educational survivals of a distant past, much like the pageantry that still surrounds a modern monarchy, signifying continuity across great cultural changes in form and substance. What does damage, once again, is the re-entry, retention and on occasion the increase of the spirit, formally expressed in the theology of franchise, of exclusive power over the means of livelihood, the fullness of grace which this misleading theology holds the rest must normally receive only from the hands of these 'lords' or from those less-than-fullness-of-the-priesthood priests who are now said to merely make the bishops present in the ordinary parishes.

Perhaps, however, in lieu of a comprehensive chronicle of how a leadership of willing slaves and of service came to be infected by the quite different model of overlordship and power, a concrete example should suffice of the manner in which the contemporary Roman Catholic leadership has dealt, not now with the channelling of the fullness of grace, but with the presentation of the fullness of truth. Recall, only for the purposes of this example, the charism (that is to say, the grace) of infallibility with which the modern Roman Catholic foundation myth maintains Jesus endowed his church. This is thought to be entailed in Jesus' promise to be with his followers in their mission to the world, so they could believe they would never betray the fullness of truth he showed to them. It is this infallibility with which Jesus endowed his church that the modern version of the Roman Catholic foundation myth claims is enjoyed in a special manner by its hierarchy, and in an even more special manner by the pope. (*Constitution on the Church*, esp. no 25)

From this way of putting the matter, one would assume that if the pope were of a mind to pronounce on some particular element in the fullness of truth, one particular item from creed or code, he would be bound to listen to the church, the whole people of God, before attempting to decide the issue for them. For, to repeat, his is a share, a special share perhaps in view of his leadership position, but a share nevertheless in the infallibility with which Jesus endows his followers in the world. Yet in the now infamous case of the morality of the use of contraception in marriage, Paul VI did consult a commission comprised in part of lay people, but he went against their witness to the truth and, worse still, successive popes have since ignored the moral decision in this matter of the use of contraceptives by the vast majority of married Catholics in the world, and have sought instead to impose a false moral precept upon them. It would be difficult to find a starker example of overlording power-play in lieu of the service which Christian leadership should supply, a service in this case of discerning the way the Spirit was moving in the lives of the faithful, to whom, after all, Vatican II had attributed the primacy in the function of infusing with Christian values the ideals and norms for all communal modes of living in the world – and that certainly comprises married life.

It is not easy to offer a satisfactory explanation for the entry of these falsifications into a Christian foundation myth or, rather, into the versions of a religion which successive forms of a foundation myth simply represent. It is even difficult to say whether the falsifications entered first as misconceptions of the grace and truth to which the religion offers an access, or as misconceptions of the communal structures of the religion and their essential, attendant liturgy. Was it that a leadership group amongst Jesus' followers, at a point at which their whole community was definitively breaking away from the Jewish religion – a point which neither Jesus nor his first followers ever appeared to have foreseen, much less intended – gradually came to feel that the continuity of their position, in face of this and all other religions, depended upon a claim that they had an exclusive franchise on a 'deposit of faith' (and of grace) to which neither the other religions nor their own faithful had any independent access? Hence the truth and grace to which they witnessed had to be deemed supernatural also in status as well as provenance? Or was it the other way round: they gradually came to think of the grace and truth to which they were to witness round the world to converts and others alike, as strictly supernatural in status and provenance and therefore the material of an exclusive franchise, itself a source of their privilege and power?

The most assiduous student of Christianity from its origins as a separate religion (that is to say, from the last quarter of the second century after Christ) would probably have to conclude that it was an inextricable mixture of both, with further complicating factors thrown in for good measure. Certainly, by the time the last Roman Catholic textbooks of theology were issued, early in the second half of the twentieth century, the 'life of grace' as it came to be called, the life in the souls of Jesus' followers as a result of God's gracious gifts, was described as a metaphysical construct, a kind of supernatural parallel to the natural life of the human being – for grace itself in the soul was defined as a 'new being', a 'new life', complete with new 'faculties' or 'principles of operation'.[2] This seems quite additional to the life which the Word incarnate in Jesus, precisely as creator, gives to all people and indeed to all things, and which is itself the revelation simultaneously of itself and of its giver, the natural life and revelation of God's continuous creation – 'and the life was the light of men.' (Jn 1:4)

If there is some kind of parallel life as the textbooks suggested, over ('super') the natural life and all its supports and healings which the gracious God pours out ever more abundantly through the creative co-operation of all God's creatures great and small, then one would expect a special group of people especially empowered to make it and its divine giver effectively present; and the eucharist, as the sacrament of this life, as the symbol which effects what it symbolises, would be an exercise of their sacred power and of theirs alone. But if, as a reading of the opening of John's gospel simply states, the life in question is life as we experience it, poured from the Source to each creature through others, with all its supports and enhancements, and all the redemptive healings which the constant turn to destructiveness by the co-creators requires, then the eucharist which Jesus instituted is the sacrament of creation, of the whole natural world and its constant divine-creaturely creation. It is the symbol (which effects what it symbolises) in the breaking of bread to others, the symbol of the present and active Spirit that receives as gift life in all its dimensions and manifestations, to pour it out to others, and thereby incidentally to reconcile and heal those damaged by the occasional turn to destructiveness, a damage done to giver and recipient alike; select soil on which the sturdy hope that life will continue to be poured out, even through the final destructiveness of death. On this reading of the texts eucharist can be celebrated by any group of people, though the followers of Jesus will celebrate it in memory of him. But no special sacred power will then be necessary in any particular group, and least of all within the fellowship of Jesus' followers.

As an example of a complicating factor which could have contributed to the gradual falsification of a foundation myth, in itself capable of carrying the fullness or truth about the fullness of grace, take a tract of theology from near the beginning of Christianity, a theology of what came to be called original sin. This particular theology of original sin comes from Augustine in the fifth century of the Christian era. It probably did not exist in this form before him. Though there were other forms of original sin theology, including the one attributed to Pelagius and to his followers and defenders against Augustine. The essence of Augustine's theology of original sin consists in talk of a transmission to all of us of a sin which our first parents incurred, transmitted by the sole and simple process of our being conceived and thus becoming members of the human race. Now the thing about that theology of inherited sin is that it makes me sinful without any act, aim or even attitude on my part. And since I did, and indeed could do nothing whatever to incur this original sin, there is presumably nothing whatever that I can contribute to ending it. The whole drama takes place in a parallel, 'supernatural' realm of reality, in some a-historical sphere that I cannot know unless I am simply told about it – and even then I have no way of understanding it.

This is another example in which the truth factor in the fullness of truth takes on the nature and status of the grace factor in the fullness of grace. For in the natural realm where grace consists in the pouring out to all of life and all the supports of life, and pouring through each to others, and sin, as active opposition to the ever active Source, consists in a creature turning destructive instead of co-creative, always at cost to oneself; forgiveness for the sinner, healing (salving, saving), redemption, reconciliation for the simultaneously damaged perpetrator and victim of the sin consists simply in a continuance on the part of God and a renewal on the part of the creature concerned of the life-enhancing co-creativity in which grace permanently consists. This view of the natural status of sin and redemption can be gleaned from a combination of various items of Jesus' own teaching: his breaking of the legalistic ties between sin and punishing suffering, particularly where he tells those who come for healing that their sins are already forgiven, for as he puts it in the Sermon on the Mount in Matthew's gospel, God continues to enrich equally the natural lives of all, makes his sun to shine alike on the good and the wicked, and refreshes equally with his rain the just and the unjust. So that the eucharist, the sacrament of creation-grace, is thereby also the sacrament of forgiveness, healing, redemption. There is a theological account of sinfulness transmitted from generation to generation which goes back to Pelagius, to take one ancient example of it, and which in the case of each new generation can be called an original sinfulness, but which does not entail anything of the essence of Augustine's transmission through the very act of conception. It is Augustine's account that would seem to involve processes which we find impossible to understand, some of which indeed run counter to our finest moral sense of justice – what kind of God would punish infants for a sin they had no part in committing? – and which require special sacred powers of special sacred persons to distribute mysterious kinds of graces over and beyond the life that God pours out to all creatures ever more abundantly and without limit of time or space.

However the current Roman Catholic version of the Christian foundation myth came about, however falsifications entered parts of it in particular, the question that now needs to be answered is this: how do these falsifications damage this major Christian communion, the other communions that share its Christian denomination and origin in Jesus the Christ, and the whole world to which it claims to witness to the fullness of grace and truth that is and always has been available in all the world? And how can such damage now be reversed? All that can be done in the present restricted context is to list the major damages done as well as the main moves already made or still possible in order to contain and then reverse the damages.

The damage which the Roman Catholic Church has done to itself by uncritical pursuance of falsifications which have crept into its current version of its foundation myth is best illustrated from three examples: two from the area of moral teaching and practice and one from the area of cultic theory and practice.

First, the false teaching on the sinfulness of all 'artificial' contraception, initiated by the encyclical *Humanae Vitae* in 1968 and persisted in by popes to the present day, did more than any other single event in recent times to cause unnecessary suffering in the lives of the minority of Catholic married couples who felt they had to obey it, and to deter in various degrees from the practice of their Catholic faith very large numbers of Catholics who knew they should not obey it. The degrees of deterrence ranged from those who simply stopped going to confession, to those who simply stopped practising, and to some who stopped believing in this Catholic faith altogether. There is not likely to be any redress in the case of this damage unless and until the Roman Catholic hierarchy admits misleading the faithful in this matter of morals, apologises for the damage already done, and seeks to re-educate itself, not simply on the methods of moral insight, but also on the nature of divine revelation and the relationship between morals, law and authority. And the likelihood of this redress being offered? Unfortunately at present it seems extremely remote. The only other possibility, namely, that both sides, the dictating hierarchy and the rebellious laity, would tacitly agree to forget about the whole sorry incident, but that the former would henceforth hear and heed the latter, seems equally remote with popes like the present one still in power and, if he can succeed in making it so, also in prospect.

Second, there is the sorry tale of the abuse by clergy and religious of the Roman Catholic Church of the most vulnerable, of children and more particularly of orphans and of others in the care of parochial clergy and religious, abuse both physical and psychological and especially sexual, the sheer worldwide range of which is still only now coming to light. The amount of damage done by this behaviour to the lives of individuals, of families and communities is quite appalling, and the damage done to the church itself is commensurate. Indeed the damage done to the church itself is exponentially increased by the manner in which the clerical establishment has handled, and still tries to handle the pullulating revelations of this outrage. First and foremost by the manner in which the responses of these handlers blatantly sought to minimise the perceived damage to the church, at the expense of healing the damage done to the victims; in the main and regularly recurring instances of covering up the most heinous sexual crimes against children of which evidence involving clergy emerged, and often even moving accused clergy away from the scenes of their crimes – to other unsuspecting communities in which it would in fact be easier for them to re-offend. By this type of immoral, if not criminal practice, these leaders were putting the church – no, not the church, for the church is the whole people of God gathered in the following of Christ – they were putting the clerical establishment which is meant to serve the people, before the people's most crucial and elementary needs and rights, the needs and rights that secure lives at least unblighted by the actions of their fellow human beings. The damage done to the church by this kind of all-too-common response is already incalculable. And yet there is more: there is that whole series of pleas designed to excuse, if not almost to justify that, together with so many other forms of self-serving behaviour – pleas and reasonings distinguished only by their degrees of shabbiness.

Examples? Shameful efforts made to scapegoat homosexuals. Pleas to the effect that church leaders, like most others, did not understand the addictive nature of paedophilia. Now there may have been some point to that plea, although it was bound to sound a little opportunistic on the lips of those who had always claimed to know, through revelation committed to them, more than anyone else about the rules of right and wrong, about sin and recidivism and degrees of gravity, and to know all of this with a certainty that could allow claims to infallibility if they decided to pronounce on such matters with full authority. But one does not need an advanced degree in the psychology of addiction to realise that many, if not most of the horrendous crimes of sexual, as well as physical and psychological abuse committed by clergy and religious have as their victims the vulnerable young, not because of any specialised addiction, but simply because these are the most easily available objects for sexual and sadistic exploitation by those who cannot control such urges. In most cases, then, this humble confession of a particular piece of ignorance amounted to no more than a shabby excuse for not doing what anyone who had reached the age of moral reason would be expected to do when such crimes against the young and vulnerable begin to be evidenced, and for doing what was too often done instead: cover the thing up and move the predator on.

Finally, from the Vatican down to the local diocese, adopting the position that the Canon Law of the church can take precedence over the prescriptions and processes of the law of the state, and in particular over the criminal law which governs the sexual crimes against the vulnerable. It is probably because in some corner of their consciences church spokespersons realise that there is no moral or legal justification for such precedence of Canon Law, that they invoke the pathetic image of bishop-father and priest-son in order to provide some semblance of reason for the precedence of church jurisdiction, although this is inevitably calculated to keep offending clergy as much or as long as possible from facing the full rigours of state law, and is therefore not unreasonably seen as another form of cover-up. So we have a Vatican spokesperson saying 'the trust of the priest-son in the bishop cannot pass through outside conditioning such as the laws of a state', an Irish theologian adding, 'the bishop is intended to be like a father. When a priest is accused of doing something wrong it is understandable that his bishop would feel defensive, just as a parent would, when confronted with the wrongdoings of his or her child', and an Irish canon lawyer, in order to make this point perfectly clear, saying, 'as a parent, you are entitled to protect your child or even to conceal him from punishment. A bishop ... does not have an obligation to see to it that his erring priest is punished in civil law. He is a kind of father figure towards his priest.' (The identity of these spokespersons is withheld in order to protect their reputations, but those who wish to verify the quotations may apply to the author of this piece for the requisite details.)

So things still go from worse to yet worse, with ever greater commensurate damage inflicted on itself, in the case of the church's responses to this second and much more grotesque moral failure before the modern world. For the attempt to use its own internal law and jurisdiction in order to deflect to any degree whatever the involvement of the law and jurisdiction of the state in order to protect its citizens, is in itself a contravention of morality and in many cases of criminal law also. And the appeal of the parent-child image used to justify such deflection, in addition to failing to justify deflection in any way whatever, simply reinforces that pathetic and pernicious image of a church in which all except the bishops or, worse still, all except the pope (from papa, father) are just children. Even the priests are children now; but perhaps even the priests themselves believe this is their true status – that would explain their general failure to live up to their pastoral responsibilities as adults in both cases of the foregoing moral failures of their church: by and large they did not stand up for their people in the case of the imposition of a false morality of contraception; and although they had more opportunity to know what was happening in their parishes along the lines of the abuses just discussed, they mostly failed in their moral and legal duties in that matter also. However, whether the clergy believe it or choose to believe it or not, the image of a church composed of a hierarchy of adults and the rest, children, is worse if anything than the image of a church composed of pastors and sheep; for the latter can allow for a church made up of adults from both hierarchical clergy and laity (adult sheep!), where the former cannot. In any case, what is interesting to note here is the manner in which that image of bishops and/or pope being father and the rest children coincides precisely with that gradually falsified version of the Roman Catholic foundation myth in which the hierarchical clerical caste, instead of being the slaves of all the people of God, became the absolute ruler-providers of obedient children. It is also interesting to note that this idea of picturing the absolute, imperial-type ruler as father of his children derived from precisely the same source as that from which the church of early times took its forms of government – the Roman emperor was entitled 'father of his people'. We should probably say in his case that this was a cynical attempt to disguise the absolute power he wielded over them, but can we really say, while eschewing all accusations of cynicism, that our 'holy father' image does not equally disguise a kind of absolute power in things sacred rather than secular, to which the only response can be one of the obedience of children? However that question is answered, we have here the clue to the next question: to what falsification of the modern Roman Catholic foundation myth can this further failure of that church be aligned?

Undoubtedly the answer must point to that falsification which consisted in the gradual adoption of the ethos of absolute power of rule and provision which came to accompany the original borrowing by the church from the Roman Empire of the latter's imperial structures – structures rightly borrowed at the time for the needs of that time – instead of gradually infusing these institutions with the ethos of absolute service which came with Jesus. This, together with the falsification of the franchise theology according to which the hierarchical caste was given sole franchise for Christ's fullness of truth and grace, as sole authentic custodians of this truth and the means of grace, for its distribution to all others. With this we have once again relations of absolute power and provision on the part of the clerical caste, with childlike obedience and passive receptivity on the part of the rest. Add to this a little-known piece of theology of the sacraments, the ordinary means of grace for the Christian, and the alignment we seek comes more clearly into view. It is known as the *ex opere operato* theology, and it means, very briefly, that the sacraments confer grace from God solely by means of their valid celebration and without any reference to the clerical celebrant's state of grace or of sin. Now of course no one is saying that this theology of church government, of truth and grace and of sacrament, causes clergy and religious to indulge in the abuses that have shocked the world (although the sense of the power of the clerical caste which comes with this theology is a widely acknowledged factor in the ability of abusers to have their way with the vulnerable people on whom they prey). Rather is the alignment more accurately described as follows: the most important thing, from the point of view of the church's very *raison d'être* in the world as this theology sees it, is to have as many as possible of these especially appointed or ordained operators of the franchise, so that if some of them exhibit vices or even commit crimes, this is scarcely ever so serious as to be made to jeopardise in any way the church's main work of dispensing grace

which, like the corresponding truth, can be dispensed in its fullness only by this clerical caste. Better to cover up even the crimes
of members of this caste, since their worst sins do not affect the
dispensation of grace in any case, than have them taint and thus
hinder the wholly essential work of the holy church. (An implicit
argument which is too easily extended to religious orders that,
even if not composed of priests, are still closely associated with
the priestly caste in the image of dispensing Christian grace and
truth.) This surely is the kind of theology that leads to putting
first the preservation of the institutional church, its procedures
and its clerical and religious personnel, even when that means
failing to report crime to those entrusted with the task of protecting society, and in this and other ways colluding in the continuance of criminal behaviour.

The damage done to the church in this second instance – in
addition, that is to say, to the incalculable damage done to the
lives of victims, their families and local communities – consists
in driving and keeping more and more people away from it,
more even than are still driven and kept away by the first instance of the imposition of a false moral teaching. And more
particularly driving or keeping more and more people away
from entering the priesthood or the religious life, at a time when
vocations continue their steep and steady decline. The plight of
several Irish dioceses, that at this present moment have no one
at all preparing for priesthood, is likely to be not reversed but
more widely imitated in the near future. And who would want
to be a bishop when, in this country as in many others, the legal
officers of the state are but beginning to investigate the negligence, perhaps at times potentially criminal negligence, of
church leaders with respect to abuse of the most vulnerable by
clergy and religious? In the United States of America in particular, the laity is being mobilised, is taking to itself at last its own
responsibility for the church, and insisting on the accountability
of the hierarchy to it, where all accountability was always the
other way round. So badly damaged is the authority of the hierarchy. But perhaps these damages to the church, understood as
clerical hierarchy, secrete the seeds of hope for a church of the
future, in which there will be popes, bishops, priests and religious, but the priests will be presidents of eucharists brought
about by the whole people and the rest real servants of the people of God rather than their power-invested overlords; and the

foundation myth will be cleansed of its later falsifications. Likely? Again, not without an unlikely theological change of heart from the present pope and his minions; unless a laity long kept passive and purely receptive can continue to organise and insist.

The professional theological critique of the ethos of church government and priesthood, of the revelation of truth, of sacrament and grace and sin, in short, the critique of the franchise theology and all of its constituent and auxiliary parts, has been under way for some time now, and needs only to be gathered together and more truly honed and more widely understood. Some few parts of it still need to be tackled: for instance, the extreme *ex opere operato* view of the efficacy of the sacraments. This is not the place to enter a full discussion of a less extreme account of *ex opere operato*. Suffice it to say, where eucharist is seen as sacrament of creation, where all participants who share bread and wine, symbolising and thus participating in the reality of God continuously gracing all with life and life more abundant and the supports of life, the sins against this co-creative activity by some or even all of these participating members, those destructive assaults upon their own lives and those of others, will never annul the life-giving agency of God, by which God continues to grace them all and by that very same activity to concomitantly and creatively forgive them, and to inspire them to grace and thus to creatively forgive each other – although the continuance of those destructive assaults on life by participating members of the eucharistic community will always cause some damage to the expected outcomes of eucharistic celebration.

Third, there is the damage done to the Roman Catholic Church by the refusal, particularly persisted in by the present pope, to allow access to leadership of that church to that half of the human race that happens to be female. This policy maintains in existence, and in excellent working order within the church's sphere of influence, a more ancient and much more widespread immorality of a dehumanising discrimination against women.[3] The defence of this sustained injustice consists in the use of the following falsifying features of the current Roman Catholic version of the Christian foundation myth: the illusion that the myth contains a historical fact, namely, that Jesus ordained a priesthood of the properly cultic kind, confined the government of his followers to this group and their successors, and that he intentionally and for all time excluded women from this priestly hierarchy. This is then cobbled together with an argument so pathetic that its very use must make any hearer suspect the desperation of the case it is meant to promote: priests are 'other Christs' in a very proper and particular sense, but Jesus the Christ was a man, ergo! In actual fact, the only people Jesus himself designated 'other Christs,' implicitly at least, were the least of his brethren, the hungry, the suffering, the imprisoned and the persecuted: 'As long as you did it to one of these, you did it to me.'

It is worth noting that this third form of damage to the Roman Catholic Church would not really be undone if in the morning the Vatican were to offer to ordain any Catholic woman who would show that she had a vocation to the priesthood as the Vatican presently understands the role and ethos of the priestly estate. For such a move would simply make women complicit in the falsifications of the myth, expressed in the imperfect theologies, and the practices which have damaged the church in the ways examined in the first and second instances above. It is clear from the previous instances that what is mainly necessary is a root and branch reform of the understanding and exercise of leadership of the Roman Catholic Church, to bring this in line with the real imitation of Christ, by defining the special priesthood as presidency of a eucharist that all those gathered in Jesus' name bring about. And if this priesthood is also to exercise a leadership role in the formulation and publication of the truth of what is going on in this common access to the fullness of God's continuously creative grace, to have it act as an organ of discernment of the ways in which the life-giving Spirit is guiding the whole community, rather than a dictatorship convinced of its forever prior and privileged entrustment with the fullness of truth. For if women were simply allowed to be ordained, and no further reform attempted, we might well be left in years to come with a rump of the Roman Catholic Church marching off down one of these sideroads of evolution, led by a woman pope, papal flags defiantly flying and drums still thumping out the same triumphal marching tune, and lasting like this to the end of time, but lasting as fossils last – for fossils, it is well to remember, are amongst the most, if not in fact the most successful forms for survival.

The damage done to other Christian churches and thereby to the whole Christian family in the world is best illustrated for brevity's sake by the official Roman Catholic attitudes and actions towards the ecumenical movement. It is clear from the document on Ecumenism from Vatican II, as indeed from the re-iteration in the recent document, *Dominus Jesus*, of the main positions there adopted, that the Roman Catholic Church has never officially recognised any goal of the ecumenical movement other than the return of all the 'separated brethern' to Rome. Now, what does the damage here is not the unreal expectation and the unreasonable demand in themselves, as much as the falsifications within the Roman Catholic foundation myth which seem to support them and which serve to show other Christian churches and the whole Christian family outside of Roman Catholicism in such a false and damaging light. These falsifications range from regarding the current Roman Catholic foundation myth as being both the only true foundation myth, and as being composed of historically factual accounts of Jesus' acts and intentions, to the franchise theology which underpins the myth's current views of priesthood, government, eucharist, grace, and the allegedly revealed truths about these and other matters already entrusted in full and final form to the aforementioned priestly hierarchy for teaching to the rest of us.

The full specifics of damage done cannot be included here. These range from the portrayal of Christian communities in the world other than the Roman Catholic Church – the Vatican would not even dignify the Protestant ones with the title of churches – as deficient vehicles of the fullness of grace and truth as a result of their breaking from Rome, to the most serious specific of all, namely, the charge that the Protestant churches in particular did not bring about eucharist and hence could not join other Christians in the one sacrament of the fullness of grace and truth-in-practice which Jesus certainly originated, and which is in any case of its very nature the principal point of entry of the life-giving Spirit, the risen Lord, into the world at any time and place. A church which refuses to share the table of the Lord even with other Christian churches is itself by that very fact a deficient vehicle of the fullness of grace and truth, engaged in a perversion of eucharist that prevents the real reconciling and whole-making presence of the risen Lord from effectively taking place.

How can such damage be undone? Partly by acknowledging the fact that other forms of the Christian foundation myth are and have always been acceptable, and particularly in this case forms which require neither the governmental structures and cultic priesthoods of the current Roman Catholic kind, nor accounts of real eucharistic presence couched in conceptual structures of substance and appearance (transubstantiation) long obsolete and indeed unintelligible to all but those trained in the history of ideas. In the case of eucharist in particular, the breaking and pouring and sharing of the bread and wine between Christian communities and to all who will take part in it, is so crucial to the Christian presence in the world that it must not be delayed until theologians of the different churches have agreed about foundation myths and about the account to be given of other related elements such as real presence. In actual fact much inter-church theological agreement on these and other matters is already in existence, though Roman Catholic leaders have been slow to either acknowledge it or to act upon it. Therefore, if this most serious damage is to be undone, the ordinary laity, the priestly people who in fact bring about eucharist, must take the initiative in the case of eucharist, like they did, also of right, in the case of the morality of contraception, and are now beginning to do by demanding episcopal accountability in the case of worldwide abuse by clergy and religious. In Ireland this truly eucharistic initiative can take the form of following their President's example: simply start going on occasion to the eucharist in the Protestant churches in your area – in the case of most of them the invitation is always already offered – participate with them in bringing about eucharist, and invite them back. In this way, and only in this way, will true Christian ecumenism begin to be, beyond the present stalemate of arid argument about governmental structures, to the immediate benefit, not merely of the Christian family in the world, but of a world itself long disenchanted with everything from the obscure theological bickerings to the often barely disguised suspicions and the harsh mutual judgments that still threaten to destroy that family. In this way also the churches will come close enough to each other and to the life-giving Spirit they are meant to embody, to realise that all have been deficient vehicles of the fullness of grace and truth, though in different ways, and to help each other by sharing bread and wine and experience and insight together to overcome these same deficiencies.

Finally, the damages done to the world at large: These are for the most part extensions of damages done within the family of Christian churches, often exacerbated when church influence extends to conditions within the world at large. Instances both general and specific are only too easy to enumerate. In general, a church that dictates moral rules rather than offer to all the service of the light it believes it has from its founder to guide our feet on the path of virtue, especially if its dictation on occasion misleads people on important moral issues (the encyclical on contraception was addressed not only to Roman Catholics but to all people of good will), and if it attempts to conceal the hugely destructive effects of gross immorality amongst its leadership corps, such a church is bound to alienate both it own members and all people of good will, to that extent depriving the world of the moral guidance and inspiration that did in fact come into the world with Jesus the Christ, if not also indeed becoming a bad kind of moral influence in the world. And more specific instances are only too easy to identify: the false teaching on contraception did even more damage when it induced objections to the recommended use of condoms to help reduce the spread of AIDS; the efforts to have the state adopt an absolute ban on divorce was bound to appear either knavish or foolish when it emerged that, first, what the Roman Catholic leadership called 'God's plan for marriage'[4] was largely borrowed from old Roman law and, second, that the Christian community always has allowed, and in its current Roman Catholic Code of Canon Law, still does allow divorce in certain circumstances. And of course the Roman Catholic church's treatment of women continues to provide good reason why secular society should see it less as a witness to truth, and more as a reactionary force with respect to the natural development of the moral welfare of human kind. Or, to take an example from damage done within the family of Christian churches: the mutual recriminations that result in mutual alienations of each other from the common table of the Lord, exacerbated perhaps by other separations in the schooling of the young, and by a mutually growing ignorance thereafter, fertile ground for prejudice thus engendered. Is it any wonder that when these coincide with ethnic divisions of various kinds, they should have to take a full share of the blame for the social discord, violence and death which occasionally erupt to shatter a community like that in Northern Ireland?

In sum, the falsifications that have crept into an otherwise

acceptable Roman Catholic foundation myth, and which lie behind such general damage done and still being done, consist in
the last resort in ignoring a feature of that fulcrum of the
Christian foundation myth with which this piece began: the fullness of grace and truth, which followers of Jesus are privileged
to see in fully human terms in the life and destiny of the incarnate Word, comes from that creator Word which is also active in
all the world at all times, and thence enlightens all. Therefore the
Christian community's service of truth and life to the world
must always be chastened by the prospect that, as it at times betrays any part of that fullness of truth and grace, it may have to
learn the error of its ways from those outside its family in whose
lives and spirits the same Word is ever present and active.

CHAPTER TWO

Church-State Relations
in an Independent Ireland

Enda McDonagh

In the context of a volume on religion and politics in Ireland today the title of this chapter is at once too restrictive and too extensive. It is too extensive because many of the significant elements in the discussion, such as those of health, of education and of law and morality, receive careful and detailed discussion in other chapters and will be largely overlooked here. The title is too restrictive because it suggests that there was only one church and one state or form of state involved. The four main churches, as they are called, Roman Catholic, Church of Ireland (Anglican), Presbyterian and Methodist, straddle the two jurisdictions in the island of Ireland. These two jurisdictions complicated the relations of the churches to the political authorities as well as to one another, particularly in the last forty years. In further restriction of the discussion the relations between church and state, of whichever tradition and jurisdiction, have been interpreted to refer only to the relations between church leaders and governments, between bishops (moderators) and government ministers, despite the churches' own self-definition of themselves as the entire believing (Catholic/Anglican etc) community. It is obvious that churches and states deal with one another frequently and directly through their recognised leaders, but their regular interactions are much broader and more subtle. Recent referenda on matters of concern to both church and state, including divorce, abortion and even Europe, have shown citizens and believers to be of a different mind from their church and political leaders.

In his recent re-assessment of John Whyte's classic work on *Church and State in Ireland, 1921-1970,* Professor Thomas Bartlett attends briefly to some of these restrictions while acknowledging that they do not generally invalidate Whyte's account. Whyte and Bartlett write as historians and their work, and that of others such as Dermot Keogh, Patrick Murray, Louise Fuller and Tom Inglis, provide essential material for the kind of theo-logical reflection and analysis at which this article aims. The fur-ther state dimension of membership of the European Union, combined with the Irish Catholic Church's membership of the European Conference of Bishops, has not received any formal attention in church-state discussion although the Irish Catholic Church has issued statements in the run-up to both referenda on the Nice Treaty, and European institutions have pronounced on previously contentious issues such as women's equality in the workplace and the legal rights of homosexuals. It is on the basis then of the narrower historical studies and of the broader and changing characters and roles of contemporary church and state, primarily within the ambit of the present Republic of Ireland, that these reflections are developed.

The Liberation of the Catholic Church
and the Emergence of the Irish Free State
In what seem to many the sad or happy days of its decline, to speak of the liberation of the Catholic Church must sound an almost pre-historic note. Yet the Penal Laws of the seventeenth and eighteenth centuries, whatever the revisionist qualifications of today, have, like the Great Famine of the nineteenth century with all its contemporary qualifications, left enduring marks on the faith and politics of successive generations of Irish Catholics down to the twenty-first century. The struggle for the civil and political liberties of Catholics, for their own education system and land ownership and the more strictly political movements for the Repeal of the Act of Union and Home Rule as well as the separatist republican movements, involving armed force if nec-essary, were frequently intertwined and overlapping while at other times they were in opposition. Both overlapping and op-position between the religious and political applied to the con-stitutional, non-violent movements like O Connell's constitu-tional campaigns and their successors and to the recurrent phys-ical force organisations from the Tone's United Irishmen of 1798 and its successors to the men of 1916 and the ensuing War of Independence. While the higher clergy, the bishops, opposed physical force and excommunicated at various times its propon-ents, the lower clergy, the priests, were often more tolerant of their own local people involved in it. By the time of indepen-dence, despite the contribution by members of other churches,

the Irish Free State was seen as the embodiment of Irish nationalist aspirations and that Irish nationalism was for many of its leaders and their supporters closely identified with Catholicism. Although the 1922 Constitution did not suggest anything like a Catholic state, the actual boundaries of the new state meant that it had an overwhelming Catholic majority thereby intensifyng the historical intertwining of nationalism and Catholicism, of politics and the majority religion.

It is against this background of such a Catholic majority among legislators and citizens, and with at least the sense of final Catholic emancipation among bishops and priests, that the new state began to chart its own course independently of its former overlord. That course included much of its British inheritance in parliamentary and court procedures as well as in its administrative personnel and operations. Within its own inheritance from both the constitutional and separatist traditions, the tenets of liberal democracy and the respect for the common name of Irishmen irrespective of creed or class, provided a strong counterweight to the potentially discriminatory power of an almost exclusively Catholic citizenry and legislature. The ethos of that citizenry and legislature was sufficient to abolish the right to divorce by private members' parliamentary bill in 1925 (a British inheritance) without much or perhaps any prompting from bishops. The constitutional ban on divorce in the 1937 Constitution may have simply carried forward this, although it was also challenged in the Senate if not as eloquently as W. B. Yeats had challenged the 1925 move.

The 1925 Film Censorship Bill, the 1929 Book Censorship Bill and the 1935 Contraceptive Bill show no evidence of episcopal interference. As Whyte and others point out, they largely reflect the conservatism of the time and not simply an Irish or Catholic conservatism. Similar provisions existed in most countries on film censorship, in many on book censorship and even in some, such as the New England states, on contraception. Yet in the immediate neighbourhood of Britain and in the minds of the many Irish Protestants who still retained strong British memories and attachments, as well as in the minds of an increasing number of disaffected writers and intellectuals of Catholic background, these moves reflected in Tom Inglis's phrase, a growing 'moral monopoly' by the Catholic Church.

Outside the realm of morality, but more clearly and

symbolically binding together Catholicism and nationalism, Catholic Church and Irish State, were the two celebratory events of the centenary of Catholic Emancipation in 1929 and of the Eucharistic Congress in 1932. They also allowed the parties divided by the Civil War, Cumann na nGael under W. T. Cosgrave and Fianna Fáil under Éamon de Valera, to profess their own Catholic loyalties as heads and members of government. Of course there was no doubt a mutual manipulation at work here between the political and ecclesiastical leaders. Symbols are not always as significant as they seem at the time. Yet there was real conviction too on both sides of the historical and contemporary connections between nation, state and Catholicism.

For most commentators, the most powerful symbol of the closeness between the new Irish state and the Catholic Church was the new Constitution of Ireland introduced by Mr de Valera in 1937. Many elements in the constitution contributed to this impression as did real and alleged discussions which de Valera had with various Catholic authorities including his friend Father John Charles Mc Quaid, then President of Blackrock College in Dublin and later Archbishop of Dublin. The preamble, not part of the constitution proper but nevertheless conveying an introductory sense of direction, begins: 'In the name of the Most Holy Trinity' and goes on to acknowledge 'our obligations to our Divine Lord Jesus Christ, who sustained our fathers through centuries of trial,' an implicit recognition of the connection between the religious struggle and the political one to be made more explicit in the very next paragraph/phrase: 'Gratefully remembering their (our fathers') heroic and unremitting struggle to regain the rightful independence of the Nation ... do hereby adopt etc ... this Constitution'.

While this preamble remains, the more controverted elements in section I, ss2 and 3 of Article 44 were removed by referendum in 1972 without episcopal comment as far as is known, excepting an *obiter dictum* by Cardinal Conway that he would not shed a tear at its removal. Its presence and its removal were alike witness to its rather empty symbolic value.

In conversation with the author in the 1960s, Mr de Valera, while he was still President of Ireland, recounted some of the genesis of these sub-sections. He knew that there was a theory that a state with a dominantly Catholic population should recognise that church as the one true church, in other words make it the established church of the state as the Church of Ireland was up to 1869 and the Church of England still was/is in England. He did not, however, wish to consult Archbishop Edward Byrne with whom he had differences over the Civil War so he went instead to the Papal Nuncio, Archbishop Pascal Robinson. The Nuncio said he could not interfere and that he (de Valera) would have to consult the leader of the Irish hierarchy, Cardinal Mac Rory, Archbishop of Armagh. The Cardinal insisted that the Constitution should recognise the Catholic Church as the one true church. Mr de Valera felt he could not that as it would be offensive to other Christians, South and North of the Irish border.

As the formula he had devised to meet these difficulties, the formula which subsequently appeared in Article 44, I, 2, was not acceptable to the leader of the Irish church, and he knew he would have difficulty in getting the whole constitution passed by the Irish electorate due to the strength of the political opposition, he decided to have recourse to Rome. His emissary, Mr Joseph Walsh of what is now the Department of Foreign Affairs, saw the then Secretary of State at the Vatican, Cardinal Pacelli, later Pope Pius XII. According to Mr de Valera the cardinal was sympathetic and said that he would consult the pope, Pius XI. The pope turned it down, seeking a similar recognition to that asked for by Cardinal Mac Rory and not uncommon in Catholic countries even then. Mr de Valera persisted. Joe Walsh was despatched to Rome yet again to go through the same motions with Cardinal Pacelli, only to be told eventually that the pope would remain silent on the matter and neither approve or disapprove. So the referendum went ahead and the constitution was adopted by the people by a fairly small majority. Any overt opposition from the church might well have seen it defeated as Mr de Valera feared.

In his Christmas message of that year, Cardinal Mac Rory offered his congratulations to the Irish people on their adoption of the new (Christian) constitution. In 1958 on the occasion of the constitution's twenty-first anniversary, Mr de Valera came to Rome to present a specially bound copy of the constitution to Pope Pius XII (Pacelli) and to receive the pope's congratulations and special blessing. Mr de Valera's constitutional ingenuity in word and action had received approval at the highest level in the Catholic Church.

In the intervening period, a lay-group of right-wing Catholics, with the name Maria Duce, supported if not inspired by the writings of a Holy Ghost priest, Denis Fahey, had been agitating for among other things the revision of the constitution to have formal recognition of the Catholic Church enshrined in it. As their activities became more extreme, they were banned by Archbishop Mc Quaid, formerly a member of the Holy Ghost Order, although in traditional Irish style they regrouped and continued their activities under another name. There were always groups of Catholics, whether they were conventionally described as right and left or as liberal and conservative, for whom the bishops did not speak. This was most obvious in earlier times on the issues of the use of armed force but it extended to a wide range of other issues such as the legislation on contraception, homosexuality, divorce and abortion on which Catholics on the liberal or left wing of the church disagreed with episcopal views. Catholics on the right wing disagreed with the views of the bishops and the Conference of Religious of Ireland on issues like social welfare, development aid, the eradication of poverty and the treatment of immigrants, refugees and asylum-seekers. A proposal by the Irish Bishops' Commission for Justice and Peace, drawn up primarily by its lay-staff, to include certain social as well as personal rights in the constitution was ignored by all the political parties except the Labour Party.

The Catholic Church in its fullness could never be reduced to the bishops and their views as leaders were not always accepted by loyal Catholics as the last word on a particular religious or moral issue. This was most sharply tested on an issue which in retrospect seems marginal to the church's previous moral concerns. The dispute over the Mother and Child Bill in 1951 which was declared by the bishops to be contrary to Catholic social teaching, brought down the inter-party government of the time after the most explicit, even obsequious acknowledgment by members of that government of the authority of the bishops in moral matters. It was in many ways a last hurrah for such authority but the dispute is discussed more fully elsewhere in this volume. A simple symbol of the changing atmosphere occurred later in the decade at the time of the Fethard-on-Sea boycott of Protestant businesses by local Catholics because of their alleged involvement with the 'abduction' of the child of an inter-church marriage. The Catholic action seemed to have the support of the local bishop as well as of the parish-priest. However, in reply to a question in the Dáil, the Taoiseach, Éamon de Valera, spoke out against it and it subsequently fizzled out. This was in marked contrast to the reaction in 1931 of both W. T. Cosgrave, then head of government, and de Valera, leader of the opposition, on the refusal to appoint a Protestant as librarian in Castlebar. Catholic politicians and citizens were no longer so behoven to Catholic bishops or clergy in public matters even when they seemed to involve religion and morality. And they were becoming more conscious of their need to rise above the religious divisions which had plagued the country for so long.

New Contexts, New Relationships
The sixties were notoriously years of change, rapid and radical, for good and for ill, in church and state, in Ireland as well as in the wider world. Still some of the old sparring between politicians and bishops continued. Even Sean Lemass, who as Taoiseach was rightly regarded as the first architect of modern Ireland, seemed to have yielded to Archbishop Mc Quaid's objections to extending the National Library into the grounds of Trinity College, which Catholics were still forbidden to attend without the archbishop's express permission. However, Lemass's implementation of the First and Second Programmes of Economic Development led to the first real economic prosperity in the history of the state, which was to provide a significant change in context both for church and state. This coincided with the media explosion which saw the establishment of Ireland's first television station, the participation by Ireland in UN peace-keeping missions and the opening of North-South dialogue in Ireland between Lemass and Northern Ireland's Prime Minister, Terence O'Neill. This opening of a hitherto isolated Ireland culminated in its admission in 1973 to membership of the European Economic Community, as it was then called. All these political and social changes offered Irish people a vision and a confidence which older, complacent and even arrogant church leaders would ignore at their peril.

By what seemed at the time a stroke of providence, the recently elected 'transitional' Pope John XXIII summoned the Second Vatican Council in 1959 and its first session opened in autumn 1962. The Irish Catholic Church played no significant role at episcopal, theological or other level in its deliberations or conclusions. However, it was followed avidly at home due to the outstanding journalistic work of Seán Mac Réamoinn for RTÉ, Louis Mc Redmond for the *Irish Independent* and John Horgan for the *Irish Times*. With further enlightened commentary in such journals as *The Furrow* and *Doctrine and Life*, many priests and people at home seemed more informed and were certainly more enthusiastic about the council debates and decrees than the bishops who attended. The major *Constitution on the Church* itself made clear the church's primary character as a people, 'the people of God', after which came the hierarchical and clerical structures of servant-leaders. In conciliar terms it was entirely wrong to reduce the church to the bishops (and clergy) even in speaking of church-state relations. As pointed out earlier in this essay this was the traditional definition of the Catholic Church which was conveniently ignored by supporters and critics of the bishops.

The Church in the Modern World document (*Gaudium et Spes*) revealed a context and method of church activity in national and global society which moved way beyond the arthritic provisions of previous church-state theory as laid out for example in Manuals of Public Ecclesiastical Law and which had underpinned episcopal and papal objections to de Valera's refusal to recognise the Catholic Church as the one true church. The two 'perfect societies', as they had hitherto been called and which were expected to have formal relations of a *concordat* style, were now overtaken by a world church and its local embodiments seeking to fulfill its mission in a society which could not be identified with the state. Meantime the state, the Irish state in particular, was being integrated into wider continental and global structures.

The Council's *Decree on Ecumenism* made any talk of a privileged state-position for one church vulnerable to serious criticism. This was reinforced by one of the clearest and most powerful documents of Vatican II, *The Declaration on Religious Liberty*. The restrictions on religious freedom of belief and practice which affected minorities in dominantly Catholic or Protestant countries for so long after the Reformation divisions, according to the principle *cujus regio, ejus religio*, (only the religion of the king or prince may be practised), was finally and radically set aside by the highest authority in the Catholic Church, the pope and council. To complete the liberating moves, the *Decree Nostra Aetate* (*In our time*) recognised the value of other non-Christian religions, pre-eminently that of the Jews and opened the possibility and necessity of dialogue with them. Archbishop Mc Quaid's comment on his return from the council that nothing had happened to disturb the faith of the Irish faithful may have been true in a way he never intended for the many who had followed the council's proceedings so eagerly. Disappointment and disillusionment at the bishops' and indeed Rome's later foot-dragging and even reversal of the council's intentions in some areas inevitably followed. Yet the great sea-change had happened. For the relationships between the Catholic Church and political authorities there was no real returning.

Yet in that very decade, two significant events occurred which ever since have dogged relationships within the Catholic Church, between the Irish churches themselves and between the Irish churches and the political authorities North and South of the Irish border. The first of these, the issuing by Pope Paul VI in July 1968 of the encyclical *Humanae Vitae*, banning all forms of contraception, was primarily a matter for relations within the church as bishops, theologians and lay-people disagreed, sometimes fiercely, on the truth and binding force of its teaching. For many committed Catholics in Ireland and around the world, it weakened the teaching authority of pope and bishops in moral matters. But it was not exclusively an internal concern. In the incipient dialogue between the churches, moral discussion particularly in the sexual area tended to be off limits, giving at times a certain unreality to the whole ecumenical enterprise. Division within the Catholic Church and between the churches on an issue of such practical import to all citizens presented difficulties to Irish politicians faced with demands for legislation on precisely this issue, the availability of contraceptives. The tangled outcome of all this is dealt with in Patrick Hannon's chapter elsewhere in this volume.

The second event or series of events began later that year in October with an attack on the Civil Rights march in Derry protesting at discrimination against Catholics and nationalists in Northern Ireland. At least this occurrence could be seen as the symbolic start of the 'Troubles' which resulted in so much death and destruction. Divisions between the churches were naturally exacerbated. The Catholic Church in bishops, priests and laity was mainly in sympathy with the nationalist cause, if frequently and explicitly condemnatory of the violent methods of the IRA.

The Protestant Churches at every level were mainly in sympathy with their own unionist people if also condemnatory of the violence from the unionist/loyalist side. All this affected British and Irish governments as well as politicians, North and South, in their search for a peaceful resolution of the conflict as in their dealings with the churches and their leaders. That is the theme of Geraldine Smyth in her chapter. It is noted here as one of the major changes in context in which churches and the state had to operate throughout this period.

Two minor episodes over the next decade or so illustrate how the 'thinking' church and the 'thinking' politician were reviewing the church-state relations in the aftermath of Vatican II and in the context of the violent divisions in Northern Ireland. On December 17-18, 1971 the Irish Theological Association, whose membership was inter-church if Catholic in majority, organised a conference on Christian Reconciliation at Ballymascanlon Hotel outside Dundalk and close to the border. It was attended by a wide range of theologians and clergy from all the churches, North and South. After some very intense and moving debates, among the conclusions it was agreed that genuine reconciliation could not be achieved where the law appeared to be discriminatory or divisive on religious grounds. 'The assembly therefore requested the executive committee of the Association to establish a working-party in the Republic and to make recommendations' on this issue. At the AGM of the ITA in January 1972, the proposal was approved and the executive asked to nominate the members who were drawn from the different churches and from different disciplines. In June 1972 the working-party presented its report to a general meeting of the Association and it was published. (*The Furrow*, June 1972)

Maintaining that the constitution should be simply the basic law of the state (its *Grundgesetz*), the committee proposed and presented a new secular preamble free of the religious and nationalist content of the present one. It recommended in the same spirit the removal of ss2 and 3 from S1 of article 44, the subsections which recognised the special position of the Catholic Church and recognised the other churches named. It also recommended removing the ban on divorce from Article 41 and the amendment of the law 'to remove the restrictions on the freedom of choice in methods of family planning'. While the report sparked off a serious debate within the Theological

Association and attracted a fair amount of publicity, its recommendations were only taken up and to some extent implemented long after the report itself had been forgotten.

Despite the position and reputation of its author, a somewhat similar fate seemed to befall the second initiative of relevance here. In the midst of the hunger strike crisis in August 1981, the Taoiseach, Dr Garret FitzGerald declared in the course of an interview on RTÉ that the Irish State 'as it had evolved over the decades was not the non-sectarian state that the national movement for independence had sought to establish, one in which Catholic, Protestant and Dissenter would feel equally at home; it had rather become a state imbued with the ethos of the majority in our part of the island'. This he could not accept. 'I want to lead a crusade,' he said, 'a republican crusade to make this a genuine republic.' If he could do that, he believed, 'we would have a basis on which many Protestants in the North would be willing to consider a relationship with us. If I were a Northern Protestant today, I cannot see how I could be attracted to getting involved with a state that is itself sectarian – not in the acutely sectarian way that Northern Ireland was … (but) the fact is our laws and our constitution, our practices, our attitudes reflect those of a majority ethos and are not acceptable to Protestants in Northern Ireland.'(FitzGerald, *All in a Life*)

While this interview resonated with the more sober terms of the ITA report and echoed what Dr FitzGerald had voiced in diverse ways and contexts before, it attracted some very sharp criticism even within his own party. His position as Taoiseach, the continuing pressure of the hunger strike, above all the use of the word 'sectarian', however justified and qualified, incensed his critics and disturbed some of his supporters. A speech in the Senate ten days later presented a more rounded account of his views. His proposal to establish a committee to review the constitution had not been implemented by the time his government fell in January 1982. By the time he returned as Taoiseach in late 1982 he had decided to give priority to the establishment of the New Ireland Forum in preparation for negotiations with the British and in which all constitutional parties in the island were invited to participate.

Of course the reference to the special position of the Catholic Church had been removed in late 1972 along the lines recommended by the ITA report. The debates on contraception, divorce and abortion lay ahead and are dealt with elsewhere in this volume. The preamble remains untouched and the proposal for a whole new constitution, which Dr FitzGerald among others has sometimes suggested, is at present at least parked.

From Church and State to Law and Morality:
The Liberal Agenda
From the mid-seventies church-state debates became almost exclusively debates about law and morality. What became known as the liberal agenda, moves to liberalise the laws on contraception, divorce, abortion and homosexuality, dominated discussion and prevailed with various qualifications. With the exception of the laws on homosexuality, these changes have been charted in other chapters. The change in the law on homosexuality, a law dating back to 1861, took a familiar form, a challenge to its constitutionality in the Irish courts, appeal to the European Court of Human Rights, victory there and a new Bill passed by the Oireachtas (1993), providing, it was claimed at the time, the most liberal provisions in Europe. A distinctive feature of this move was the lack of Dáil debate or indeed public controversy. The ethical and legal problems occasioned by biological developments such as *in vitro* fertilisation have yet to be resolved despite the long-established practices of some of these activities. Such issues are the subject of a special article by Maureen Junker-Kenny in this volume.

The liberal agenda, as understood here, dealt with personal freedoms or individual rights, particularly in the areas of sexuality and human reproduction. The disputants usually blamed the other side for being over-preoccupied with such matters. In truth 'liberals', 'conservatives' and media in the debate reflected a natural if sometimes unhealthy interest in the sexual doings of our citizens; natural because sexual activity and human reproduction are critical to the survival and thriving of a society; unhealthy because so many other matters critical to the survival and thriving of society, such as domestic, criminal and 'political' violence, could be overlooked or marginalised by the concentration on sexual issues. Whether, now that the liberal agenda in such matters is more or less complete, other neglected matters will come to the fore is uncertain. The continuing disclosure of child sexual abuse, particularly by clergy, seems certain to overshadow the corruptions of wealth and the degradations of poverty among other critical social concerns.

Women's Rights

One of the major issues involving church and state in the second half of the twentieth century was that of the status of women. While women in Ireland enjoyed the vote from the 1918 election on the same terms as men (unlike their situation in some European countries), and they actively participated in the struggle for independence, their representation in public life and in the workplace was limited by the ethos of the time and discrimination in regard to pay.

Article 41 of the 1937 constitution, on the family, reflected what women critics at the time regarded as an oppressive or at least restrictive ethos in regard to women. Section 2 has two subsections which read as follows:

1. In particular, the state recognises that by her life within the home, woman gives to the state a support without which the common good cannot be achieved.

2. The state shall, therefore, endeavour to ensure that mothers shall not be obliged by economic necessity to engage in labour to the neglect of their duties in the home.

Apart from the removal of the ban on divorce, this article remains in place although the status of women within and without the home has moved on quite a bit. The government's establishment of the Council for the Status for Women in the late fifties began a change which only really took flight with the various forms of the Women's Liberation Movement/feminism from the late sixties. Despite the participation of committed Catholic lay women and religious sisters, the church as a whole or in its official pronouncements did not play a significant role. Indeed it was regarded as at least a silent opponent of women's rights with its official position still very close to that of Article 41. This emerged particularly in the debates leading up to the referenda on divorce, where the primacy of the family and the potential damage to the good of society (the common good) were frequently stressed by official spokespeople for the church, although not only by these. It was assumed by many supporters and critics that Article 41 reflected Catholic social teaching and may have been directly influenced by the drafters' clerical advisors. Given the general situation in the twenties and thirties and Mr de Valera's views as expressed in the Dáil debate on this article, clerical advice was hardly necessary. It remained true, however, that little support was forthcoming from bishops and clergy as the rights of women continued to be asserted and achieved. In fact, in response to the pressure from women's groups, the Irish courts and European institutions rather than the Irish legislature were the chief promotors of women's rights. The symbolic climax to the development of women's rights in Ireland came with the election in November 1990 of the first woman as President of Ireland, Mary Robinson, who had herself as politician and lawyer been engaged in the struggle for greater equality for women. The change over the decades was reinforced at that same symbolic level with Mary Robinson's successor, the current President, who is also a woman, Mary MacAleese.

The Catholic Church at any level could not be untouched by all this. Catholic lay and religious activists ensured that voices of women were more effective in changing attitudes and activities and even structures in minor ways like the introduction of women as eucharistic ministers and more belatedly (for trivial reasons) as girl altar servers. More serious moves saw women achieve limited responsibility in church commissions like that of Justice and Peace or agencies such as Trócaire. The appointment of women to church marriage tribunals, and more recently the appointment of Judge Gillian Hussey to head the independent Audit Committee to report on how far dioceses and religious orders have implemented the official guidelines on clerical sex abuse, is perhaps the most striking of all. (This committee, overtaken by events, has since been stood down). Naturally perhaps the Conference of Religious of Ireland (CORI) have had women taking major responsibility in every area of its work. While much of the official church recognition of women has been born of necessity, it would hardly have happened at all if Irish society and then the Irish state had not led the way. For both state and church changes in the wider society usually provide the lead and, in this socio-moral matter at least, the state responded more quickly.

The most serious challenge by women to the present structures of the church is the movement for women's ordination. While this movement gathers momentum worldwide it has a strong following in Ireland, operating under the name BASIC (Brothers and Sisters in Christ). In July 2001 BASIC organised the first international Catholic conference on women's ordination in Dublin. Some years earlier it held its own national conference at which the keynote speaker was the Professor of Law at Queen's University, Belfast and later President of Ireland, Mary MacAleese. The interaction between the socio-political and the ecclesial through the activities of lay Catholics still operates, as frequently now in the 'liberal' as in the 'conservative' direction.

The Social Agenda
While political leaders over recent decades have been promoting with varying degrees of commitment the liberal agenda as described above, and church leaders have often been resistant to it, what might be called the social agenda of fairness in society through redistribution of resources, combating poverty, improving the conditions of the deprived and excluded such as travellers, those with disability, immigrants and asylum seekers, has been promoted largely by voluntary organisations including church organisations like the CORI Justice Desk, the Justice and Peace Commission and the St Vincent de Paul Society. Similarly, the pressure for a fairer world by assistance to the developing world has come mainly from voluntary and church organisations like Trócaire, Concern and Goal. Of course politicians and government agencies have played an increasingly important role but much of the inspiration, information and implementation has come from these civic and church bodies. Why the church and its agents might feel happier with social rather than liberal issues requires further analysis.

In the law and morality debate in which political and church leaders have been frequently engaged in recent decades, some changes of emphasis and terminology have been significant. While the constitution speaks of 'personal rights' and these have been expanded judicially to include rights implicit in the constitution such as the right to privacy, today the usual term is human rights. And while the wider Catholic Church of the nineteenth century was sharply critical of the concept and term 'human rights' as destructive of all authority including divine authority, in the late twentieth century, at least from Pope John XXIII's encyclical, *Pacem in Terris* of 1963, the whole Catholic Church including the Irish church has been a staunch promoter of human rights and in some critical regions of the world one of their most effective defenders. This does not mean that there are not sharp differences about what constitutes a human right in specific instances, as in the foetus's right to life versus the mother's right to choose. And there is a very broad debate spanning secular and religious circles about the status of social and economic rights as listed in the UN Declaration of Human Rights. Church leaders and spokespeople tend to support the equal status and justice-ability of social and economic rights with those of civil and political rights, while politicians and civil lawyers tend to deny this, with the notable exception among others of Mary Robinson, UN High Commissioner for Human Rights 1997-2002.

At the socio-moral level of analysis, the divide turns on the more individualist attitude to society of those who would deny the full legal impact of social and economic rights, as against the more unified and inter-related concept of society of the advocates of social and economic rights. 'Solidarity in unity' is another current expression used by mainly religious commentators to overcome a rampant individualism. It was on this basis that the Irish Episcopal Commission for Justice and Peace proposed including four social and economic rights in the Constitution (*Re-Righting the Constitution*, Dublin 1998). The present Article 45 on such matters is specifically denied the possibility of vindication in the courts. In a different idiom, the traditional concept of government and law was directed to the good of the whole community or 'common good', the term used in age-old definitions of law and in the preamble to the Irish constitution, but now in retreat before an aggressive individualism coupled in Ireland with a certain antipathy to terms thought to be peculiarly Catholic in provenance. The term 'natural law', which had been thought to transcend religious affiliations and to embrace the whole range of human morality and rights, has suffered a similar eclipse partly due in Ireland to the Catholic Church's claim to be the official interpreter of natural law. As the recent church-state antagonisms diminish, these terms and concepts, or related ones, will recover their real value and usefulness.

A couple of further issues should be mentioned even if it is impossible to deal with them adequately here. Socio-moral issues and their legal implications must now, it is widely recognised, cover environmental protection. A certain amount has been achieved legally in Ireland although much of this has been under pressure from Europe. Apart from members of the Green Party, few politicians have taken this issue beyond their own backyard. The church, clerical and lay, has been equally negligent in recognising the moral and indeed deeper Christian significance of respect for the earth. Priests like Sean Mc Donagh have given an important lead without attracting much support from mainstream Catholics at any level.

The last point in this hasty coverage of issues in law and morality concerns the current debate arising out of the clerical sex abuse scandals on the relation between Canon Law and Civil Law. Unless arrogance and stupidity prevail on either side, this is a pseudo-problem. Of course the church has the right constitutionally and legally to manage its own affairs and discipline its own personnel. Where, however, these personnel are accused of civil crimes and there is no suggestion that such criminal laws are contrary to the moral law and human rights, then the church authorities have a moral obligation to co-operate fully with the civil authorities in the investigation of these alleged offences. Canon 1395 par 2, which deals with such offences by clerics as child sexual abuse, creates no difficulties itself for this co-operation, whatever particular interpretations might suggest. And natural justice, a term shared by church and state, would demand protection as far as possible of the reputation of the accused as presumed innocent until found guilty, while at the same time, in accordance with the church's own guidelines, protecting children against the danger of possible further abuse by removing the priest from pastoral, chaplain or other hazardous duties. The solution to these practical problems demands good faith and willingness on the part of church and state but should not be all that difficult. Recent dilatoriness on both sides, but particularly on the church side, has aggravated the dangers to children, increased difficulties for the accused, damaged the credibility and leadership of the church and created unnecessary tensions between church and state.

Re-envisioning the Church and its Mission in Society
Much of the co-operation and the tension between church and state derived from an earlier vision of church and state as two powers, the spiritual power or church and the temporal power or state. This vision had originated with emancipation of the church by the Roman Emperor Constantine in the fourth century and its establishment as the church of the Empire by the Emperor Theodosius later that century. What came to be known as Christendom, the union of throne and altar, of the powers spiritual and temporal with, in church eyes, the priority of the

spiritual, continued through the centuries. Through the East-West divisions of church and Empire, the divisions of the Reformation and the Counter-Reformation in the sixteenth century and the rise of the nation-states, the vision of the two powers and the actuality of their co-operation or antagonism persisted. Even after the American and French Revolutions and through the rise of democracy, there lingered in many European countries this vision of two powers. However, their relationship might be reversed with the civil power now the dominant one. In the new independent Ireland, despite its massive Catholic majority which had before independence known the reality of an established church, that option of establishment was not taken. However, the vision of spiritual and temporal powers as characterising church and state was unconsciously and, as we saw, sometimes consciously at work. There was in the first fifty years of the new states, South and North, an informal establishment of the Catholic and Protestant churches. Christendom lingered on.

It still does, at least in the attitudes and practices of many church leaders. What Tom Inglis has charted in his book, *Moral Monopoly*, with the sub-title *The Rise and Fall of the Catholic Church in Modern Ireland*, treats the Irish church and more particularly its episcopal leaders as a social (quasi-political) power, as reliving the vision of Christendom. In that sense the church was bound to fall as politicians became more independent and self-confident and politics itself more secular.

Vatican II provided at least partly for a church which could carry out its evangelical mission without depending on or restricting state activity. It was genuinely seeking a way out of the Christendom inheritance, which had become such a burden to the universal church over almost two centuries both in countries supportive of it and in countries hostile to it. The documents already listed, particularly *The Church in the Modern World* and the *Declaration on Religious Liberty*, show that the church was catching up with the democratic revolution in politics and with other aspects of the modern world. Some contemporary critics of Vatican II see it as having gone too far and as having sold out to 'modernity' just when 'postmodernity' was replacing modernity's belief in scientific rationality and inevitable human progress. Vatican II's supporters respond that, as Chesterton said of Christianity that it hadn't failed because it had never really been

tried, Vatican II had never really been tried because of official resistance to it, particularly in Rome. That is a debate for another
occasion. The present task is to sketch some vision of church
which will free it to fulfill its gospel mission in a society which is
at once heavily secularised in its structures, attitudes and practices and yet with many of its members explicitly or implicitly in
search of one or all of the following: some ultimate meaning for
life, a foundation for morality and some kind of transcendent or
spiritual experience.

A possible framework for the sketch of church in society required here might involve three of the major characteristics of
biblical literature, of the biblical peoples, Israel and the Christian
community, and of the major biblical figures, for Christians their
founder and continuing head Jesus Christ. These characteristics
of the literature, the peoples and the leaders may be termed the
priestly, the prophetic and the kingly or, in the equally authentic
term relevant to us, the wise. New Testament literature and
Christian commentators have frequently spoken of Jesus as
priest, prophet and king while remembering the injunction attributed to him in the gospel of John as he stood before Pilate
that his kingdom was not of this world. A primary quality of the
good king in the Hebrew scriptures was wisdom and much of
what was spoken of as 'wisdom literature' was given kingly au-
thorship, as with David and the psalms, while the wisdom of
Solomon was legendary. In Jesus, in his person and teaching, divine and human wisdom recurred without any pretensions to
the kind of earthly kingship which some of his contemporaries
and even some of his close disciples expected up to the very end:
'Wilt thou at this time restore the kingdom of Israel?' There was
never at any time a hint of the kind of kingdom which many in
Israel expected and desired and which Christians subsequently
promoted in various versions of Christendom.

The followers of Christ as constituting a priestly people, with
its New Testament origins, was restored to its primacy in Vatican
II's *Constitution on the Church*. This people embodies the mystery
of God's presence to the world at large. And it is the whole people which embodies the presence of God, not the religious officials of whom Jesus was very critical in his day and who were
deferred to a later chapter for consideration in Vatican II's treatment of the church. Immediate challenges arise for the church as
to how it is to be made visible and effective as primarily a com-

munity of the believing and baptised, and not be perceived as an episcopal or clerical body. In some reactions to the (partial) democratisation, declericalisation and demystification set in train by Vatican II, a restorationist spirit has been at work. Episcopal and clerical primacy, prestige and power have once again been stressed and so has a return to older forms of liturgy and of clerical and religious dress. Often the reason advanced for these moves is the restoration of the sense of mystery, of the transcendent and divine in life and liturgy.

It would be foolish to deny that the sense of mystery and of the transcendent is weakening in church life and liturgy and that the council as implemented so far has done little to renew that sense. But the weakening was already at work, at least partly because the pre-Vatican II church had not confronted the positives as well as the negatives in the changing and secularising world around it. That church had preferred to stay with forms which spoke increasingly of myst ification rather than mystery and consciously or unconsciously betokened human power rather than divine grace. In a renewed vision and structure of church, the sense of transcendence and mystery which people need and which so many despair of finding through the present power structures, the liturgy and activities of the Christian community, must help keep the whole society open to a liberating transcendent and refuse the temptations of the parallel social powers characteristic of Christendom.

The temptations of the priestly dimensions of the church to seek power and the associated prestige and property in society should be offset by the prophetic voices in that community. Prophets in the Hebrew scriptures were particularly critical of the neglect by the religious leaders and their associates of the poor and excluded in their power-seeking and wealth accumulation. One of the most cherished names for Jesus has been that of prophet. His refusal of the trappings of wealth and power gave substance to his prophetic teaching. Indeed his self-emptying even to death on the cross, as described in St Paul's Letter to the Philippians (chap 2), provides a permanent prophetic critique of the worldly aspirations of religious leaders, with their seeking of the first places in synagogue, church or civil forum. At the more obviously moral level, the traditional prophetic calls for justice and peace provide a final basis in the divine Creator, the ultimate and absolutely Other, for the equal respect due to human creatures in their dignity as images and children of God, and for the respect due by them to all creation in its rich diversity. Such a prophetic community, in deed as well as in word, will bear witness within society to the highest aspirations and attainments of human beings and offer a necessary and continuing critique to the individualist self-seeking of the strong at the expense of the weak. Only where the prophetic voice is effective can the priestly people authentically worship and witness to the transcendent and incarnate God of Jesus Christ.

Prophets have their own temptations. Power and prestige also beckon for them if in more subtle forms than that of conventional fame and fortune. Their summons to the others to change and be converted may well disguise from themselves their own self-seeking and their own need for conversion. In themselves or certainly in the community they serve, these temptations may be overcome by wisdom, personal and communal, human and divine. The wisdom literature of Israel borrowed heavily from surrounding cultures while integrating that wisdom into its own faith in Yahweh, the one true God of Israel. The Israelite, Jesus of Nazareth, inheritor of that wisdom tradition, enlarged and deepened it in his parables and proverbial sayings, while ultimately subjecting it, in Paul's vision, to the divine wisdom which despite their protestations led him to lay down his life for his friends. In the end divine wisdom may sometimes look like human folly. Yet as a protection against self-indulgent or simply irrational prophetic pretensions, human as well as divine wisdom may be needed. Living in this world but not finally of this world demands that disciples of Jesus be wise as serpents and not just simple as doves, in a typical 'wisdom' saying of Jesus himself.

In its attempt to cope with the modern world, the church must wisely evaluate and accommodate. In a fresher vision of church and world, the ambiguity of each becomes clearer. The sense of mystery, divine and human, in creation and creator evokes the priestly response not just of Christians but of people belonging to every religion and none. It is the Christian responsibility to engage in wisdom with these other traditions in order to expand the awareness and understanding of the mystery of God's presence in the world among themselves and among their partners in dialogue. Wisdom provides protection against the mystificatory conservative temptation of the priestly, and against the self-indulgent radical temptation of the prophetic. It has its own temptations of course to yield to worldly accommodation and ease in face of the authentic demands of true worship and inclusive justice. Wisdom's resistance to these temptations requires the challenge and support of the priestly and prophetic in the church.

The vision of the church as a priestly, prophetic and wisdom community, in the senses described, helps to locate it in the broader society without immediately prescribing reforms in structure. Assuming the priority of the believing people after the teaching of Vatican II, and adhering to the basic service structures which originated in New Testament times and have developed in response to inspirations and needs with inevitable accommodations and compromises, wisdom suggests that a clean break with the Christendom mentality is necessary. That really means an end to clericalism, to the caste system of bishops, priests and religious with their power and privileges. They will be integrated as servants into the believing community. This of course suggests that they be chosen as in the past by the believing community they are to serve while confirmed in the unity of the whole church by local bishops and by the church's traditional symbol of universal unity, the Bishop of Rome. There need be no formal relations with the political powers. The church's mission in society, of promoting a meaningful and moral life, will be effected through all its members with their priestly, prophetic and pastoral wisdom gifts, who enter wholeheartedly into the familial, social, economic, cultural and political life of the society. Catholic Christian citizens, drawing on the inspiration of their faith community, should be full and free citizens in promoting the human rights and the common weal of all members, more immediately of their own civil society but ultimately of the whole globalising world. Their distinctive civic attribute might well be their concern for the excluded and discriminated. Their ecclesial leaders will no longer have any civic role beyond the role of citizen and the freedom to preach the gospel and serve their people.

The Emerging Paradigm: Religion and Society

To some extent any new vision of church in society is continually being overtaken by events. Vatican II has been criticised by radicals in Latin America and by conservatives in Europe for accommodating itself too much to the liberal and largely unbelieving European middle class. Trying to fit the universal church into such a context could only distort it according to these two sets of critics, otherwise utterly different in their analysis of the past, and in their prescriptions for the future church. The analysis and prescription of Vatican II had, in the *Declaration on Religious Freedom* and in its less substantial documents on ecumenism and inter-faith dialogue, prepared the way to some extent for the situation which has developed since. The obvious vitality of the major religions in the world has given, as mentioned earlier, many sociological scholars cause to rethink their belief that secularisation, European style, was unstoppable around the globe. The fundamentalist nature of some of these religious groups is obviously a cause for great political as well as religious concern.

Of more relevance to this discussion is the sheer plurality and variety of religious communities in most countries including Ireland. In some recent debates in Ireland it was almost assumed that the pluralist society to be desired would be simply a secular society with religion a purely private and personal reality in so far as it existed at all. Of course many religious and non-religious commentators saw the inherent contradiction in equating pluralist and secular in this context. It will be more difficult to make the equation from now on with the growth in the Muslim and other religious communities. In fact, to speak of a secular society may soon be as outdated as speaking of a Catholic or Christian society. Part of the difficulty here has been the tendency in the nation-state to identify society and state. In face of a much more diverse society at home with so many more connections abroad and in face of a growing sense of the necessity and power of voluntary organisations and interest groups, the state will have to be distinguished much more sharply from the society it serves in its legislative, judicial and administrative roles. In that situation, the Catholic Church will have more Christian freedom and less social power. For the sake of religion and morality it will have to foster effective dialogue with other churches (ecumenism) and with other faiths (interfaith dialogue) and indeed with those of no religious faith but with a sense of the need for human meaning and civic morality. By then the debates of the twentieth century may seem as obsolete as those of the fourth, the century of Constantine.

CHAPTER THREE

The Protestant Churches in Independent Ireland

Kenneth Milne

Those with an appetite for statistics will find much to interest them in the multitude of government reports on the Established Church of Ireland that were presented to crown and parliament in the course of the nineteenth century. Indeed, it has been claimed that the result of all these commissions and committees was that the British parliament was as well informed about the operation of the Irish church as it was about any institution in the whole empire.[1] It was these very statistics that, in an early manifestation of the part that numbers could play in the formulation of public policy, provided the critics of the Church of Ireland with the ammunition they needed to subvert its established position. The statistics so laboriously collected and collated revealed the inequitable and inefficient manner (to the nineteenth-century whig mind) whereby the resources of the church were administered, and demonstrated, what had previously only been suspected, that the Established Church did not command the loyalty of a majority of the population in a single county of Ireland.

Always a minority church, its constitutional origins lay in the understanding of church-state relations prevalent in the immediate post-Reformation period when terms such as 'minority' were of little significance. As Jacqueline Hill has argued, with special reference to the Protestant control of Dublin Corporation that lasted well into the nineteenth century, 'how important were majorities in politics before the end of the eighteenth century?'[2] By the 1920s the Church of Ireland was not arguing in terms of political theory, but the union with Great Britain still provided a potent sense of security for the religious minority, and the Protestant community was, irrespective of denomination, largely unionist in sentiment. The established status of the Church of Ireland, it should be remembered, survived until 1871, which was within the living memory of many who were alive in 1922.

Which is not, of course, to say that all Protestants were unionists, even with a lower case 'u'. Many were not, and could claim to have a lengthy lineage in the annals of Irish nationalism and radicalism that stretched back to the founders of the republican movement in the eighteenth century. To be more precise, the bearers of some of the great names, such as Tone and Emmet, though of Protestant, indeed Anglican stock, shared with their continental contemporaries a high degree of religious scepticism. But among them were also such devout northern members of the Established Church as Thomas Russell, a founder of the Society of United Irishmen. Napper Tandy, of the parish of St Werburgh, Dublin, was secretary to the Dublin Society, and a group of young Protestant lawyers from St Michan's parish were prominent in United Irish circles in the city. Recent commemorations of the 1798 insurrection have uncovered much evidence of Protestant, including Church of Ireland, involvement on the insurrectionary side in Wexford and Wicklow as well as in Antrim and Down. Of course, as has been well said, liberal Protestants were interested in the rights of Catholics, not the rights of Catholicism!

So far as the rise of cultural nationalism is concerned, one need not subscribe entirely to W. B. Yeats's somewhat hyperbolic claim that the minority to which he expressed himself proud to belong 'created most of the modern literature of this country', in order to see the point that he was making.[3] The most pertinent conclusion to be drawn from the long list of Protestant names among those who repose in the Irish nationalist pantheon is that it enables Protestants to dismiss the claim, now little heard, but once quite frequently aired, that to be truly Irish one must be Roman Catholic. Douglas Hyde's Irish credentials can scarcely be called into question![4]

Yet the claim that, by definition, Protestants are somehow less Irish than others derives, presumably, from the well-attested fact that the great majority of them traditionally saw their Irishness as belonging in an imperial setting. The General Synod of the Church of Ireland made clear its position when home rule legislation appeared to be imminent in 1912. The president of the synod, Archbishop Crozier of Armagh, while claiming that 'our church knows no politics', endorsed the view expressed by Dr George Salmon in 1893 (a time of similar apprehension), that what was at stake was 'the political annihilation of the Protestants of Ireland'.[5] On the eve of the general election of 1910, when home rule for Ireland was a major issue, eleven former moderators of the Presbyterian General Assembly published a manifesto declaring that the Union was in the best interests of all the people of Ireland.[6] Great numbers of the male members of the Church of Ireland and of the Presbyterian and Methodist Churches, lay and clerical, signed the Solemn League and Covenant in September 1912 and those who did not were undoubtedly out of sympathy with the mass of public opinion in their churches. There were, likewise, exceptions that proved the rule among Methodists, for instance, but the Methodist journal, the *Christian Advocate*, made it clear that the official policy of the church was against home rule.[7]

However, once the establishment of the Irish Free State was achieved, Archbishop J. A. F. Gregg of Dublin gave a strong and timely lead to Church of Ireland people, publicly exhorting them to give their loyalty and goodwill to the new state.[8] Similarly, the General Assembly of the Presbyterian Church called on members in the Free State 'to co-operate wholeheartedly with their Roman Catholic fellow-countrymen in the best interests of their beloved land'.[9] By 1949, the year in which 'Éire' formally became a republic and left the Commonwealth, Gregg was Archbishop of Armagh and Primate of all Ireland. Again he gave a strong and unequivocal lead in ensuring that state prayers used in public worship in the Republic should reflect the constitutional reality. Intercessions for the crown, that had for centuries evoked a warm response from Church of Ireland congregations, were henceforth to be restricted to use in Northern Ireland for, as the archbishop put it, 'in our prayers, above all, there must be reality'.[10]

Inevitably, the affairs of the state church, as the Church of Ireland was for over three hundred years, were inextricably linked with those of the body politic, and it would be impossible to treat seriously of any phase of Irish history in the early modern or modern periods without encountering the rôle of the Established Church. Much the same can be said of the rôle of the Roman Catholic Church from 1922 onwards. Yet the Protestant presence was still of some significance. An off-the-record remark made to a Church of Ireland bishop by a Department of Education official in the early years of the state that 'if the Protestants didn't exist, we'd have to invent them', was taken to imply that, however small in number, the very existence of a Protestant population inhibited government (or so it could claim) from certain courses of action that could have been regarded as discriminatory.[11] Perhaps politicians (or, more likely, officials), concerned to reduce their vulnerability to hierarchical pressure, occasionally found it convenient to play the Protestant card. Generally speaking, however,where educational matters were concerned, Protestant, or at least Church of Ireland, commitment to the maintenance of the denominational system chimed in perfectly with the policies of the Roman Catholic Church, and there was universal encouragement for the occasional incidence of positive discrimination in favour of small Protestant schools which was to everybody's advantage.

On a wider canvass, Éamon de Valera's consultations with Archbishop Gregg while framing the 1937 Constitution were substantial and no mere matter of form.[12] As we now know, de Valera's article 44.1.2, acknowledging the 'special position' of the 'Holy Catholic Apostolic and Roman Church as the guardian of the Faith professed by the great majority of the citizens', fell short of what many influential voices, both in Dublin and Rome, would have liked,[13] and presumably owed much to his wish that the minority population should find the new state inclusive. Which is not to say that the minority population had invariably felt this to be the case.

Many Protestants were distinctly uncomfortable, to put it mildly, with the new state's close adherence to Vatican precepts where the social regulation of society was concerned, and most Protestants (if not, indeed, most citizens, however inhibited they may have felt from saying so) were out of sympathy with a policy on the Irish language that at least in rhetoric intended the replacement of English by Irish as the vernacular. Since, therefore, the Irish Free State was explicitly Catholic in social regulation and aspired to be Gaelic in culture, it is little to be wondered at that the Protestant presence withdrew into itself.

The litany of incidents that lent credibility to those who had claimed that home rule would be Rome rule, in practice if not in theory, has often been rehearsed. They include the Dunbar-Harrison case of 1930, when the suitability of a Trinity-educated Protestant woman for appointment as county librarian of Mayo was in question,[14] the Tilson case of 1951, when debate raged around the legal status of the promises made by the partners in an inter-church marriage,[15] and the 1957 'boycott' of Protestants in Fethard-on-Sea, another 'mixed marriage' issue.[16] They are part of the history of this state. That they happened should be recorded, if only so that subsequent generations should realise that the Protestant experience in the twenty-six counties has not been universally happy. Similarly it is important to refer from time to time to the impact of Roman Catholic marriage regulations on Protestant demographic trends here. Almost every Protestant knew about this particular Protestant grievance: not so many Catholics did, and it is necessary that they should do so, if only to explain, at least in part, what appeared to many Catholics to be a manifestation of a superiority complex. F. S. L. Lyons conceded that such an attitude was to be found among Protestants, and said it was 'simply a part of their *mystique* as a governing caste and if it seemed to those outside the charmed circle to be an entirely unjustified arrogance, it was largely an unconscious arrogance'.[17] In some cases it probably was such, even on the part of those who had little cause for *hauteur*. But the almost self-imposed apartheid to which Protestants clung owed much to the *Ne Temere* decree of the Roman Catholic Church which required both partners in a mixed marriage to undertake, in writing, that the children of the marriage would be brought up in the Roman Catholic faith. The 'Protestant dance', and 'Protestant table-tennis club', usually under parish auspices, were seen as a protection against those relationships that in 'mixed' company could so easily lead to a marriage where the Protestant parents and grandparents would be, in a sense, marginalised, at least so far as the education and religious upbringing of the children were concerned. Inter-church marriages still call for much sensitivity, especially in rural areas, but the growth of ecumenical understanding and indeed of liturgical convergance, which are of comparatively recent vintage, have done much to reduce the pain. As has the relaxation of Vatican requirements, though the Protestant churches will not be satisfied until parity of esteem is acknowledged.

In seeking to account for Protestant withdrawal from much of public life, one should not overlook the part played by the cases of terror perpetrated against Protestants in the War of Independence and the Civil War, though they most commonly suffered for their unionism or their landlord past, than for their Protestantism. Bloodless revolutions are rare, and in those years terrible things were done to defenceless people, southern Protestants and northern Catholics alike. However, whereas *Ne Temere* survives in Protestant folk memory, the atrocities of 'the Troubles' have not lingered on, which surely says something about the relative scarcity of such events, however dreadful at the time, and the brevity of the period that gave rise to them.[18]

All in all, it is scarcely surprising that the Protestant minority maintained a relatively low profile in national affairs in the early years of the state. Leon Ó Broin was a Catholic public servant of considerable standing in Irish society. His ecumenical instincts were never in doubt, and he played a major part in the Mercier Society, an inter-church theological group that met in the years 1941 to 1944.[19] Ó Broin remarked to the present writer on more than one occasion that people tended to underestimate the impact on Irish Protestants of finding themselves on the losing side in a revolution and the psychological trauma of such an experience. After all, Civil War memories endured for generations and continued for decades to bedevil not only the political life of the country, but also personal relationships between individuals. That Protestants for the most part withdrew from public life was hardly to be wondered at. Fortunately for them (and perhaps also for the country), there were other facets of life to which they could contribute, not least the commercial, professional and philanthropic. There may well have been instances when opportunities for public service, and therefore the potential for influencing events, were on offer, but not availed of. Garret FitzGerald referred in his autobiography to the tradition of having at least one Protestant judge in the High Court and to the fact that during his second term as Taoiseach, 'none of the senior Protestant barristers we approached were able to accept appointment when the occasion arose'.[20] And that was in the more relaxed period of the 1980s. It should also be borne in mind that in the fraught atmosphere of the early decades of the state, opportunities to contribute to public debate may have been missed. When the thorny matter of censorship was scrutinised by a 'Committee on evil literature', established in February 1926 by the Department of Justice, it included Professor W. E. Thrift, member of Dáil Eireann and fellow of Trinity (an unusual combination then as now), and eventually provost.[21] The committee, which took cognizance of birth control information, sought church opinion, but (officially at least) little was forthcoming, for reasons about which we can only speculate. When his views were sought, Archbishop Gregg simply offered to answer any questions that the committee cared to put to him. His offer was not taken up.

The Church of Ireland leadership may well have considered any attempt to influence the course of events to be a waste of time. Though relations with government were conducted with *gravitas* and courtesy, it is worth remembering that the representatives of both sides would previously have lacked that social intercourse between prominent members of society that does so much to oil the wheels of government. One issue on which the Church of Ireland had strenuously expressed its views was that of the introduction of compulsory Irish to the school curriculum. A high-level deputation to the Minister for Education, seeking some derogation where Church of Ireland schools were concerned, got nowhere. In fairness, however, it must be noted that this was not a matter of religious conviction (though there were religious overtones to aspects of the language question) and the language itself was something on which the Protestant community was divided, if very unevenly.[22]

While a certain withdrawal, perhaps even exclusion, from public affairs was evident, it would be unjust to accuse Protestants of losing entirely their sense of social responsibility. Nor was that confined simply to looking after their own. Important initiatives in Irish society, such as the Civics Institute with its playgrounds for the children of working mothers, was a case in point. (Though there were instances of Catholic clerical criticism of such endeavours as undermining family life by encouraging mothers to work.) Protestants continued to play an active part in the St John Ambulance Brigade of Ireland and other voluntary public services, and participated in such emergency services as the A. R. P. and Local Defence Force, set up during the Second World War. The Irish Countrywomen's Association held attractions for Protestant women and many rose to positions of trust. It was in the interests of young farmers to throw in their lot with Macra na Feirme, and many of them did. Less to be expected, perhaps, was the support for Muintir na Tíre, given that its founder was a Roman Catholic priest, Fr John Hayes. This organisation received significant support for its programme of rural development from Protestants, including the encouragement of Bishop Phair of Ossory, who was reported as saying in the course of Kilkenny Rural Week in 1960 that he wished to see 'a truly happy people', taking pride in the state and with a desire to contribute to its well-being and prosperity.[23] Nor should Quaker social initiatives be overlooked, prominent members of that society like Victor Bewley having been to the fore in conscientising the public as to its responsibilities towards the travelling community.

The rôle of the Protestant school in easing the very considerable strains, indeed shocks, experienced by the Protestant community in the Free State can scarcely be exaggerated. The records of the General Synod of the Church of Ireland and its Board of Education provide abundant evidence of the manner in which the church regarded the schools under its patronage as in some ways providing an ark to shelter Protestant children from the prevailing winds of cultural change that swept across the educational system of the twenty-six counties, whereby Gaelicisation of society was a priority and the teaching of Irish history a handmaid of that process.[24] For this reason, the Protestant school has had a particularly significant part to play in the life of the Protestant community as a vehicle for educating children in its religious, cultural and political traditions. Which may not be far removed from the theological underpinning more usually associated with the Roman Catholic Church as the rationale of its commitment to church schools. Of course, the southern minority's attitude to its schools owes something to the fact that it is a tiny minority of the population, and there well may have been a time when it was thought that its very survival depended in large measure on its schools. Certainly the survival of the Protestant teaching profession, particularly at primary school level, was at stake. The Church of Ireland has dedicated a great share of its resources to education. Particularly in the 1960s, the Church engaged in a major overhaul of the system to fit it for the great changes then being introduced by the state. When the General Synod established committees to enquire into the state of secondary (1962) and primary (1964) schools, it had in mind securing the wellbeing of that majority of its pupils that attended schools under Protestant management. The Secondary Education Committee that emerged from these investigations, whereby the other Protestant churches that had an involvement in school management joined with the Church of Ireland to set about the renewal of Protestant secondary schools, sought to ensure that

Protestant children were not educationally disadvantaged by attending the schools of their parents' choice. While in time the Secondary Education Committee became the agency for the distribution of state aid to assist with secondary school fees, that was not the rôle envisaged for it originally, and it needs to be remembered that these initiatives came about when emigration was high, not least among Protestants. The equipping of Protestant children to take their place in Ireland, rather than as emigrants to other shores, was what was at stake. Furthermore, when so-called 'free education' was introduced in 1967, the Secondary Education Committee gave priority to the less well off when distributing state resources, at the cost of considerable unpopularity within its own community.[25]

We are recalling a time when secondary education was, for the most part, equated with that of the grammar school, and when the minority of Protestant pupils who received post-primary schooling regarded it as a stepping stone either to university (for there was little else on offer at third-level) or to admission to the more traditional professions of law, medicine and accountancy. Yet there were those in the Protestant community who, looking ahead, could see that the world of employment was changing, and that it was irresponsible for their community to neglect to provide its young people with a vision of the changing employment opportunities that would come about as the number of places in the traditional commercial and financial enterprises contracted and new areas opened up. It was to this end, at a time when school career counselling was virtually non-existent, that the Church of Ireland took the unusual step of publishing a careers book to educate pupils, parents and teachers to the need to take their eyes off the traditional sectors, and to look more widely at the emerging opportunities for work in Ireland.[26] In his foreword to the 1969 edition, Archbishop Simms of Dublin outlined the purpose of the book (which was distributed free to all Protestant secondary schools) as follows:

> It is hoped that this book will aid both teacher and parent to guide those who are preparing for their future work in life to see the elements of vocation, adaptability and dignity in the many different occupations which a society, urban or rural, industrialised or agricultural, offers to those who, while concerned with earning their living, may also have a sense of joy and fulfilment in serving their country.[27]

Commentators frequently attribute the groundswell of unrest on the part of the Catholic community in the North to the impact of education and in particular to the opening up of university education to students irrespective of means and the opportunities that this gave to Catholics. But education has had a subversive influence on the old order south of the border as well, which is not always recognised. No doubt television, Vatican II and the EU have played their part, but education has been the paramount agent of change. A society that was for the most part educated only to primary level has been replaced by one with expectations of secondary education of some form or other, while a very considerable number of students now have third level ambitions. Inevitably, the workings of public opinion have undergone considerable change. In this new situation, the Protestant community has itself undergone a two-fold change: not only have its members benefited individually from the growth in educational opportunity (for, let it not be forgotten, there is such a thing as a poor Protestant), but as a community, it has found itself in an increasingly congenial society. Above all, it has enjoyed (which is not, perhaps, too strong a term) the increased opportunities for social integration and for sharing religious experience and has found confidence in the discovery that criticism of authority no longer marks it off as being in some way dissident, anti-Catholic or anti-national. A greatly altered political and ecclesiastical environment has come about through the interaction of various agents of change, propelled even faster by what is sometimes perceived as a growth in secularisation in the train of enhanced economic property. The stark contrast that for so long obtained as between social welfare provision in the six and the twenty-six counties, a cogent argument against the unification of Ireland in unionist eyes, has in large measure ceased to be the case. A new generation of Protestants shares in the general feeling of confidence that pervades society in the Republic. Furthermore, this new generation has, insofar as it thinks about it at all, a confidence in its own situation, and this, I would maintain, owes not a little to having, perhaps unconsciously, come to terms with its past or, rather, its forebears' past.

It is, of course, a moot point whether it is preferable to be exposed to no history teaching at all than to bad history teaching. And few would argue that the teaching of history in either part of the island has been all that it might have been. Both jurisdictions have regarded the place of history in the school curriculum as, in part, a moral one: to the nationalist it was part of the process of nation-building, not least where the promotion of the Irish language was concerned, and to the unionist, in like manner, a means whereby loyalty to Northern Ireland and the British connection would be inculcated and supported. The Catholic population of Northern Ireland for the most part attended schools closely linked with their church, and in which Irish history was cherished. But the history taught in those schools maintained by local authorities, largely Protestant in enrolment, was of a different kind. To quote from the official history of Stranmillis College, Belfast: 'There were inescapable difficulties in attempts to avoid ideological bias especially in the teaching of Irish history, so syllabuses tended, like textbooks, to concentrate on English history...'[28] Despite the fact that curriculum development, particularly at primary level, has done much to introduce pupils in Northern Ireland to the history of their immediate environment, and giving due recognition to the ideals of those who promote in schools the concept of Education for Mutual Understanding, it is incontrovertible that Protestant children in the twenty-six counties have, and always have had, considerably more knowledge of Irish history than their co-religionists in the six counties. It may not always have been soundly taught, but at least they knew, so to speak, the essential grammar and vocabulary of Irish history, and the more fortunate, of late, have been taught very well indeed. A result of this has been an awareness of how their community was traditionally perceived by others. How accurate this perception was is another matter: the point at issue here is that they knew about it. A lack of even basic knowledge of Irish history has put northern Protestants at a considerable disadvantage. Nationalist interpretations of the course of Irish history, however valid, can be questioned, but not by those who know no history. Protestants in the Republic, or at least those of them who cared about such things, have been able to take advantage of the very considerable re-thinking that has been applied to much Irish history. While not seeking to defend the indefensible, they have been in a position to question the questionable. This exposure to the ongoing debates in Irish history has impacted not alone on how the Protestant community sees itself historically, but also on how, for instance, the Church of Ireland understands its past, warts and all.

Professor Alan Ford, evaluating the importance of church history, has written about the part played by historians as follows:

Their work relates to a real and vibrant tradition, and has to come face to face with the conflicts and myths created by those traditions. Historians, by the very act of writing, participate in the task of interpreting and shaping these traditions both for their own and future generations. As a result, once the complexity is welcomed and accepted, and the dangers of prejudice and the necessity for self-awareness recognised, religious history has a capacity to make a particularly rich and stimulating contribution not merely to the field of Irish historiography, but also to Irish society as a whole.[29]

In this manner, church historians, as well as others, have contributed to a mutation in the climate of opinion where the Irish religious past is concerned. The psychology of society at large has begun to undergo change, and bring the freedom that comes when, however painfully, long-cherished but increasingly untenable positions are abandoned, making way for a refreshing wave of confidence.

The voting patterns of Protestants since the inception of the independent state are not documented. However, there would seem little doubt that they were for the most part pro-treaty and supportive of the early Cosgrave administrations. While what might be termed the cornerstones of both the 'confessional' and 'Gaelic' states were laid in those years, it has to be remembered that issues such as contraception and divorce, and to some extent censorship, though fiercely debated from the nineteen seventies onwards, were not so generally discussed in earlier decades. Rigorous attitudes to family planning and divorce were not confined to the Roman Catholic Church, and the operations of the censorship board concerned few outside literary and intellectual circles.[30] (Admittedly, as Protestant churches shifted their positions, a day did come when publications relating to family planning, published by such impeccable Anglican sources as the Mothers' Union, *could* have fallen foul of the Gárda, but there were no prosecutions!) Again, Cosgrave was not de Valera, the *bête noir* of those who supported the Treaty.[31] Protestant attitudes to de Valera, the archetypal republican, and his party, Fianna Fáil, softened with the years, as he was perceived to take

a strong line against sectarianism when he felt that the integrity
of the state was concerned, such as in the Tilson and Fethard-on-
Sea cases, and there is general agreement that Protestant support for Fine Gael was severely damaged when John Costello's
government took Ireland out of the Commonwealth in 1949.
Such initiatives as Garret FitzGerald's 'constitutional crusade' of
1981 in some measure restored the confidence in Fine Gael lost
in 1949. Archbishop Armstrong of Armagh responded by describ-
ing the Taoiseach's speech of 9 October 1981 as a 'courageous'
step, but no more than a step,[32] while Archbishop McAdoo of
Dublin said:

> ... the Taoiseach's ideas deserve to be seriously considered
> right across the political spectrum by all Irish men and
> women who long to create confidence and to bring about rec-
> onciliation between those whom the events of the last decade
> have so tragically polarised.[33]

It has been said that FitzGerald's capital so far as Protestants
were concerned diminished when he espoused the cause of
those who called for a referendum on the insertion a 'pro-life'
clause in the constitution,[34] but confidence in his goodwill and
integrity hardly faltered and have, if anything, been boosted by
subsequent disclosures of 'low standards in high places' in Irish
political life.

While the southern minority of modern times scarcely receives (or merits) the volume of research into its affairs that was
lavished on the Established Church during the nineteenth century, yet it does attract a surprising amount of attention, most,
though by no means all of it, from historians. Michael Viney
coined the phrase 'the five per cent' for a series of *Irish Times*
pieces in the 1960s, and others have followed in his footsteps.[35]
The Church of Ireland in particular appears to have exercised a
certain fascination for those Irish commentators who travelled
to Rome to cover the Second Vatican Council, for it seemed that
nearer home was an institution that bore some of the marks of
the kind of church that they envisioned for Irish Roman
Catholicism. They attended the General Synod with refreshing
enthusiasm and reported its transactions with considerable acu-
men on radio and television and in the press. That Irish
Protestantism failed to live up to their (somewhat unreal) expectations was, in part, simply because the Protestant churches, not
least the Church of Ireland, being human, do not invariably live

up to the ideals made possible by their ecclesiologies. Another factor was the growing inter-communal distrust in Northern Ireland. It was not long before media coverage of the General Synod had moved its focus from matters liturgical and ecclesiastical to things political. These were, indeed, years of considerable church debate on forms of public worship, but the cameras seldom lingered on that part of the agenda, sharing (and helping to create) the palpable sense of drama that accompanied debates on political matters.

There is little doubt that the minds of General Synod members were preoccupied with 'the northern situation', which vitiated the progress of ecumenical dialogue. Not, of course, that these matters were unrelated. The growth of ecumenical sentiment, so welcome in some quarters, was far from welcome in others. Irish Anglicanism operated in a political situation that was as tense as that in any part of the communion, with the possible exception of South Africa. Great credit is due to those Protestants, both the leaders and the led, who resisted the opposition to ecumenism. It was in this highly-charged atmosphere that the ground-breaking inter-church meetings between the leaders of the Roman Catholic Church and of the member churches of the Irish Council of Churches were initiated in 1973.

Of the many strands that combined to create the troubled community situation in Northern Ireland, two were clearly discernible: the resentment of many Catholics at the discrimination to which their community was subjected (well documented by official enquiries) and the apprehension of many Protestants that their particular identity was under threat. In a crisis situation, when the chips were down, Protestant public opinion in the north was little divided. In face of a common foe, as so often in the past, two of Wolfe Tone's classic categories of Irish Christian, 'Protestant' (by which he meant Anglican) and 'Dissenter', stood shoulder to shoulder as unionists, perceiving the 'Catholic' as nationalist, if not indeed republican. In each of the three traditions were many who deplored what was happening. But it was a fact of life, and the fragile nature of the political settlement reached under the terms of the Belfast agreement of Good Friday 1998 makes it clear that we are not out of the wood yet.

This chapter has been taken up with matters southern, which, indeed, impinge on matters northern. What many unionists perceive to be the negative aspects of the Belfast Agreement are but part of the picture. Irish nationalism has dropped its constitutional claim to the territory of Northern Ireland, aspiring only to a unity by consent. Traditional anti-partitionist rhetoric has been officially discarded, and one may venture to suppose that Catholic public opinion in the Republic is for the most part glad to relax its gaze on Northern Ireland, satisfied with the status of the northern minority that has now been achieved.

Southern Protestants likewise are hopeful that the terrorist threat to their northern co-religionists has considerably abated, and like many of their Catholic neighbours, have reverted to that rather detached attitude to things northern that was customary before 1969. To an outside observer, it may seem perplexing that these southern Protestants were not in the van of the movement (such as it was) to unite the country. Surely the prospect of a united Ireland in which their numerical presence and political influence would be strengthened was appealing? But for the most part they took little interest in northern affairs.

Perhaps, this was because, in years gone by, they could see little advantage for their northern counterparts in coming under the rule of Dublin. But today it is more likely to be because the southern Protestant lacks that sense of belonging to a sundered community that has so fortified the northern Catholic. To be more precise: Protestant sentiment in the border counties of the south has been distinctive, and has indeed given evidence of identifying with the other side of the frontier. The survival to the present day of the loyal institutions in Cavan, Monaghan and Donegal attests to this. But elsewhere in the southern state, such has not been the case, nor would such sentiment have enjoyed the degree of reality that propinquity to Northern Ireland has given it in the northern counties.

There can be reasonable objections to the use of terms such as Protestant and Catholic to designate what are at heart political positions, but such usage has come to be accepted as shorthand. We have referred above to Tone's use of 'Protestant' to signify members of the Established Church of Ireland and, in common parlance (and to the natural irritation of members of other Reformation traditions and of some Anglicans also) an Irish 'Protestant' betokens a member of that church, the generally accepted explanation for this usage being that Anglicans were the aboriginal Irish Protestants, some of whom passed through the Reformation experience in Ireland or came to the country at a time when the term 'Protestant' was commonly used to betoken the Established Church. There are certain marks common to the churches of the Reformation: an emphasis on scripture as containing 'all things necessary to salvation', for instance, and worship in the vernacular. But there is no 'Protestant Church' as has been well put by Peter Brooke: '... Protestantism is not a religion. There is no such thing as 'the Protestant Church' (except in the popular use of the term to refer solely to the Church of Ireland).'[36]

This anomaly was addressed in a General Synod report on sectarianism, when treating of the relationship between the Church of Ireland and the Orange Order:

The Orange Order declares itself to be:

'composed of Protestants, united and resolved to the utmost of their power to support and defend the Protestant religion.' The Church of Ireland is strongly supportive of efforts to promote the visible unity of the church. However, there is as yet no single body of doctrine uniting all those churches and groups calling themselves Protestant. The Church of Ireland reserves to itself the responsibility of defining, defending and interpreting in the light of Holy Scripture the Faith it has received.[37]

The Church of Ireland makes no claim to be 'the Protestant Church'. On the contrary, one can detect, certainly among younger members of the church in the Republic, a preference for the term 'Church of Ireland'. While 'Anglican' is now much more generally understood and accepted within the Church of Ireland than used to be the case, it is not how most parishoners would describe themselves in an Irish setting. (It has, of course, an appeal for those who have difficulty with the name 'Church of Ireland', itself inherited from establishment days.)

The foregoing semantic digression is more relevant to our purpose than might at first appear, when we look ahead to consider the benefits to Irish society that might accrue from the variety of religious traditions that now exist here.

Much depends on the minority having been 'integrated' rather than 'assimilated', integration meaning a reciprocal acceptance of 'belonging' inclusive of distinctiveness, assimilation representing a dilution of distinctiveness to the point of disappearance. But now we must ask, disappearance into what? The

Ireland of the twenty-first century differs greatly from that in which so many of the inherited attitudes in our society were formed. Terence McCaughey has written 'Protestants [and here the word is admissable] in Ireland should be the Christians who exercise the freedom afforded to them by not having to operate within the constraints involved in the Roman obedience, in order to say and do things which may help all of us towards a wider and more urgent discipleship.'[39] He has also stated that 'Calvinism has been the dominant form of Christian presence in South Africa among the Afrikaners and in Ulster among the Protestants.'[40] For better or worse, Anglicanism has been, and remains, the predominant form of 'Protestant' presence in the twenty-six counties of the Republic of Ireland. Numerically, the membership of the Church of Ireland in the Republic is much greater than that of the other Protestant churches. Furthermore, the Church of Ireland has a high profile, particularly in the capital city. The national cathedral of St Patrick is situated there and church administration centred there. Dublin is where the clergy of the Church of Ireland are prepared for ministry, and Dublin is the customary meeting place of the General Synod and most of its committees and councils. Nor is that profile restricted to the capital. Even where numbers are small, for reasons of history and in no small measure because of the continued presence of ministry, both episcopal and parochial, the Church of Ireland is frequently the most visible (sometimes only) Protestant presence and participant in local society. It is therefore to be expected that the Church of Ireland should have something to say to that society. But while Calvinism has a distinctive doctrinal system, what distinguishes Anglicanism is not a distinct corpus of doctrine, but its method of 'doing' theology. This has become increasingly evident in recent years, in no small measure due to the work of Archbishop Henry McAdoo. In the opening words of the preface to his seminal work, *The Spirit of Anglicanism*, MacAdoo wrote :

> Anglicanism is not a theological system and there is no writer whose work is an essential part of it either in respect of content or with regard to the form of its self-expression ... The absence of an official theology in Anglicanism is something deliberate which belongs to its essential nature, for it has always regarded the teaching and practice of the undivided church of the first five centuries as a criterion.[41]

McAdoo was a key figure, co-chairman, of the Anglican-Roman Catholic International Commission that resulted from a Common Declaration of Pope Paul VI and Archbishop Michael Ramsey in 1966. The ultimate purpose of the commission was and remains, 'the restoration of complete communion in faith and sacramental life'.[42] Lamentably, it would seem that ARCIC might never have existed, to judge from the level of public debate in the country on issues pertaining to Church of Ireland and Roman Catholic doctrinal differences. This disappointing (to put it mildly) amnesia has been especially apparent in discussion in the correspondence columns of the national press on such issues as that of President Mary McAleese receiving Holy Communion in Christ Church Cathedral, Dublin, and, more recently, the Dunboyne school affair. What can only be termed travesties of both the Roman Catholic and Anglican positions have marked debates that showed little sign, to date, of theological awareness.

Unlike those other Irish churches conditioned by the Reformation, the Church of Ireland retains what used to be called the 'historic episcopate' and its public worship is conducted according to set forms that follow a detailed pattern of the liturgical church year. It is an episcopal church with synodical government, in which the elected voice of the laity is strongly represented and crucial. Anglicanism is wrestling with the concept of 'authority' and acknowledges that there is much hard thinking to be done. But the Church of Ireland would be guilty of a *trahison des clercs* were it, in its dealings with the temporal powers, to neglect to demonstrate that its form of governance is not that of the Roman Catholic Church in miniature but rather is a representative, synodical one. While a convergence of Roman Catholic and Anglican theological thinking, such as ARCIC has presided over, is to be welcomed, a convergence of ecclesiologies is something to be treated with caution. In situations where Anglican teaching can appear to be in some disarray, the capacity to seek a form of 'magisterium' may have some appeal. Anglican churches are frequently accused of speaking with an uncertain voice and of giving a hesitant lead, and one can understand why this accusation is made. Yet such tentativeness is inevitable if what is glibly called 'freedom of conscience' is to have any meaning at all. There are non-negotiable articles of faith and practice, but even here questions of definition legitimately arise.

In a modern state such as the Republic of Ireland, where the forms of authority that previously bound society are questioned, and often disregarded, it is at least useful to put forward the idea that authority does not have to be exercised in the traditional mode.

Churches continue to be consulted by government. Approaches to government by ecclesial bodies tend to be welcomed, especially when they are ecumenical, but the Protestant contribution to public discourse on behalf of society as a whole is limited by scarcity of human and other resources. Can the Roman Catholic Church aspire to exercising a leading, yet inclusive rôle in Christian witness in the Republic of Ireland? It is well placed to do so by virtue of its numerical strength and the dedicated expertise of such organisations as the Conference of Religious of Ireland which other churches admire but cannot hope to match. Certainly, there are instances of inter-church consultation and co-operation when common interests are clear (and when an ecumenical voice is more likely to be heard). But at a time when the prophetic Christian voice needs to be heard in Ireland more than ever before, the 'scandal' of our divisions is no mere piece of ecumenical jargon.

The very size of the Roman Catholic Church, and the place that it holds in the hearts of many Irish people, ensure that its policies largely determine the fortunes of ecumenism here. Consider, for instance, the blossoming of inter-church relations in the immediate aftermath of Vatican II. Which is not for one moment to suggest that all obstacles to union come from Rome, or at any rate, Maynooth. It will be recalled that when attending the New Ireland Forum at Dublin Castle in 1984, representatives of the Roman Catholic hierarchy revealed that, had there appeared to them some hope of success, they would have considered seeking a derogation for the Irish church from some aspects of the rules governing mixed marriages.[43] Here was an acknowledgement of the divisive nature of those rules, and that such an approach to the Vatican was even considered is encouraging. More than that, it is consistent with the Vatican *Decree on Ecumenism*, issued in 1964, which referred to the 'hierarchy' of truths, the value of joint theological study, and the importance that all Christians 'since they bear the seal of Christ's name' must work together in social matters.[44]

Similarly encouraging is the eirenic tone in which the larger

Protestant churches now express their position *vis-à-vis* the Roman Catholic Church. The Church of Ireland has affirmed that '... in our search for unity in truth we continue to encourage growth in personal and community relationships between members of the Church of Ireland and people of all Christian traditions in Ireland, including those of the Roman Catholic Church.'[45] The Presbyterian Church, while not seeing much evidence of the radical changes that would be necessary to make any significant reconciliation between the two churches possible, 'rejoices' in the better relationships which are now experienced between Roman Catholics and Protestants in general,[46] and the Methodist Church has declared that 'joint worship, prayer and study has become an established fact in relationships with Roman Catholics', and that this has been an enriching experience for those involved.[47]

Such authoritative expressions of goodwill, like the hierarchy's statement at the forum, are not to be discounted. They betoken attitudes that are far in advance of those that existed fifty years ago. F. S. L. Lyons has already been cited. It is tempting to refer again to that essay of his, in which he quotes a statement by Henry Harrison, the doughty Parnellite who survived until 1954. According to Harrison,[48] the minority's hopes of exercising influence in the new state depended on 'whether they would prefer to rest upon their special position, which sometimes gives rise to comment and criticism, or to emerge into the broader paths of normal citizenship ...' Allusion has already been made in these pages to the challenge that faced the Protestant community of achieving integration rather than assimilation, and a good case can be made for claiming that integration has won. Perhaps a similar choice faces the ecclesiastical strategists?

CHAPTER FOUR

In the Middle Ground and Meantime:
A call to the Churches in Northern Ireland to find themselves on the edge

Geraldine Smyth OP

It is now twenty-one years since Eric Gallagher and Stanley Worrall in their prophetic study, *Christians in Ulster*, assessed the part played by the churches, and posited 'the Irish question' as 'the ultimate challenge to Christianity'.[1] While one may not hope to emulate their distinguished work, one can still profit from it, and in revisiting it, take some bearings from it. In their concluding chapter, entitled 'Churches on Trial', and in response to their question, 'What more might the churches have done?' they posed another rhetorical question: 'Might they not have adopted a more positive line of action to the process of secularis-ation that is beginning to take root in Ireland as it has already been doing elsewhere?'[2] In this observation, they pointed to 'the irony about the situation in which some of the more positive results of the secularising process – for example the principle of ignoring religious or political views in all contexts where they are irrelevant, such as employment, sport, social life, are just what Ireland needs to lessen its inter-communal tensions.' Gallagher and Worrall also noted that secularisation was regarded by the churches 'as a menace.' The churches showed an obdurate face in seeking to maintain their traditional rights and influence over all aspects of public life. The authors contended (quoting John Harriot) that the churches' wonted stance was one of draw-ing back from every issue where 'institutional sacrifice might be offered' and might make the necessary difference in a divided society. Some (deserved) recognition is accorded to the church's role when acting in the role of Good Samaritan during the worst times of civil strife and sectarian crisis, or when taking on the go-between role of shuttle diplomacy (*vis-à-vis* government, pol-itical parties and paramilitary organisations).

So, what has changed in twenty years? Certainly the political landscape has been transformed beyond recognition. Not even these prescient authors could have foreseen what can now be viewed as the single most significant change in the troubled history of Ireland and Britain – the signing in November 1985 of the Anglo-Irish Agreement by An Taoiseach, Garrett FitzGerald and Prime Minister Margaret Thatcher. That there could be meaningful ceasefires in the Autumn of 1994, followed by the signing of the Good Friday Agreement months later, and the establishment of a precariously stable power-sharing government in Stormont, proportionately representing the unionist-loyalist and nationalist-republican population were prospects then hidden from common mind and prophetic imagination.

To say that the churches have played little direct role in the achieving of such political transformation is no understatement. What then has been their social-political role? What, if anything, have they learned from secularisation and modernity about the respective roles of state, society and church or about the changed public significance and social forms of the church? Where do they find their place within contemporary society in Northern Ireland in this post-conflict period known as 'the peace process'? How can the churches hope to express themselves in theological and spiritual ways that meet the needs and aspirations of people caught up in unprecedented change, not only locally, but regionally and globally?

In exploring such questions, I shall first attempt an overview sketch of the socio-politico-religious context, offering some comment on the way religion functions in what Frank Wright termed an 'ethnic frontier society' – one in which relationships have been shaped and maintained in mutual deterrence. I shall then propose some theoretical approaches that have the potential to interrupt the patterns of mutual deterrence, if not reconcile the conflicting interests in this meantime period between conflict and reconstruction. Next, I shall focus on the church in its various social forms, through a critical and self-critical reflection on the social and theological place of the church in the public sphere on the threshold of this new millennium.

Socio-Politico-Religious Context:
Turning from Deterrence to Engagement
The first ceasefires in September-October 1994 interrupted what had been an almost unbroken wave of violent conflict stretching back for a quarter of a century. It is as difficult to forget as it is to

recapture those heady days and the disbelief that the end of the nightmare might be at hand. In retrospect, we know that it was not the end, but the beginning of the end. Despite the temporary breakdown in the IRA ceasefire (1996-1997) and subsequent breaches in loyalist paramilitary ceasefires, despite the unconscionable terror of the Omagh massacre, the peace process continues. The gains of the Good Friday Agreement have held, with the increasingly sturdy political arrangements on a threefold axis (Northern Ireland Assembly at Stormont, the North-South Ministerial Council and the Council of the Islands) have been operating to a degree of effective practice, that belies the intermittent posturing and histrionics in Stormont. The Parades' Commission continues to hand out balanced, though rarely popular, adjudications. De-commissioning has taken some significant steps. The stinging nettle of police reform has been grasped, and important new measures initiated of public recognition and redress towards victims and survivors. Within the larger scheme of things, we are indeed at the beginning of the end, even though, up close and more immediately, the sense lingers of being caught between two worlds – 'one dead, the other powerless to be born'.

It is important to keep proper perspective, therefore. We are still caught in what one conflict-transformation analyst terms, 'the accordion phenomenon', that dynamic in the de-escalation period of a protracted conflict in which the felt effect of the antagonists' coming into closer contact and exchange provokes the nervous reflex pull-back to familiar positions of securer distance.[3] This helps to explain, following the Good Friday Agreement, some intense residual manifestations of cultural separatism associated with marches and parades, with its now cliché-ed rhetoric of civil and religious liberties. Summer after summer, old conflicts are re-staged with accompanying paramilitary displays, sectarian violence and even killing. These have spread, possibly by orchestrated intent on the part of paramilitary groups in parts of Belfast, with few enough successes to report in mediation. Each group mirrors the intransigence of the other. In this reaction formation, there is a rebound to positions of safe cultural distance, a pattern of public mutual blaming, with each group digging itself into redoubtable positions of separate identity on ever-higher moral elevations.

Withdrawing Sanction for the Claims of 'Redemptive Violence'

Thus, in Northern Ireland's 'ethnic frontier society', relationships on many fronts have been structurally antagonistic. Whether turning upon views of the legitimacy of the state, human rights, cultural esteem, or political gain of any kind, within this pattern, one group seems axiomatically to structure itself and its political stance in opposition to the other group, each harking to Dublin or London in political terms and to its respective church tradition for bolster and ballast.[4] For much of the past century, social, economic and political relationships have been constrained by the threat of recurrent conflict, re-inscribed by religious justifications – whether through appeal to the Exodus-Promised Land-Covenant tradition on the part of Protestant unionists, or to the Victim-Resurrection-Martyr tradition on the part of Catholic nationalists. Even in periods between overt conflict, a negative peace reigned, a 'tranquillity of mutual deterrence'. This pattern was disrupted by the Civil Rights Campaign in the late 1960s and early 1970s, challenging state and civil society alike and calling time on a politics of the *Pax Romana*, where the victor dominated and the vanquished acquiesced. Notwithstanding the non-violent nature of this movement, politicised paramilitary conflict flared and spread. Now, clearly, there must be an eschewing of the pre-1969 unionist hegemony, and of any inverse majoritarian nationalism, for both can offer nothing but the false 'tranquillity of mutual deterrence'.

Walter Wink, in his interpretation of the biblical concept and symbolism of 'the Powers of this world', argues the need for a de-mythologising of the spurious claim that violence can deliver peace. Drawing on the work of René Girard, Wink construes salvation history as a long, faltering journey of God's chosen people away from thraldom to a culture of sacral violence to the transforming event of Jesus' voluntary self-giving on the cross, as the final sacrifice. Wink moves between different discourses, at ease in zones where culture, religion, violence and conflict transformation intersect, displaying some fluency in the diverse grammars of biblical theology, cultural mythology, political ideology, and making a trenchant critique of the positivist global systems of economics and geo-politics. With reference to the history of the twentieth century, he exposes the illusion of violence as effective or redemptive, in terms of religiously sanctioned violence and the self-defeating machinations to limit violence by the 'sacral control' of modern day victimisation rituals. Following upon the identification and killing of a scapegoat, a holding-period of deterrence is thus usually guaranteed, but is doomed to achieving but a temporary respite. This period of pseudo-tranquillity gives way to repetitions of the sacral violence, thus fuelling the relentless cycle of mimetic vengeance rather than bringing the promised redemption.[5]

The churches in Ireland need to examine this sacral legitimising of the cycle of violence. It is futile simply to condemn the violence 'out there' in an act of self-distancing. Rather is it imperative to discover how we Christians and churches are implicated in maintaining the violent dynamic, in segregated social locations, and through clinging to those identity-forming symbol structures which sustain old rivalries and scape-goating patterns that tend inexorably towards victimisation of 'the Other', with tribal notions of being a chosen people, of martyrdom as liberation, and of selectively adapted doctrines of salvation by exclusion. In such instances, false memory is kept alive through quasi-religious re-enactments of past or future triumph.

In the subsequent sections I wish to examine these cultural dynamics more closely, using a three-fold framework which takes the three anthropological realities of the human need for truth, identity and freedom as points of reference. In terms of this framework, one can also search out the conscious and unconscious ways in which such cultural dynamics are translated into three analogous theological and ecclesiological stances: which fail in faith, by asserting truth-claims in absolutist terms rather than in humble searching; which refuse the risks of hope, by sculpting group identity into custom-made tribalism rather than living icons of community, and which privatise the practice of love in opting for self-centred versions of freedom, rather than the open-ended hospitality to the outsider and stranger. Exploring these three axes of truth and meaning, identity and belonging, and the integration of social freedom and responsibility, one can argue more precisely for the withdrawal of the sanction of Christian discourse for relationships of mutual deterrence. This will demand of churches a three-fold movement of de-centring ('institutional self-sacrifice'): first involving self-critique and active recognition of other churches and traditions; second, symbolic gestures of repentance and empathy towards the other church; and third, new patterns of interdependence expressed in ecumenical relationship and hospitality. In this movement, churches are drawn beyond passive legitimation of violence to an active reconciling role in the process of peace-making.

Church in Society: Social Visions and Social Forms of the Church
Before returning to the threefold hermeneutic outlined above, some further observations must be made about the need for the churches to reclaim their social vision and examine their own conduct as social realities and sacred institutions which have long served to mirror and re-inscribe with mythico-sacral potency the historical patterns of mutual disregard, exclusion, and hostility. It is perhaps this very mythico-sacral potency which has disguised from the churches themselves the reality that they have frequently operated less out of an ecclesial vision of service, than as self-interested social entities.

In order to understand the theological and ecclesiological significance of the church in this 'meantime', it is necessary to acknowledge the ideological and sociological dynamics that come into view in our contemporary context in which so often the present and future are held captive by a closed history, and 'time' is allowed to overwhelm 'space'. Here, we seek specifically to find some new perspective on the church within a society in major transition. How can the church be the community of the New Creation, opening up to a new era, seeking a new social location, reshaping a theology that can engage both politics and life in its fullness?

In a useful study, Martin Marty quotes Karl Woyjtyla (later, John Paul II) who asserts that the church possesses both a 'special interiority' and 'a specific openness.'[6] The special interiority relates to its focus on Jesus Christ, and the common faith and sharing of its members, united across different contexts, in communion with all those who have gone before them through the ages. This interiority opens them to communion with God, and its specific language relates to worship and to witness. If this were the only mode of being and of language, the church would be in danger of becoming a sect, engaged in insider talk, taken up with its own growth and identity, keeping its back to the world.

The church, however, is also endowed with the gift of openness and connection to the world. This engagement takes place not wildly, but according to a certain discipline. Hence it is a 'specific' openness which does not break faith with its intrinsic life and being. To be open without discrimination runs the risk of cultural assimilation or of being swept hither and yon by the wind of prevailing ideology. While needing to be vigilant and not suffer the loss of its soul or squander its heritage to secularism, it is called to be open to the signs of the times. The church, for its own gospel integrity, must acknowledge horizons wider than itself and its own tradition. It is, in fact, impelled by its own vision and ethos to turn itself outwards and to address itself to the secular world (cf Isaiah 49; Matthew 24). Thus could Karl Barth (perhaps the first twentieth-century *contextual* theologian) urge Christians to hold the Bible in one hand and a newspaper in the other.

Many see the days of formal Christianity as numbered, at least in the Western world. There is no lack of statistics to corroborate the impression of falling practice – whether in regard to lowering attendance at church worship and slackening participation in church-related pursuits. Closer examination of the evidence, however, shows what is far from an open and shut case. This is not to argue simplistically that Christianity is alive and well in the West. Nevertheless, prophesies of twentieth century secularists that religion would soon be seen offstage by modernity and secularism, that dependence on religious symbol-structures would be cast off as people came of (modern) age, have not been fulfilled.[7] In Ireland, what seems to be emerging in such surveys is a) a continuingly strong avowal of religious experience as central to people's lives; b) an increased questioning of institutionalised religious practice and authority; c) a thin rather than 'thick' Christian culture (Geertz) expressed without a formal knowledge of Christian teaching; with only a tenuous understanding of the Christian substance of personal prayer and public worship; and a significant decrease in involvement in voluntary and social outreach.[8] There are serious implications here both in respect of the churches' actual self-understanding and also of their social forms. By implication, historic church divisions in Ireland are less and less viewed as justifiable on theological and doctrinal terms (whether on the basis, ironically, of the formal success of ecumenical dialogues, or by default, because of the advancing trend towards doctrinal ignorance and apathy). Such divisions – and particularly the more hostile expression of these divisions – will be explicable as little more than badges of cultural identity or political affiliation, untenable in meaningful theological terms.[9] It can be proposed, then, that if churches do indeed have a contribution – in partnership with other bodies – to the shaping of a middle ground between church and society, it needs to be grounded in a critical and self-critical quest for truth and meaning; in hope-filled public gestures of solidarity with those who are suffering; and in taking risks to cross boundaries both in expressions of social freedom and ecumenical outreach that include and liberate.

While this paradigm may seem ideal, it offers a horizon within which the church can understand itself as an eschatological sign of God's purpose for the world, as called and sent by Jesus Christ to embody in its own community narrative and outward relationships the vision and values of God's reign on earth. But it is a paradigm which can also be correlated to this-worldly social forms.

Martin Marty sheds light on this, proposing that in its social expression, Christianity (as any religion) can be seen to organise itself to differing degrees according to three forms:

1) a totalist form which sets out to impose itself on every aspect of a person's life – religious, personal, familial, social, political, economic.

2) a tribalist form which tries to counter the ubiquitous inroads of secularism by a re-inscribing of identity and the boundaries of identity in rigidly exclusive ways, in terms of separation from outsiders. This can involve shunning, antagonism, strong ethno-religious hostility, and even ethnic terrorism.

3) a privatist form which embodies the individualist turn that would frame everything in terms of individual choice, consumer control and free market economy, and reject the need for communal dimensions, whether in terms of constraint or support.

Marty demonstrates that the 'totalist' and 'tribalist' forms are based on an intense emphasis on the primacy of interiority. By contrast, the unencumbered privatist form, while seeming to stand for unlimited openness, actually shuts down the bases of a shared system of meaning and of belonging. Pressed further, it yields a de-centred individualism.

Arguably, this typology suggests distortions of the ecclesiological vision and values of confessing, belonging and witnessing such as proposed above. But, given the need, as argued, for the churches in Northern Ireland to pursue a self-critical hermeneutic of their social role, one finds here useful co-ordinates on the way to becoming peace-making churches in this new millennium.

Searching Together for Truth to Live by
The church is a community that offers people a context for encounter with and search for truth. As a community confessing faith in Jesus Christ, its creeds and symbols of faith emerged and have until now operated to give such meaning to the community of believers, who are above all an interpreting community, and know themselves in the light of the living memory of Jesus Christ who spoke of himself as the way, the truth and the life. For Václav Havel, 'living with/in truth' was a cornerstone of both his political vocation and spiritual aspiration, both challenge and gift.[10] Truth is not only the first casualty of war, but is elusive in the time following the conflict amid the struggle for the mutual understanding that leads to peace. It is not only politicians who have refined the art of combining the evasive answer with the self-justifying explanation. Across the board in public life (including those to the fore in the 'public church'), one observes a desire to hold on to the un-examined proposition or dominant opinion in preference to thoughtfulness and open-ended conversation.[11]

It is often remarked that the churches in Ireland have lacked vision, adopting an approach to truth that has encouraged acquiescence, while phrasing certain of their beliefs in ways that could be read as legitimating regnant ideologies of Orange and Green. On the Roman Catholic side, conservatism was consolidated by an absence of adult formation in biblical and theological understanding, and an approach to doctrinal truth that relied on unquestioned authoritarian propositions. For Protestants, truth claims were rooted in biblical claims to righteousness, interwoven with a history and ideology that stressed triumph and superiority in quasi-sacral terms. These were delineated in reciprocal antagonism and have functioned towards a favouring of religious absolutes which moved easily into the realm of political dogmatics and positivist accounts of history. Upheld by selective memories of 'chosen traumas' and 'chosen glories', one's own church's truth claims were cast as inerrantly right and those of the other unquestionably wrong. Thus, too, each group has vied with the other in constructing a calculus of pain wherein the suffering of one's own community at the hands of the other always weighed heavily in one's own favour. Thus, denominationally favoured doctrines, the large-scale canvas of history and small-scale record of local memory were infused with a totalising power. Yeats's comment is chillingly apt:

We had fed the heart on fantasies,
The heart's grown brutal from the fare;
More substance in our enmities
Than in our love ...[12]

In 1993, the Opsahl Commission (of which Eric Gallagher was an eminent and wise member) challenged both Roman Catholic and Protestant churches to make some self-limiting moves towards the other for the sake of contributing to peace and reconciliation. This was seen to involve respectively re-visiting doctrines and truth claims which operate according to cherished absolutes, whether in regard to Roman Catholic impositions upon interchurch marriages, or Protestantism's historic formulations against the Roman Catholic Church.[13] Recently, some have called for the setting up of a Truth and Reconciliation Commission in Ireland. It is a timely call, although it is hard to see how it would function, until there obtains an embedded constitutional consensus, not to speak of settlement. Certainly protagonists in South Africa's Truth and Reconciliation Commission saw the pre-establishment of a Government of National Unity as a *sine qua non*.[14]

The moment is now, nonetheless, to read the signs of the times and plant the seed of the idea, gleaning hope from other places once bogged down in despair. There is scope for some ground-breaking action in this regard, in which churches have a role: for example in moving to interpretations of history, liberated from the absolutist hermeneutics of the single vision. Now is the time to retrieve historic models and exemplars that refused the 'final solution' of overwhelming the Other into accepting the ascendant culture. Required rather are positive acts of recognition of the Other which assume no short-cuts through the philosophical field of 'the one and the many'. Church historians and theologians need to make further contributions alongside others, to develop an inclusive theology of memory, self-critical reflection and mutual accountability; joint educational projects aimed at mutual understanding and co-operation. The second centenary celebrations of the 1798 uprising represented a moment of opportunity and some churches, writers, political leaders and community artists did rise to the occasion, creatively co-operating to recover the memory of the uprising in terms of its best ideals. They sought to liberate memory, whether from Protestant amnesia or from Catholic Gaelicisation, and from its captivity to the later superimposed ideology of physical force Irish Republicanism,[15] and also liberating the Protestant United Irishmen from the historic limbo to which they had been condemned – in Tom Paulin's glum phrase – to 'endure posterity without a monument'. Clearly, in the 'mean-time' in which churches now find themselves, the forging of a reconciled society will much depend on the de-commissioning of set minds and the relinquishing of one-sided certainties in favour of truth that is complex, many-in-one, sustained by a baptised imagination and capable of living in the tensions of paradox. One thinks here of Yves Congar, the twentieth-century Dominican theologian who suffered at the hands of church authorities not well-endowed with such capacities. Reflecting on truth as a project of reconciliation (and quoting the physicist Nils Bohr) Congar asserted that, whereas the opposite of a true proposition is a false proposition, the opposite of one profound truth may be another profound truth.

In the context of the peace process, we can call to mind the differing emphases in churches of the Reformed tradition and the Roman Catholic Church in regard to doctrines and practices that have taken on new levels of contentiousness in the context of political conflict – for example, misconceptions about how the other church approaches the forgiveness of sins or funeral rituals (occasions to celebrate the life of the one who has died and comfort the bereaved; or occasions to pray for forgiveness of sins on behalf of the one who has died, and comfort the bereaved). The writings of the Interchurch Group on Faith and Politics have provided some clarification here, in showing how stereotyped mutual interpretations have provoked no end of confusion and hurt. Sharing more freely our respective understanding of such doctrines can only be of benefit. It would be helpful too for Protestants and Catholics to explore together what they hold deeply in common, alongside specific differences. Helpful here is Paul Tillich's interpretative paradigm of 'Protestant Principle

Catholic Substance', which gives some explanation of the differentiated preference of Roman Catholics for additional sacramental and devotional substance in the expression of their faith, and of Protestant preference for greater simplicity, clarity and austerity in the same regard.[16]

It is a sociological axiom that internal differences tend to be suppressed in times of conflict. Churches in Ireland are currently confronting an unwonted pluralism and divergence from within. This throws into bold relief fundamental issues of authority and participation. In those very situations where a prophetic voice of truthfulness is needed, such voices are often marginalised. An illustration may avail.

In 1997/8, the Glencree Centre for Reconciliation conducted a follow-up enquiry to the Opsahl Commission's specific challenges to the churches. Those of us on the panel receiving submissions from churches and church bodies, as well as other individuals, noticed that almost all those presenting, although generally the appointees of their church, felt constrained to begin with a disclaimer, that what they had to say did not represent the consensus view of their church. While there was usually a tough-mindedness on the part of each group of contributors, one also sensed a weariness arising from their long struggle in the task of promoting mutual understanding, as too, a self-doubting as to how far they were supported, as to how far their church was imprisoned within structures. This question of authority was almost palpable: the authority of experience, the authority of the gospel, or of a given church's tradition (with its preferred hermeneutical keys), and of how to stand authoritatively amid the plurality of positions within local congregations, or within different levels and offices of jurisdiction. In respect of the churches functioning as social entities, one was aware of the tension between gospel authority and the dynamics of human power.

The disclaimers, the fact that there were no senior church representatives present, and that the 'delegates' were usually drawn from the most significant of their church committee structure, left the panel with the impression that the church authorities were not prepared to take such an independent process with either seriousness or trust. Even taking into account the reality of different structural approaches of church order across traditions, the impossibility of accessing views that bore a mod-

icum of official authority bespoke the churches' increasing in-
capacity to transcend their own institutional weight. What I
have described as 'a structural density and procedural deficit'
was clearly evident.[17] At a time when politicians are failing to
galvanise the trust necessary for overcoming nightly hostile
attacks across community interfaces, it is to be lamented that
churches likewise are failing to speak and act with authority.
The voice that should speak boldly of peace and justice prevari-
cates and is not heard.

It is a modern pastime in Ireland to rail gratuitously against
church leaders and structures. That is not the intention here.
Churches in Ireland, as anywhere, are themselves grappling
with the tension of remaining faithful to a founding vision
through changing generations, and struggling to ensure that
ecclesial institution and gospel charism are held in relationship.
Swelling the chorus of disapproval avails nothing, and we who
are members of the church are all implicated. One recognises the
dilemma, but if churches wish to influence reconciliation in the
public domain, they need to find meaningful ways of speaking
with an authority appropriate to their tradition and calling, and
to be more visible with interchurch initiatives. Until this malaise
is addressed churches will find themselves speaking in code or
behind closed doors, contributing little to the desperately needed
public practice of dialogue, failing in their vocation to live within
the truth.

Zygmunt Bauman, writing from the perspective of a sociolo-
gist confronting the challenges of modernity and postmodernity
to the human need for truth and meaning, offers some apt insights which may be used here by way of summarising this section. Speaking of truth as a social relation, he contends that the
pursuit of truth in recent centuries as a means to universal
claims and a 'design for certainty' has been a project of dominance and the subjugation of otherness, justified in terms of
order overcoming chaos, but leading paradoxically to the emergence of ever greater ambivalence and alterity.[18] In a context
where all are called to self-reflection and to some more humble
and dis-interested approach to truth, the place in one's belief system for contingency rather than certainty becomes significant.

We are currently witnessing the collapse of many steadfast
certainties in Northern Ireland, in the face of which – and as the
level of social anxiety and insecurity rises – those in positions of

political or religious influence have a crucial role to play. Too often, they replay old dogmas, exploit people's fears, rather than encouraging their communities to participate in shaping the new vision and allowing their distinctive values creative play in the process of change.

Perhaps the primary role of leaders in times of social upheaval is to be interpreters of the change, and to help their communities to make sense of the losses in the light of a compelling vision rooted in faith.

Contingency as the Condition of Hope:
Letting go of the Losses; Discovering a New Belonging
Whenever groups feel betrayed at the collapse of a system which in former times was or seemed all-sufficient, that is the time for political, civic and church leadership to help them *to make sense of the losses*. But so too to help them *to grieve for the losses*, to learn hope in accepting vulnerability as the hidden path to life on the far side of contingency – whether in the light of the life, death and resurrection of Jesus Christ, the insights of human sciences, or even the pragmatics of political pressure. Sometimes, as Bauman says, we can transfer contingency from the vocabulary of 'dashed hopes' into that of the 'opportunity', from the language of domination to that of emancipation.[19] Citing Agnes Heller, Bauman urges the need for accepting contingency and making of it our destiny:

> A society has transformed its contingency into its destiny if the members of this society arrive at the awareness that they would prefer to live at no other place and at no other time than the here and now.[20]

These words touch into the underlying challenge of the peace process as concerning people in their differences of faith and politics seeking to discover new meaning, to find hope for living beyond domination, and to risk sharing the same space. There is some echo too of Jesus' intimation of the grace of truth, even when it is bitter: 'The truth will set you free.' It will demand a turning away from the dry cisterns of a past golden age in favour of the cold-water contingencies of the here and now. The church too is a community of *belonging*, whose members gather and celebrate the life, death and resurrection of Jesus Christ. An identifying characteristic of Christian discipleship is the hope generated through standing together in the gap of suffering, and letting go to what feels like chaos and collapse, entrusting one-self to the deeper, fuller life that may be emerging (Matthew 10:38ff; Philippians 2:3-11).

In the contemporary resurgence of identity politics from Belgrade to Belfast, community leaders are called to steer a course that upholds particular community belonging, without falling prey to exclusiveness; that enables their people to express trust, encouraging them to surrender security whenever it has degenerated into an end in itself. This process recognises the necessity of boundaries but also the need for re-defining bound-aries in face of changing situations. Churches, like any other social group, need to be bi-lingual – confident in the identity-forming processes of their own internal language and symbolic practice – yet able to communicate with those who operate ac-cording to other grammars of confession, celebration and wit-ness, but with whom other social and cultural realities are shared. Walter Brueggemann, adverting to a paradigmatic bibli-cal story (2 Kings 18-19), develops the double metaphor in this regard of an intimately coded language for use within the wall of one's own community, and a different more public language of communication across the wall with those (erstwhile ene-mies) beyond the wall with whom we must parley for the sake of the well-being of the group and indeed the common good. Given that the church is called to a specific openness and to an inward and outward orientation, this seems self-evident. Churches today are equally liable to lose themselves in sectarian self-iden-tifications or through immersion in secularist ideologies or the compulsion of consumerism.[21] There are examples to hand of churches beset by fundamentalist religious reflexes, while es-pousing to the point of idolatry the prevailing political ideology. South African churches have admitted as much, and in Ireland churches have let themselves stay captive to 'the false allure of benign apartheid' – as well as to its more malignant forms.[22]

There is scope here to make but brief observations on the role of churches in identity formation, identity securing and identity transcendence. It is not uncommon for those who urge diversity as a welcome enrichment to point to the more frequent phenom-enon in Ireland of 'identity-in-opposition', whether within or between communities. Embattled communities typically culti-vate identifying features to distinguish themselves over against the Other, while neglecting resources within their tradition which would enable them to confront the perceived threat more creatively. Vamik Volkan (adducing Freud's 'narcissism of minor differences') illustrates the peculiar, even tragic lengths to which opposing protagonists of a protracted ethnic conflict will resort in bolstering group cohesion or satisfying aggression through the narcissistic cultivation of such small differences.[23]

As official institutions, churches here have through custom or comfort identified with the pervading culture, whether of nationalist or unionist hue. They have derived some self-import-ance as rallying-powers. Rather than lifting their eyes beyond their own boundaries to interpret the new signs with prophetic vision, they have too often failed to tackle the causes of the sec-tarian cancer gnawing away at the vital substance of church and society.

Thus, much of the social activity of the churches is linked to church space and property, tribal in effect if not intention. So, for example, in the case of the Loyal Orders, chaplains have tradi-tionally been appointed and church property used. Comparably, Catholic nationalism has been sacralised at religious graveside commemorations,[24] and there has traditionally been strong clergy support of nationalist sports bodies.[25] While there are indeed valid arguments to be made in favour of the existent available choice of denominationally-based education, some of the docu-mented evidence, in the early years of the Integrated Schools Movement, of punitive attitudes and practices of some church pastors towards the founding members of this movement are shaming: the ignoring of requests for a meeting; the withholding of the normal opportunity for children to make First Communion and Confirmation; the un-preparedness to appoint chaplains, amounted to non-recognition of the new sector, showing such stances to be determined by sectarianism rather than impelled by a confident catholicity. Speaking at a confer-ence sponsored by the Faith and Politics Group, 7 March 2000, Garrett FitzGerald observed:

> While it is true that at the highest level the main churches in Ireland have endeavoured to ... co-operate in rejecting and resisting violence, on both sides there has also been a far too ready political identification with their own flocks, which at times has involved unambiguously political statements by one or other church. Moreover insistence on maintaining religious divisions in society, e.g. through the educational

system, together with the Catholic Church's insistent application of its mixed marriage code, even in the muted form that
this now takes, have been most unhelpful in Northern
Ireland.[26]

Appealing for a sense of historical perspective in overcoming
four- to twelve-hundred year old cultural divisions, the former
Taoiseach urged that these divisions ought not to be exacerbated
by appeal to religion, and that 'Christian churches should be
healing forces rather than ancillary sources of continued bitter-
ness and division.' Making comparison between Northern
Ireland, Yugoslavia and the Ukraine in regard to this general ecclesiastical unhelpfulness, Dr FitzGerald doubted whether, 'in
these areas of deep-seated division the various churches... are
doing as much as they might be expected to do as Christians to
heal divisions and to practice the Christian love they preach' (p
22). Today, one awaits without high expectation the response of
the churches to recent research, illustrating the reality that children as young as two are being socialised into sectarian attitudes
and speech with deepening intensity with each year of age. This
research confirms the need for attending to the two most influential formative contexts for children – the family and the
school. Will the churches see that these grim findings might
have a specific message for them? Are they too blind to see; too
imprisoned within confessional structures to notice?[27]

Yet, that is the increasing perception as evidence mounts.
Garrett FitzGerald echoes the Worrall and Gallagher reference
to the churches' tendency to avoid issues where 'institutional
sacrifice' was demanded. So too, the University of Ulster research (Duncan Morrow *et al*) gives similar conclusions about
the churches' slowness to accept responsibility. Clergy who
were interviewed, while acknowledging a need for social interaction with the 'other community', ascribed little importance to
interchurch relationships, often expressing expectations that the
other group should change first.[28] This testifies once more to an
ecclesial self-understanding rooted in self-sufficiency and the
doctrinally ill-founded belief that churches somehow are ex-
empt from the self-examination and systemic change demanded
nowadays of virtually every public body from the civil service to
the police.[29]

The research of Cecelia Clegg and Joseph Liechty demonstrates the churches' responsibility for securing sectarianism,

despite their strenuous disavowals. Cecelia Clegg and Doug Baker are now offering those at different levels of church leadership some formal and systematic opportunity for institutional self-reflection, inter-church meeting and partnership in transforming sectarianism.[30] One way of construing this is to see the social form of the church in the North as captive to its divided history, too prone to sacrifice the present to the past, and insufficiently prepared to give shared leadership on how to co-operate practically within the contested space and make of it a common civic home. Recently, when I asked a highly committed Christian, active in the field of peace education and ecumenical reconciliation, as to whether there were any new signs of churches becoming more seriously committed *as churches*, there was a long pause, and then the observation in a tone suggesting that it gave her no pleasure to admit it: 'The churches just aren't there.'

Working in Partnership for Social Freedom?
Reconciliation in the Public Sphere
In this post ceasefire period, Northern Ireland has more fully experienced many aspects of modernity which the Troubles had disguised. It is now witnessing the privatisation of religious freedom, pluralism in social choices and the professionalisation of public action. There, as more widely in the West, leaders are judged, not alone on their capacity to 'function' in a professionally competent manner within their specific sphere, but also on their ability to perform effectively and make a public impact on problems arising in other specialist spheres (such as economics or politics) – acting as representatives and contributing in a contemporary society where influence is no longer determined by social (or religious) stratification, where inherited authority and hierarchies controlled knowledge and secured their own ruling interests.

This does not simply mean that the churches, and especially those in positions of social responsibility, can find themselves pulled in opposite directions – inwards and outwards (the need to be 'bilingual' has already been noted). So also, in this time of change, it is essential that churches no longer pretend to claim the total field of people's lives, that they acknowledge the complexity of their members' commitments, and welcome the differentiation of knowledge and interests within and across communities. They can facilitate people's contributions beyond the old religious hierarchies and social stratifications, and be prepared themselves to work collaboratively with other bodies in the construction of the public sphere. This will require humility and some openness to being themselves changed through honest searching, dialogue, and willingness to engage creatively in civic ventures of reconciliation.[31] Almost ten years into the peace process, there is still a sense of precariousness, of life in the balance, and churches are called to enter into processes of reflection, self-surrender and solidarity, without which neither social nor ecclesial transformation can be sustained.

I would argue that the witness dimension of mutual understanding, dialogue and co-operation *between the churches* is intrinsic to the possibility of socio-political transformation, and also at the heart of what it is to be the church of Jesus Christ. The flourishing of the churches and their mission will depend on their willingness to engage within a changing social paradigm that is not governed by the unquestioned centre-holds of authority, but according to a highly differentiated system that is plural in perspective, multi-centred in regard to the exercise of freedom and constraint, and in which communities live in overlapping, multi-layered contexts of responsibility, decision and risk.

Those in pastoral leadership must be aware that they are socially located, alongside politicians, educators, the media, social movements and the leisure industry in appealing or competing for people's involvement. They need to recognise that they can no longer expect to operate as the controlling centre, as an unassailable given in the lives of their congregations, still less in public life. If the churches are to be able to exercise their role as churches in what one social theorist has referred to as our 'runaway world', it is urgent that they gain some purchase on what is happening at this deeper structural level in the social system, to accept that they are part of that whole process of upheaval and transformation, not apart from it. To fail to do so would be to betray their inner call and jeopardise their public mission. Jesus proposed that the church was to be a community whose members would be recognised by their love of others, for their willingness to reach across the boundaries of race, gender and social difference, open to the stranger and ensuring justice for the oppressed.

As intimated earlier, churches seem unable or unwilling to

risk themselves in involvement in processes beyond their direct
control, or afraid to give a lead in projects that require critical
self-examination or social questioning, or that would demand
sustained boundary-crossing with other churches in response to
community crises, or to the call to share convivially the life of
Christ's New Creation. It can be acknowledged that, encouraged
by EU-based visions of social inclusion, cultural diversity, empowerment and reconciliation, and helped by outside facilitation, some individual churches and church-based partnerships
have begun to move in this direction, and are in some instances
taking their place alongside the many groups and movements in
joint efforts to overcome sectarian existence and violence, to
generate expressions for community creativity, and release the
springs of social vitality gone underground in the sheer struggle
to survive the wasteland days of the Troubles. But these are still
the exception, lamentably, when the key to a way forward for
churches is via partnership and participation. Grasping after denominational autonomy is the way of false freedom and isolationism, a sign of modernity gone wrong, rather than the mark
of reconciliation and justice proclaimed by Jesus as the sign of
God's reign on earth.[32]

The churches can also draw freely and learn from the insights of other professions and sectors, from academic and com-
munity-based research, from the imaginative initiatives of
artists, from the commercial or Trades Unions sector, or new
voluntary initiatives on social and economic need. They have
much to learn from the perseverance of women's and community-
based projects, which have often prepared a prophetic way for
others – including churches and organs of state – to follow. Yet,
one must still lament the absence of strong structural church
support or involvement in such initiatives of spiritual comfort
and compassion as, 'An Crann/The Tree', a project rooted in
personal narratives of pain by those who had survived trauma
or bereavement.[33] It was such initiatives as this, or another
memorial exhibition, entitled 'The Cost of the Troubles', which
paved the way – eventually – for the semi-state consultative
commissions to engage the issues of reparation to relatives of
victims, and processes of memorialisation. So too, in respect of
the 'Healing Through Remembering Project', one must again
pose the question, 'Where were the churches?'

The recently published report of the 'Healing Through

Remembering' project represents a salutary gathering together of proposals for public rituals and processes of truth recovery, the healing of memories, and ways of celebrating people who have broken new ground in the process of recognition, reconciliation and justice. Such recommendations, emerging from the consultation process, as memorials, an annual Day of Reflection, public and collective commemorations, social policy, education initiatives, community and intercommunity interactions, represent a wealth of ideas for thoughtful, compassionate and creative engagement from many individuals and organisations. Fr Kevin Mullen, a priest deeply involved in the trauma of the people of Omagh, was one of the commission members. Too, the 'Four Church Leaders' gave interviews, and there were submissions from the Irish Council of Churches, and from a few theologians. But there is no sense emanating from the report of the churches' integral involvement. The suspicion again arises that the church committees which did make submissions were marginal rather than central to the respective churches' structures of political and social responsibility, carrying little institutional weight. The vast majority of submissions came from civic rather than ecclesial bodies, and were couched largely in a language devoid of religious or ecclesial resonance. Did the churches as churches once more miss the moment?

Given the nature of the issues and given the traditional role of churches in the 'cure of souls', in the practice of symbolic rituals of healing and transformation, or of the journey from death to new life, this must give Christians and churches pause for self-examination: why the absence of an overtly religious idiom and of any specifically church-related role or proposal? Was it those with decision-making power or influential church groups who balked at the challenge; afraid that the mirror might be held up to institutional practice or past complicity; faint-hearted at the prospect of showing themselves inept in the handling of painful tensions and delicate choices regarding inclusion and exclusion; fearful, perhaps that the expectation of sharing of platforms or pulpits would expose political ambiguities and theological differences within their own ranks – or worse still that the cost would entail loss of members, or necessitate compromise of dearly-nursed but dying custom? Were the churches perceived to be too politically aligned, or indeed incapable of making the necessary institutional sacrifice? Are churches now deemed marginal to the main issues, out of touch, irrelevant? Have they been replaced, because they had already in fact vacated the public space, leaving gestures of repentance, forgiveness and the restoration of justice to more courageous secular groups? Is their role more properly a more modest one, alongside, among others, rather than leading? Do churches know that they are missing and not much missed, that in the sad perception of the peace agent – 'The churches just aren't there'?

Whatever the answers to these questions – and one suspects that they will be complex rather than simple answers, positing still more questions – the distinctive involvement of the churches *vis-à-vis* such public enterprises of reconciliation and the creation of a new society has changed little in twenty years. Judging from this 'Healing Through Remembering' report, as from that of the Glencree Believers' Inquiry or of the Opsahl Commission already mentioned, the lack of any deep-seated impetus to change confronts us, as it did twenty years ago in the pages of Worrall and Gallagher's *Christians in Ulster*. In ways, churches continue to act as if they were at the centre, whereas they are more often positioned on the sidelines, making the same old signals, unaware that the rules of engagement have changed, or that many of the players have been replaced. Churches are not to be found at the heart of the human action and passion, in the zones of marginality where people cry out for healing and new life. The distinctive Christian voice has fallen as silent as Zachary's, but no new birth seems at hand.

In this 'mean-time' between violence and peace, there is a pressing need for churches, and not just the many committed Christians, to take their place alongside other groups and organisations, collaborating with them in building a new 'middle-ground', letting their voice be heard in free debate, ready to listen across boundaries, within and without, and especially to those on the far margins. There are many with the gifts and competences within the churches from whom those in authority in the churches could profitably learn and be enriched. This was Christ's vision of a community of discipleship. Paul's image of the church as one body with many members and different functions, under the power of the Spirit working unto good (1 Cor 13:12-31) is unequivocal. The overtones here of the body politic can be read as implying the need for church groups to work in partnership with, rather than in opposition to other social movements and public bodies. This does not mean that they should lack confidence in speaking out of their own wisdom and faith, ready to draw from their store-house things both new and old – theological, ethical and liturgical riches that can deepen the process of living within the truth, sharing creatively from their symbolic resources in the wider task of reconciliation. It explicitly calls them to risk themselves in co-sponsoring projects characterised by openness to the Other, participation and a free exchange of life between centres of power and the sites of struggle. Perhaps the key question for churches is whether they now bunker down inside their chosen trench or discover themselves with others on the edge.

CHAPTER FIVE

Interpreting the Divorce Debates: Church and State in Transition[1]

Linda Hogan

The unique intertwining of the Irish state and the Catholic Church is nowhere more evident than in relation to marriage and the family. Although one may interpret recent Irish history as involving the gradual separation of the Irish state and the Catholic Church, the situation in relation to marriage is rather more complicated. It is more complicated because of the evidence from the divorce debates of the 80s and 90s that affinity with the church's position on divorce was far stronger than any commentators had expected. Moreover, since the vast majority of marriages in the state are still contracted according to Catholic norms, political discussions of the nature and regulation of marriage have inevitably been conducted in the context of this cultural and demographic dominance. The unspoken assumptions that shape Catholic thinking on marriage have thus been embedded in the social fabric of Irish life so that recent attempts to untangle the theological from the political in relation to marriage have had to negotiate difficult territory.

The encounters between the churches and the state on marriage and divorce have certainly been divisive. Two referenda to delete the constitutional ban on divorce were held within ten years, once in 1986 and again in 1995. Despite opinion poll indications early in 1986 that 61%[2] favoured the deletion of the constitutional ban on divorce contained in Article 41.3.2, the first referendum was defeated by 63.5% to 36.5%. In 1995 it was only carried with 50.3% voting in favour and 49.7% voting against. This was by any calculation an extremely narrow margin. Moreover, while the major clash between the institutional Catholic Church and the state was on the introduction of civil divorce, issues of nullity, bigamy and mixed marriages further complicated the field. The debates of the 1980s and 1990s were fascinating for many reasons. On the one hand we were grappling with complex sociological issues. They ranged from the effects of marital breakdown, to the renegotiation of the roles of men and women within marriage, to the changing demographics of a country that had emerged from decades of economic stagnation and isolationism. At the same time we were confronting again the cultural dominance of the Catholic Church and the implications of that for the rights of minorities, the common good and the value of pluralism. These distinct issues were enmeshed in the debates of the 80s and 90s. As a result the question of the appropriate state response to marital breakdown was transformed into a debate about the relationship between the Catholic Church and the Irish state, especially given Catholicism's unique position as the religion of the majority of citizens.

The Political Situation
With the enactment of the 1937 Constitution of Ireland, the boundaries between ecclesiastical and civil law in relation to marriage were blurred. This blurring is still evident in the normal practice of holding only one ceremony, during which the sacramental and civil aspects of a marriage are contracted. In the Irish state religious officiators also act as registrars of civil marriage, thereby becoming the main state officials for marriage. Moreover, since the majority of marriages are contracted in the Catholic Church, it is Catholic priests who in the main act in this dual role. This is in marked contrast to the practice in most countries where the ecclesiastical and civil aspects of marriage constitute two separate ceremonies, reinforcing the point that for many people marriage is both a religious and a civil event. But in Ireland, both actually and symbolically the two are elided. There is no doubt that this conflation of church and state has deeply affected the social construction of marriage and was especially problematic when marital breakdown occurred. Until 1995 the only way to end a marriage in Ireland was by obtaining a nullity decree, either through a civil or ecclesiastical process, or both. Judicial separation formalised under the Judicial Separation and Family Law Reform Act 1989 did provide a further mechanism for dealing with marital breakdown, but it did not free individuals to enter another marriage. The situation improved, however, in 1995 when Article 41.3.2 of the Constitution was repealed.

Yet because of the coincidence of civil and ecclesiastical law the politics of annulment was complex. During the no divorce years in Ireland there was a huge increase in the numbers of couples seeking church annulments. This led to the suspicion that annulment was being chosen more because it was the only way to end a marriage rather than because it was a true description of the relationship from the beginning. This suspicion was accentuated when the church gradually extended the 'psychological grounds' on which it believed that a person may be unable to enter into a marriage. Moreover, Sheila Rauch Kennedy's book *Shattered Faith* provided further claims that nullity procedures within the church itself were being abused so as to provide divorce for Catholics under another name.[3] From the 1970s onwards a significant number of couples availed of church nullity procedures, although they had no effect in civil law. Sometimes couples also sought a judicial separation to formalise the maintenance and support aspects of the annulment. Since a church annulment had no standing in civil law, it had no impact on the status of children born, since in the eyes of the state they were born within a legally contracted and still extant marriage. Moreover, the status of the children of the annulled marriage was not affected in canon law either. Repeating the earlier Code of Canon Law, the 1995 code states that parties seeking a declaration of nullity of their marriage should be assured that 'should their marriage be declared invalid, the status of children born of that marriage is in no way affected.'[4] Earlier, in Canon 1137, it states that such children 'are always regarded as legitimate'. Some who sought church annulments may have feared that their children would then become children born outside of wedlock. However this was not the case in either canon or civil law.

However, in Ireland a further complication pertained. The absence of civil divorce prior to 1995 meant that in cases where marriages were annulled there was no mechanism for dissolving the civil contract of marriage. Even if the church declared the first marriage null and void, in the eyes of the state the original marriage was the only one it recognised. Therefore couples who married in church after their first marriages were annulled were, in the eyes of the state, in bigamous unions. Neither the second spouse nor any children born had any rights in relation to support, maintenance or inheritance. In other jurisdictions couples usually have the civil aspects of the first marriage dissolved and are therefore free both civilly and ecclesiastically to enter into a second union. However, the absence of civil divorce in Ireland meant that this was not an option. Of course there were some situations in which a couple could apply for a nullity decree from both the civil and ecclesiastical courts. However, according to Rosemary Horgan, 'the draconian legal consequences attaching to nullity, including the higher burden of proof, and the length of such proceedings' meant that this was not an option chosen by very many.[5] The fact that those involved in these second unions were not prosecuted, while welcome on pastoral grounds, further reinforced the strength of the symbiotic relationship between the Catholic Church and the Irish state. The introduction of civil divorce meant that at least this anomaly could be dealt with and the situation regularised much in the same way as is done by Catholics in most other countries. There is no doubt that through these decades Article 41.3.2 had great significance in that it was regarded as a *de facto* privileging of Catholicism since resistance to civil divorce is characteristic of, if not unique to the Catholic Church. Reformed churches differ in their approaches to the remarriage of divorced persons and a number have, in recent years, relaxed their rules to permit the remarriage in church of divorced persons. However, even before this change they mostly supported the provision of civil divorce on the grounds of the autonomy of the state and the requirements of the common good.[6] Thus although what some might regard as an unhealthy closeness between the civil and sacramental aspects of marriage still pertains, the introduction of civil divorce has been a significant milestone in effecting a change in relations between the Catholic Church and the state.

During the referenda debates there was much discussion of the likely impact that the introduction of civil divorce would have on the institution of marriage, without any mention of the impact of ecclesiastical divorce. No doubt it is still too early to reach meaningful conclusions on this issue. Moreover, it will be difficult to assess the impact that a remedy for breakdown has on marriage, when there was no prior investigation of the impact of marital breakdown itself or the anomalies of the Irish situation on the institution of marriage. Still more difficult will be to isolate this aspect amid the diverse causative factors that shape societal trends. Notwithstanding the issues relating to marriage itself, the debates also provide an interesting lens through which to investigate the nature of a church in transition and a state rethinking its inherited relationship with that dominant church. The issues raised by each of these transitions go to the heart of the nature of Irish society in the late twentieth century and, although many merit reflection, it is on the theological aspects of the debates of the 1980s and 1990s that the remainder of this essay will be focused. I will limit the discussion to two of the key concerns, one relating to the church's relationship with the wider society, the other focused on an internal church matter. The first is the issue of pluralism, minority rights and the common good. The second is the nature of the Catholic hierarchy's articulation of its position on divorce and the significance that has for the broader church.

Pluralism, Minority Rights and the Common Good
Since its foundation the relationship between the Irish state and the Catholic Church has gone through many changes. The general view[7] is that the 1937 constitution sedimented a particular version of that relationship in which the demographic dominance of Catholicism was reflected in the country's political, legal and cultural infrastructure. One example is the 1937 constitution which inserted a ban on civil divorce, thus diminishing the rights that Irish subjects held under British rule whereby citizens could petition Westminster Parliament to dissolve a marriage on certain restricted grounds.[8] The intervening decades provided other examples of the workings of this unique relationship, one which was detrimental to both church and state. These intervening decades also wrought changes in a different direction within Catholic theology, particularly in terms of how pluralism was approached. Changes in the church's attitude to religious freedom and consequently to different religious traditions facilitated a less antagonistic reaction to pluralism. Yet, although one could not regard the history of these decades as one uninterrupted narrative of progress, nonetheless there was a gradual softening in the church's attitude to religious (even if not to moral) pluralism.[9]

In the Irish context the submissions of the Catholic bishops to the 1984 New Ireland Forum and the interventions during the 1986 divorce referendum campaign provide an insight into the evolving thinking on pluralism, minority rights and the common good. In consulting on how a lasting peace and stability could be established, the Forum attempted to deal with the perception that the Republic was in some respects a sectarian state in which the values and rights of the Protestant minority were neither respected nor promoted.[10] All the churches were invited to make submissions and the Catholic hierarchy, with the aid of some Catholic lay people, did so in February 1984. The core of the Catholic Church's position hadn't changed much. It insisted that it did not seek to have the moral teaching of the Catholic Church become the criterion for constitutional change, or to have Catholic principles enshrined in civil law. What they did seek however was the right 'to alert the consciences of Catholics to the moral consequences of any proposed piece of legislation ... while leaving to the legislators and to the electorate their freedom to act in accordance with their consciences'.[11] The issue of divorce figured largely in the submission, both because there was a growing expectation that the government would call a referendum to delete Article 41.3.2, and because it was one of the most glaring examples of Catholic principles being enshrined in civil law. Here the hierarchy's response was guarded. It would not say whether it would oppose the deletion or not and its consistent line was that if it did oppose it, it would be on the basis of the harm to society, rather than on the basis of church teaching. In the event the church did strongly oppose the referenda both times, although at the official level it was very careful to avoid telling people how to vote. Throughout the hearings the value of pluralism and the rights of minorities were invoked in the abstract. Yet when the church delegation was questioned about how the values of pluralism and minority rights might be embodied in practice they were reluctant to develop their position. For example, no serious consideration was given to the possibility that civil divorce for those whose consciences and religions permitted it may be a legitimate embodiment of the value of pluralism. Instead the limitation of the common good was invoked as a restriction on pluralism and minority rights.

A notoriously ambiguous concept, the common good has been endlessly invoked in Catholic ethics to limit expressions of difference. Yet the understanding of the common good throughout the bishops' submissions was seriously deficient, particularly because it implied a kind of majoritarianism that is anathema to the common good. For example, Dr Cassidy explained 'the common good is all about people, [that it is] about the greatest happiness of many, many people, [that it is about] the values and institutions which inspire and sustain us in our daily lives'.[12]

However, one would have to question this understanding. The common good is not in essence related to numbers, rather it is about the harmonisation of different values in the attainment of a just and cohesive society. The common good is not about a trade-off between the rights of minorities and those of majorities but rather about 'construing the relationship of the individual to society so that the limits and possibilities of both individual and communal well-being are preserved, and in which the appropriate responsibilities and obligations that exist among individuals are clarified and articulated'.[13] It could be possible to argue that the common good is served by requiring couples whose marriages have broken down to stay married, even if they are permitted to separate. However, one would have to argue that this kind of witness enhances the stability of marriage, despite the fact of separation. Yet the church never made this argument nor did it try in other ways to show how the maintenance of the marriage bond, despite the breakdown of the marriage, was crucial to the preservation of the common good. Instead it vaguely referred to the common good, implying that this required the sacrifice of the rights of minorities for the overall good of society. The common good and the overall good of society do not mean the same thing. The overall good of society implies a kind of utilitarian calculus that runs counter to the concept of common good. Moreover, the inevitability that people will disagree about the substance of the common good was not conceded in the bishops' submission. The assumption was that the content of the common good is knowable and unambiguous. There was no teasing out of the different ways in which the common good might be protected and enhanced. Nor did the church give any consideration to the possibility that the common good might be better served by the provision of civil divorce for those whose marriages had broken down and whose consciences allowed it.

Remarkably for a universal institution, the church's deep knowledge of the diversity of human life has never been reflected in the substance of its understanding of pluralism. Nor has the value of pluralism ranked very highly in the church's priorities. It appears to be the value that is sacrificed most quickly, the one that immediately and always gives way to other 'more important' values. For example, when Dr Daly addressed the issue of the Catholic members of the electorate informing their consciences he said, 'We cannot expect voters to leave their consciences behind them when they go to the polling booth. Inevitably we would expect that those who freely accept the teaching of our church will vote according to their consciences ... we ... have the right to carry out our duty to impart the moral convictions, the moral teaching of our church to our own members.'[14] The implication here, confirmed in the later debates about divorce, is that 'imparting the moral convictions and the moral teaching of the church' is in tension with the value of pluralism. The value of pluralism does not seem to count among those moral convictions that the church feels obliged to impart. Instead it is marginal, welcomed only when it is not a hindrance to other issues. But would not the Catholic believer be attending to the beliefs and values of the church by valuing pluralism and giving due consideration to minority rights? Indeed throughout the different divorce debates one might argue pluralism was only granted lip-service. It was not deemed to be constitutive of the church's 'moral convictions and the moral teaching'. As a result it was given very little weight when the thorny and difficult issue of balancing the various goods or values was considered.

Catholic Teaching, Divorce and Dissent
The ambiguity of the church's own position on divorce was also raised during these years. There were (muted) discussions of the changes in church teaching over the centuries, although the hierarchy only reluctantly acknowledged this fact. Nor was the wide-ranging internal theological debate within the church given much attention. Yet within Catholicism from the beginning, divorce (as opposed to annulment) has been accepted in certain contexts. If one begins with the assumption that monogamy without divorce is the law of the gospel then, even within the gospel itself, there is a perceptible change.[15] Known as the Pauline privilege, the absolutist ban on divorce was modified to allow converts to Christianity to remarry if their spouses had not converted. Moreover, it was radically extended in the sixteenth century so that slaves taken from Africa could remarry, even though there was no way of knowing whether absent spouses would abandon them or not. On their behalf, Pope Gregory XIII dissolved their old marriages and declared them free to enter second marriages 'lest they not persist in their faith'.[16] The Petrine privilege also admits of an exception if one or other party is unbaptised. Moreover, in the 1920s Pius XI ex-

ercised jurisdiction over the marriage of two non-Catholics. He dissolved their marriage on grounds other than the Pauline and Petrine privileges.[17] It is true that within Catholicism the number of contexts in which divorce is permitted is small and one should not overstate the case. Yet there is significance in the fact that these exceptions were introduced and extended in the history of the church. This suggests that other exceptions might be contemplated in the future, or at least that this cannot be ruled out. Clearly the teaching on divorce is neither exceptionless nor unchanging. Yet throughout the divorce debates of the 80s and 90s the significance of this aspect of church practice was dismissed on the grounds that it was exceptional.[18] However, this misses the substantial point that the church's teaching on divorce, like all its moral teaching, is part of a developing tradition, which is constituted by both continuity and change.

The tragedy of marital breakdown, coupled with the recognition that the church's teaching has undergone change, has caused some Catholic theologians and pastors to question the magisterium's refusal to extend the grounds on which divorce and remarriage might be permitted. In particular this has involved reinterpreting the biblical texts that appear to prohibit divorce. Many biblical scholars claim that Jesus' teaching on divorce needs to be interpreted as gospel rather than law; that his absolute prohibition was subversive of societal norms which discriminated against women; and that the biblical authors felt free to adapt Jesus' teaching to their own situations.[19] Theologians like Kevin Kelly also draw inspiration from the Church of England's Marriage Commission's 1978 report which recognised that although all couples should strive to reach a level of oneness of an indissoluble marriage bond, not all do achieve this. That report maintains that marriages ought to be indissoluble, but rejects the doctrine that marriages by definition cannot be dissolved.[20] Eastern and Orthodox practice which holds 'that a marriage can die ... but those who are left alone as a result of it ... may still find salvific life in the loving union of a second marriage'[21] is also drawn on in this regard. Such strands are regarded as fruitful in the search for a theology of marriage that is true to the spirit, rather than to the letter of Jesus' teaching on divorce.

These internal discussions are not new in Catholicism. Since the 1950s when Herbert Doms' book *The Meaning of Marriage*[22] (actually published in 1935) became the catalyst for a renewal of the theology of marriage, these issues have been debated within the church. Yet this important aspect of the church's tradition was completely ignored in the documents and statements that issued from the Bishops' Conference. While it may be unrealistic to expect the Bishops' Conference to discuss the detail of these dissenting voices, the fact that they were not given any value is discouraging. Within the church there are differing points of view, among bishops, theologians, laity and priests on many moral issues. The nature of the moral enterprise makes this inescapable. That the church has not yet found a way of living fruitfully with the existence of these disagreements is disappointing, but not surprising. It is not surprising because the institutional church continues to work from a paradigm that prizes external conformity rather than faithful dissent. Moreover, the submissions and the interventions in the divorce debates also raise the issue of who speaks for the church and for whom the bishops speak. The Christian moral inheritance is not an unchanging, timeless or exceptionless tradition. Rather the church is a complex and ambiguous organism with a rich inheritance of moral wisdom, revelatory texts and core principles and values. Thus the idea that one might have one voice speaking for all and representing these diverse aspects of a single tradition is completely inappropriate. So too is the idea that there might be only one unambiguous and exceptionless answer to the issue of divorce and remarriage. Clearly this contradicts both the nature of the Christian moral tradition and the existing history and doctrine of the church.

Conclusion

As a result of its demographic dominance, the Catholic Church's teaching on divorce and remarriage has maintained an unhealthy supremacy in the civil life of Ireland. The representation of that teaching as absolutist and exceptionless has denied the diversity of belief within the church and has silenced dissenting voices. It is true that the church insisted that it required no special treatment from the state. However, in informing the faithful of its moral principles the church failed either to convey the diversity of its own tradition or to remind people that demographic dominance in itself can present a threat to the common good. Nowhere in these debates did the church consider that its moral principles would best be embodied by the enhancement of minority rights, respect for pluralism and the introduction of civil divorce as a remedy for marital breakdown. The fact that these did not enter into the church's discussion suggests that, although it was not seeking special concessions, neither was it concerned about the impact of its own demographic dominance on the state.

The debates of the 1980s and 1990s suggest that both church and state were undergoing change, internally and in their relations with one another. Within the church there was a move away from the appeal to moral doctrine and towards an appeal to consequences and to social harm. The official approach of the church was that although it had a principled objection to divorce, it was on the basis of harm to society that it was opposing its introduction. Although it is very difficult to verify the claim that civil divorce is more undermining of the institution of marriage than irretrievable breakdown, separation, annulments and bigamous unions combined, it appears from the evidence of both referenda that this was a position that many people found convincing.[23] The strong presence in the political debates of lay Catholic organisations whose perspective could be regarded as conservative also represented a significant change. So too did the church's claim to value pluralism, although this could be regarded as more superficial than substantial. There were also changes in the positioning of the church within society, particularly in the years between the two referenda. This was occasioned to a great extent by the exposing of the Catholic Church's institutional failures regarding the abuse of children. There were also financial and sexual scandals. Thus with its reputation damaged, the extent to which the church was listened to as well as the manner in which the debate was conducted changed significantly. One only has to recall the exchange between Proinsias De Rossa, Minister for Social Welfare and the Archbishop of Cashel, Dr Clifford. As noted by Tom Inglis 'it would have been unthinkable even ten years [previously] for a left-wing minister in a Fine Gael-led coalition to call a Catholic archbishop a liar, and get away with it – without either any Fine Gaeler repudiating his remark or another bishop rallying in outrage in their colleagues defence'.[24] Yet this is precisely what happened.

The divorce debates of the 1980s and 90s thus provide us with a lens through which to examine two powerful institutions undergoing major changes both internally and in their external relations. These debates, however, are part of a larger and more complex story whose significance has yet to be analysed. Although one might interpret the changes negatively as signalling the decline of an institution, I am inclined to interpret them in a more positive light. Instead one could understand these years as one phase in the renegotiation of relationships and the return to a more appropriate position for the church, that is as one interest group among many. Furthermore one can hope that they also represent a regrettably divisive stage on the way towards a pluralist and multicultural state in which the civil rights of a morally, ethnically and religiously diverse population are respected.

CHAPTER SIX

Legislation on Contraception and Abortion

Patrick Hannon

The inclusion in this volume of a chapter entitled 'Legislation on Contraception and Abortion' may need explaining, at least so far as legislation on contraception is concerned. For it will probably come as a surprise to people under the age of thirty that there was or is any law in this matter, and that the present legal situation is the outcome of a process which started in 1973 and ended only in the early nineties; and that the topic exercised politicians and indeed the public generally, often to the point of acrimonious controversy. The issue of abortion legislation is of course still current, but again the reader needs to be of a certain age to recall its origins, and even the reader of a certain age is likely to have forgotten the detail of what has transpired to be a very complex matter indeed.

The chapter's inclusion in a volume in honour of Dr Garret FitzGerald reflects the fact that, as Taoiseach and otherwise, he participated both in the political processes which have led to the present situation and in the public debate which attended them. A particular reason is that the law on contraception and abortion in the Republic has generally been taken as evidence of the kind of Catholic 'sectarianism' thought to be an obstacle to a solution to what came to be called the Northern problem. More generally, the history of the Republic's laws in these matters is at one level part of the history of relationships between (especially) the Catholic Church and the state, and of the impact of religion on social life.[1]

Whether, or to what extent, the laws in question have impinged upon the developments which have culminated in what is now called the peace process is debatable, and indeed it is difficult to know how at this stage one might tell, if only because the solution to the problem has long ceased to be thought of in terms of the removal of obstacles to reunification, and there are other quite identifiable obstacles to the achievement of a lasting peace. But the history of the legislation does say something of the story of the relationships between church and state, and especially the relationships between the Roman Catholic Church and the state in the Republic.

But this in turn may seem to be of little more than academic interest now. It is a cliché of commentary on modern Ireland that its evolution has seen the waning of the influence of 'the Catholic Church', meaning the bishops, and perhaps the clergy. And the history of legislation on contraception and abortion is often cited as part of the evidence for this claim. For in the space of three decades, the law has moved from a situation in which it could be said to have reflected Catholic moral teaching on the morality of contraception and of abortion to a stage where it no longer does so, certainly not in the case of the former and not at all clearly in the case of abortion. But there is so much other evidence of the apparent waning of Catholic influence that it is hardly necessary to take particular notice of this.

Yet the history of this legislation continues to have its own interest and its own particular significance. For it reveals change in the self-understanding of the Catholic Church, and change in the way in which its leadership understands its role *vis-à-vis* both the church's membership and the wider society. I would want to maintain that the change is on the whole for the better, and that it contains the potential for constructive participation in the shaping of our society's future. But I would wish to argue also that even more change is needed, and that only when it is accomplished can the church – or, better, the churches – be a credible bearer of its own good news, and a source of spiritual and moral energy in the Ireland that is in the making.

This is of course a large theme, and there are many aspects of it which can only be mentioned here. At the heart of the task facing the Catholic Church is the massive challenge posed by the scandals disclosed during the past decade. The work of recognising the import of these, and of responding appropriately, is likely to absorb the energy of leaders and members for a long time to come. And this work will take place against a background of, as it seems, a continuing secularisation, not all of which is benign. It takes place also against a background in which the church at large is both in crisis and – with a few apparent exceptions – in paralysis. And its background in Ireland includes the fact that heavy shadows have fallen also on other institutions of state and of society, and there is a general collapse of trust to a degree dangerous to the polity's health.

Others have written, in this volume and elsewhere, of these larger dimensions of the contemporary challenge. Here I shall focus on what has happened to the laws which are the subject of the chapter, and on the response of Catholic Church leadership and membership, and the way in which their response has both reflected and shaped a changing ethos. I hope in particular to point to some positive features and some limited gains in the changes which have taken place. But first, a brief history of the legislation.

Contraception

Strictly speaking there was no law concerning contraception, but rather laws concerning the availability of contraceptives. The core of these was the prohibition by the Criminal Law Amendment Act 1935 of the importation, sale and manufacture of contraceptives. Such was the situation prior to a challenge to the constitutionality of this prohibition, first at the High Court and then on appeal to the Supreme Court, taken in 1972-73 by Mrs Mary McGee, on the ground that it infringed her right to marital privacy. The challenge failed at the High Court but was partially successful on appeal, for the Supreme Court found that there is indeed an implicit right to marital privacy in the constit-ution, and that the ban on importing – as distinct from selling or otherwise distributing – contraceptives infringed that right in Mrs McGee's case.[2]

Catholics had in any case come to question the correctness of an absolute prohibition on the use of artificial contraceptives and, notwithstanding the reiteration of traditional teaching by Pope Paul VI in *Humanae Vitae*, Irish Catholics were among those who by the end of the sixties thought that there should be some reform of the law. But efforts to introduce legislation by way of Private Members' Bills in 1971, 1972 and 1973 were un-successful, and it is clear from the record of Dáil and Seanad de-bates that among politicians generally there was little interest in promoting liberalising measures. It was clear also that attempts to promote such measures would be opposed by the Catholic bishops.[3]

Meanwhile, of course, the contraceptive pill had arrived upon the scene; its prescription or sale could evade the charge of illegality by reference to its potential for regularising the menstrual cycle. But it was not difficult to see the hypocrisy in this; and when the anomaly to which the McGee judgment gave rise was met by the setting up of family planning clinics which made contraceptives available free of charge (for it remained illegal to sell them, though clients were encouraged to give a donation toward the upkeep of the clinic), the case for reform was overwhelming. For good reasons and bad, this proved more easily said than done, and it was not until 1979 that the exceedingly cautious but nonetheless innovative Health (Family Planning) Act was passed. And it took almost a decade and a half more before the law finally settled in its present form.[4]

Abortion

Prior to 1983 the law concerning abortion was that set out in sections 58 and 59 of the Offences Against the Person Act 1861, both of which appear to rule out abortion absolutely. But the meaning of section 58 was considered in the English case *R v Bourne* (1939), and it was accepted that an abortion to preserve the life of a pregnant woman was not unlawful. Macnaghten J also ruled that where a doctor was of the opinion that the probable consequence of pregnancy was to render a woman a mental or physical wreck, he could properly be said to be operating for the purpose of preserving the life of the mother. No court in the Republic has relied on this judgement, and in *Society for the Protection of the Unborn Child v Grogan and Others*, Keane J – now Chief Justice – expressed the view that 'the preponderance of judicial opinion in this country would suggest that the Bourne approach could not have been adopted in this country consistently with the constitution prior to the eighth amendment'.[5]

The eighth amendment resulted from a referendum held in 1983 and involved the insertion into Article 40.3 of the following provision: 'The State acknowledges the right to life of the unborn and, with due regard to the equal right to life of the mother, guarantees in its laws to respect and, as far as practicable, by its laws to defend and vindicate that right.' This makes explicit what a number of judgements – including that in *McGee* – appear to have considered implicit, namely a constitutional prohibition on abortion. Its proponents were not satisfied that existing constitutional law was adequate, and they feared in particular that judicial interpretation at some future time might find abortion lawful.

A number of cases concerning the interpretation of this amendment ensued in the years following. These had to do in the main with the provision of information on or referral to abortion services available in other jurisdictions, and have their own interest. But a more fundamental issue, and one of more interest here, came to be considered in 1992 in what became known as the X case: the meaning and scope of the phrase 'with due regard to the equal right to life of the mother'. X was a fourteen year old girl who became pregnant as a result of an alleged rape. She and her parents wished to travel abroad so that she could have an abortion but, the matter having come as it were incidentally to the attention of the Director of Public Prosecutions and the Attorney General, an injunction was obtained restraining her from leaving the jurisdiction or from arranging or carrying out an abortion.

On appeal to the Supreme Court, however, a majority of the judges held that if it were established as a matter of probability that there was a real and substantial risk to the life – as distinct from the health – of the mother, and that this risk could only be averted by terminating the pregnancy, such a termination would be lawful. The Court accepted the evidence given in the High Court that the girl had threatened to commit suicide if compelled to continue with the pregnancy, and it judged that this threat constituted a real and substantial risk to her life, and on this basis the injunction was lifted.[6]

The Supreme Court's decision was controversial, not only because it had found abortion to be lawful where there was a real and substantial threat to the life of the mother, and that suicide constitutes such a threat, but also because some *dicta* of the majority suggested that the right to travel could be restrained in order to prevent an abortion taking place where there was no threat to the mother's life. The government decided that a number of issues to which the judgement had given rise merited resolution by referendum.

The first of these was what came to be known as the substantive issue – the nature and scope of the prohibition of abortion – and it was proposed that an amendment should be inserted as an addition to Article 40.3.3 (the provision added in 1983): 'It shall be unlawful to terminate the life of an unborn unless such termination is necessary to save the life, as distinct from the health, of the mother where there is an illness or disorder of the mother giving rise to a real and substantial risk to her life, not being a risk of self-destruction.' The second issue was that of travel, and an amendment was proposed in the wording 'This sub-section shall not limit freedom to travel between the state and another state.' A third proposal concerned the provision of information and it read: 'This sub-section shall not limit freedom to obtain or make available, in the state, subject to such conditions as may be laid down by law, information relating to services lawfully available in another state.' The amendment concerning the substantive issue was defeated, those concerning travel and information passed.

The defeat of the proposed amendment on the substantive issue left untouched the most fundamental question, and critics of the X judgement of whatever hue remained dissatisfied. Those who had thought the eighth amendment to have copperfastened the right to life of the foetus from conception were bound to be unhappy about the recognition of the threat of suicide as a ground for the lawful termination of a pregnancy. Those who opposed the amendment because they wanted a more liberal law could not have regarded the decision in X as going far enough. And even those favourable to the acceptance of the threat of suicide as a ground had to be uneasy about the absence of legal regulation, including regulation concerning the time within which an abortion in circumstances of threatened suicide might legally be obtained.

Sporadic public debate took place throughout the nineties, and the various interest groups, depending upon their standpoints, called for legislation or for a new referendum. The Constitutional Review Group gave some consideration to the issues at stake in their report published in 1996.[7] Having set out the principal problems arising from the wording of the eighth amendment and from the decision in X, and having sketched a number of approaches toward a resolution, the report concludes: 'While in principle the major issues discussed above should be tackled by constitutional amendment, there is no consensus as to what that amendment should be and no certainty of success for any referendum proposal for substantive constitutional change in relation to this subsection. The Review Group, therefore, favours, as the only practical possibility at present, the introduction of legislation covering such matters as definitions, protection for appropriate medical intervention, certification of "real and substantial risk to the life of the mother" and a time-limit on lawful termination of pregnancy.'

The Review Group's option for simple legislation was not in the event followed. In 1997 a new government took office, and soon afterwards the Taoiseach indicated that it was intended to publish a Green Paper which would set out the issues, provide a brief analysis and examine possible approaches toward a resolution of the problem. A cabinet committee oversaw the work of an interdepartmental working group, and submissions were invited and received from all interested parties. It was felt necessary 'to stress that the purpose of inviting submissions was to inform the process of the preparation of the Green Paper on the range of issues surrounding the debate on abortion and to obtain the views of individuals and organisations thereon, and not to conduct a plebiscite or a weighing of public opinion on the course of action the government should take'. In the light of public and parliamentary discussion of the paper, it was decided to hold a referendum, and this took place in March 2002.

What the twenty-fifth amendment proposed in essence was to roll back the decision in the X case and to remove the threat of suicide as a ground justifying termination of pregnancy. But the manner in which this might be accomplished was in the circumstances inevitably complicated, and the text of the amendment involved a combination of constitutional principle with what would ordinarily be statute law. The text was daunting *to look at*, though not, on a closer look, so very complex as some critics insisted. But for another type of critic it suffered from a more serious flaw, for it defined abortion as 'the intentional destruction by any means of unborn human life after *implantation* in the womb of a woman' (italics added). This was bound to arouse the scepticism of those who hold that the human being's rights as a person, and in the first place the right to life, accrue at the moment of conception. In a low poll (42.89% of an electorate of almost three million) the amendment was defeated by about ten and a half thousand votes, opponents being not only those opposed to rolling back the decision in X but also those who considered that to support the measure would amount to a betrayal of the principle of the sanctity of life from conception.

The Stance of the Catholic Bishops

So much for the recent history and present state of the law concerning the availability of contraceptives and on abortion. What, meanwhile, has been the stance of church authority in the debates which have accompanied the changes summarised above? On the face of it, what has been happening is a move away from a situation in which specifically Roman Catholic beliefs were expressed in the law of the land to one in which this is no longer the case. And this, on the face of it, supports the impression of a waning of Catholic influence, or at least the diminution of the influence of the Catholic bishops on law and governance in the state. The matter is, however, somewhat more complex than that.

It may be as well at this point to remark that some characterisations of Irish Catholicism (and indeed of Irish religion generally), and some accounts of the influence of 'the church' in Irish life, are not helped by a lack of historical perspective. On some accounts one might be forgiven the impression that the Irish Catholic was until recently an unusually biddable type, and indeed Brian Fallon has written of a strong 'culture of obedience' in the decades between 1930 and 1960. But, as Fallon observes, this was also true of many other countries at the time.[8] Moreover, on the topics which are the subject of this chapter, there was probably no great difference in the substantive beliefs of the members of at any rate the several Christian churches.[9]

Take the law on contraceptives as it was before the developments recounted above. This did of course reflect Roman Catholic teaching concerning the use of artificial contraceptives, and there can hardly be any question of its not being evidence of Catholic influence. But it needn't be supposed that in 1935 the measure required the support of an intervention of bishops or clergy, for it is unlikely to have occurred to any Catholic legislator of the time to question a teaching so long in place and reiterated strongly only five years previously by Pope Pius XI in the encyclical *Casti Conubii*. And neither is it clear that the prohibition would have been felt as imposing a heavy and alien burden by other Christians in the state. Christian opposition to the use of artificial contraceptives had a long history, and it was only in 1930 that the Lambeth Conference – the views of which would have impinged upon the membership of the Church of Ireland – had declared their use permissible.[10]

Nor was there anything unusual about the persistence of the

prohibition of abortion under the Offences Against the Person Act 1861, an enactment in the first place of the Westminster Parliament. The Green Paper's summary of abortion law in other jurisdictions in Europe, and in Australia, New Zealand, Canada and the United States is essentially a narrative of liberalisation, mainly in the 1970s and 1980s, of laws which were on the whole as restrictive as our law was under the 1861 Act. Nor is the Catholic Church the only Christian Church in the Republic which considers abortion morally wrong; nor indeed are Christians the only people whose ethical code opposes the intentional destruction of unborn life.

I mention these facts not to deny or minimise the reality of the influence of Catholic teaching on the law of the Republic, but to make the point that debate about law and morality is misstated whenever it is presented in terms merely of a contest between Catholics and the rest. The reconciliation of individual freedom with a common good is a task for every legal system, and not an eccentricity of the Irish, Catholic or otherwise. When our debates have been transmuted, as they so regularly are, into issues of the relationship between church and state, false polarities are created and the true nub of the matter has become obscured or lost.

There was a time when Catholic theology might reasonably be fixed with a good deal of the blame for this kind of misconception. Teaching concerning religious freedom and about the relationships between church and state gave rise easily to the conclusion that where Catholics were in a majority, Catholic faith and morals should be promoted and defended by the law, or at least that the law should contain nothing which was at odds with official church teaching. When Dr Noel Browne wrote to Taoiseach John A. Costello that 'from the beginning it has been my concern to see that the Mother and Child Scheme contained nothing contrary to Catholic moral teaching', he was giving expression only to what would naturally have been expected in the Ireland of the time.[11]

A New Approach
But change was in the offing, a change stimulated in great part by changes within the Catholic Church itself. The Second Vatican Council (1962-65) dramatically re-envisioned the church, but of course it was only articulating a vision which had been in

the making for many decades. There was to be a new 'openness to the world', a 'dialogue' with other Christians and faiths and philosophies, a recognition of the baptismal vocation of every member to witness to the values of the gospel of Jesus Christ, and of the irreplaceable significance of the lay member's witness – and of a 'lawful autonomy of secular pursuits'. The church was 'not just the pope and the bishops', but the whole 'People of God'; ministry was service, of the gospel and of the whole church. And the mission of the church was to proclaim and celebrate and assist in the establishment of God's reign of justice and peace and love.[12]

This vision is of course as yet unrealised, and in some matters scandalously unrealised. But its influence was from the first perceptible, even if often minimally, and it was the background to the evolution of a new way of seeing the role of the Catholic Church in Irish society, and a new mode of address on the part of the bishops when they came to intervene in public debate. Coincidentally in terms of the focus of this chapter, this new mode of address made its appearance in 1973, in a statement of the Conference concerning legislation intended to change the law regarding the availability of contraceptives in the aftermath of the *McGee* decision. The mode's main features have characterised every intervention of the bishops in debates during the past three decades about what is now usually called social morality.

The main features are three. First, the bishops distinguish between morality and law, and reiterate church teaching concerning the moral issue. In the 1973 statement they recall the teaching of *Humanae Vitae* on the use of artificial contraceptives. Second, they concede that the question of what the law should be is a question for the conscience of the legislator or the voter. In 1973 this was the import of the dictum that 'there are many things which the Catholic Church holds to be morally wrong and no-one has ever suggested ... that they should be prohibited by the state', and of their asking the legislators to balance the pros and cons of the measures proposed. Third, the bishops offer their own view of the legislation; and in the case of contraception (as of divorce) they have supported their own view by reference to certain malign social consequences which they anticipate the changes will bring.[13]

Signs of Hope?
Sceptics have said that this is only a slightly more sophisticated way of trying to ensure the enforcement of Catholic morality by means of the law of the land. Obviously the bishops have wished that the positions which they took or endorsed would prevail – it would be odd if they wished otherwise; and critics of a different sort complain that they have conceded too much. But in stating the right and the responsibility of legislator or voter to decide on the form which the law should take, they enunciate a principle which challenges each lawmaker and voter to take responsibility for the future of our society. It would be the height of irresponsibility if, under any pretext, this challenge is not taken up.

It was taken up and followed through in an unexpected way in the recent referendum on abortion. In their statement the bishops again recalled the key principle in Catholic moral teaching: human life is sacred from the moment of conception, and nothing can ever justify the deliberate killing of an innocent human being. They were frank in their criticism of the legal situation which the X case brought about, welcoming the proposed amendment as 'a significant improvement'. Naturally they advert to the definition which sees implantation as the point of entry of the law's protection of the unborn. But it remains their conviction 'that the new proposal represents a considerable improvement on the existing situation, and that it does not in itself deny or devalue the worth and dignity of the human embryo prior to implantation'. And so '[i]n dealing with what appears to be a limited or imperfect measure, we believe that, in the context of *The Gospel of Life* (#73), Catholic voters should feel free in conscience to support this measure, even if it is viewed as less than might have been desired'.[14]

Among the opponents of the amendment were some who continued to believe that the measure left life vulnerable between conception and implantation, and they will have contributed to its defeat. It is difficult to see how, wishing to be 'pro-life', these voters opposed what in all the circumstances is the best that from a pro-life standpoint is likely to be achieved, and it was simply wrong of some of them to suggest that the bishops' stance was at variance with the pope's teaching. But their disagreement is the kind of price which is paid when, as it must be, the freedom to exercise one's own judgement according to conscience in matters which are debatable is acknowledged. And it is surely a gain in moral maturity, if one may say so without appearing to patronise (or to seem naïve), that they felt free to exercise their judgement in this manner.

It is evidence of progress also – whatever one may think of the substance of the matter – that it was lay people who took the initiative which resulted in the referendum of 1983. As one who subscribes to Catholic teaching on abortion, this writer is pretty incurably sceptical about the likelihood of finding a formula which will do what the sponsors of the eighth amendment intended; witness both what happened in the X case and what had to be proposed – unsuccessfully – in the attempt to undo it. But the initiative signified an assumption of responsibility by lay members of the church in a matter of urgent concern in lay experience, even if what was attempted might be thought to have been ill-starred and even if, arguably, it may also be said that the bishops (along with the main political parties) were too hasty in their endorsement.

But the bishops' endorsement of this initiative and, in general, of the continuing agitation for a new referendum following the X case raises another kind of question. How is it that 'conservative' movements and initiatives are more likely to secure episcopal backing than 'liberal'? This is reminiscent of the question, how is it that 'liberal' dissent is always silenced or dismissed, 'conservative' hardly at all? It will not do to answer that of course liberal dissent is what injures faith or morals or the unity of the church, for what is excessively conservative has the same potential. The question cannot be taken further here, but it may be remarked that a leadership which habitually fails to heed informed and conscientious questioning from whatever quarter is doomed to lose touch with the true *sensus fidelium*.

A third and final sign of progress in modern Irish experience is that (at last) the level of public discussion of religious and moral matters has greatly improved. Contrast the slogan-wielding and name-calling which passed for debate in the 1983 referendum campaign with the main contributions to the debate in that of 2002. There were many reasons for the poverty of debate in former times, not least the virtually total absence of theology from the university. But this was in part a symptom of a deeper and more pervasive malaise, what can now be identified as a clericalism which excluded lay experience and lay competence, the cost of which is proving to have been much greater than its effect upon the quality of thought and debate about religion in the public forum.

At the end of three decades then, of which it is usual to say that they have seen a waning of Catholic influence in social affairs, there are discernible what from a Catholic theological standpoint are some gains. And these are gains not just in terms of the church's mission or of its institutional interests but in terms of the future health of society and of life in the *polis*. Without overstating the gains or underestimating losses, one might see in the debris of the present the prospect not of death but of a new kind of life. The churches as churches, heralds of the gospel, servants of gospel and of the community, may yet contribute in fresh ways to the shaping of a new Ireland. But not before a painful rebirth.

CHAPTER SEVEN

Church-State Relations in Primary and Secondary Education

John Coolahan

One cannot understand the interface of church and state relationships in contemporary Ireland regarding education without an awareness of the historical context in which they were formed. As state support emerged for a more general provision of education in the nineteenth century, the issue of the control of schooling became a very contentious one. Politicisation and socialisation were among the aims of the state in the promotion of schooling, but the churches viewed the schools as vital areas for denominational control and influence. The clashes involved form a significant feature of the political and social history of the nineteenth century, with the churches, and particularly an increasingly confident Catholic Church, proving to be the victors. The shaping influences of the configuration of modern Irish schooling are rooted deep in nineteenth-century experiences. The balances of authority and control achieved at this earlier period have proved to be very durable. It is only within the last generation that these began to be seriously challenged and in the context of society undergoing accelerated social, economic, cultural and religious change, that a new configuration is in the process of being forged. Local control of schooling, particularly in terms of staff appointments, religious instruction and the ethos of schools, was a major policy concern of the churches. This chapter examines three eras in relation to that policy which might be termed – winning control, holding control and sharing control.

1. Winning Control

In the early nineteenth century, against a background of intense denominational animosity and political division, the education of the young became a significant political issue. The traditional hegemony of the Established Church was being confronted by a demand for the equal acceptance of the rights of all citizens to a state-supported education in accordance with their religious affiliations. A landmark effort to establish this position was the Fourteenth Report of the Commissioners of the Board of Education, 1812, which sought to devise a schooling system that would induce all children to receive the benefits of education 'as one undivided body, under one and the same system, and in the same establishments'. It set out the essential principle which should underpin such a scheme 'that no attempt shall be made to influence or disturb the peculiar religious tenets of any sect or description of Christians'.[1] This daring stance against a prevailing climate of proselytism, was adopted by Lord Stanley in 1831 as a guiding premise for the national school system. Announcing a state-supported primary school system, Stanley stated that a main aim of the system was to unite the children of different denominations, with the schools being open for combined literary and moral instruction for four or five days a week, while separate denominations' religious instruction could take place at times outside of these days. The new Commissioners of National Education were to assist local initiative in the provision of schooling, and applications from mixed denominational local groups were to be especially favoured. Predictably, however, the churches opposed a mixed denominational system, and long and bitter struggles took place to re-shape it to being a denominational one. While the system remained *de jure* a mixed system, it became *de facto* a denominational one – Akenson states that this had become a reality early on. 'By approximately mid-century, the national school system had become a denominational system',[2] but pressures to make it more overtly denominational continued throughout the nineteenth century. State support for denominational teacher training colleges from 1884 was a further major concession to the denominational emphasis. In a pastoral letter issued in 1900, the Catholic hierarchy formally acknowledged the success in remodelling the national school system from the original plan:

> The system of National Education ... has itself undergone a radical change, and in a great part of Ireland is now, in fact, whatever it is in name, as denominational almost as we could desire. In most of its schools there is no mixed education whatsoever.[3]

The vast majority of the schools came under the control of managers of a particular denomination. The manager appointed teachers almost invariably of his own denomination, the pupils attending were predominantly of the same faith as the manager and teachers, and the manager ensured that as far as possible a denominational ethos prevailed within the schools, whatever the formal regulations stated. The national school system, up to the current generation, has been by far the predominant mode of formal schooling for the great majority of the Irish people. As the twentieth century opened, it was clearly established that while the state controlled the curriculum, operated an inspection system, paid the teachers and was responsible for most of the costs of school provision, a great deal of authority rested with the local manager, almost always a clergyman, on teacher appointment, religious instruction, ethos of the school and general oversight of the work of the school at local level.

With regard to secondary education, the relaxation of the penal laws in the late eighteenth century led to the emergence of Catholic secondary schools set up by diocesan authorities and religious congregations. These came on stream alongside existing Protestant secondary schools which benefited from endowments. The secondary system was the product of private enterprise and it established a strong tradition of ecclesiastical control of such schools. In 1838 the report of a Select Committee, chaired by Thomas Wyse, proposed a state supported secondary system, on the mixed denominational principle of the national school system, but no action was taken. The 1850 Synod of Thurles clearly enunciated Catholic opposition to state encroachment on educational provision and opposed the newly state-established Queen's Colleges. In this context, the report of a Royal Commission in 1858, proposing the financing of secondary education on the mixed education principle and the redistribution of endowments to all secondary schools, adopting this principle was not likely to win support. A resolution passed at a Catholic meeting in Cork in March 1859 put the opposition succinctly when it stated: 'No form of intermediate (secondary) education is suited to a Catholic people, unless it be granted to them in separate schools, and in terms always strictly in accordance with the teaching and discipline of the Catholic Church.'[4] The condemnation by the bishops in 1863 of attendance of pupil teachers at the Model Schools of the Commissioners of National Education was in alignment with this attitude. In 1867 Cardinal Cullen articulated the guiding principle for the following century when he stated:

It is quite necessary that we should preserve our intermediate educational establishments in their present independence
and free from all government control.[5]

This did not prevent the Catholic authorities from pressurising
the government for state finance for their secondary schools.
The political problem at the time was, could a mechanism be
found whereby the admitted financial needs of secondary education might be met without, at the same time, giving assistance
directly from public funds for denominational education?

The Intermediate Education Act of 1878 provided this mechanism. Under the terms of the Act, a Board of Commissioners
would administer a public examinations system on the basis of
which managers of schools would be issued with payments related to the success rates of pupils in the examinations, the funds
coming from funds available following the church disestablishment in 1869. Once the schools fulfilled the examination requirements, including the exercise of a conscience clause, and the
pupils passed the examinations, the schools were left altogether
undisturbed in relation to the conduct of their affairs.
Interestingly, in the lead up to the Act, church representatives
had indicated opposition to state funds for school buildings and
to a state inspection system considering that this would give the
state too much potential influence. The Act of 1878 was to have
very long-term consequences for the character of Irish secondary schooling, and it remained the legislative framework for
secondary education until political independence.

The last great conflict between church and state regarding
schooling took place in relation to the Education Bill of 1919/20,
on the eve of independence. This was a major Bill intended to reform the administrative structure of Irish education by estab-
lishing a central Department of Education, with an Advisory
Council, County Education Committees and local boards of
management for schools. Individual school managers were to
retain the right to appoint teachers and to safeguard the teaching of religion.The Bill gave rise to bitter controversy. Among
key protagonists were the Catholic Church authorities who
vehemently opposed the measure, and Protestant Church representatives who favoured it. In the event, the Bill was withdrawn
in December 1920, a week before the Government of Ireland Act
was passed, which established the partition settlement.[6] The
Catholic Church had fought and won too many educational

battles under the old regime to let its position be undermined, as it saw the situation, during the last gasps of that regime.

2. Holding Control

Despite its defeat, the Education Bill controversy cast a long shadow over educational development in both parts of the island. In the South, the very strong pronouncements of Catholic churchmen against the Bill alerted politicians within the Irish Free State, sundered by civil war, that education was an issue to be 'handled with care'. In case there was any doubt, the Catholic Clerical Managers Association issued the following statement in October 1921:

> We feel confident that an Irish government established by the people for the people ... will always recognise and respect the principles which must regulate and govern Catholic education. And, in view of pending changes in Irish education, we wish to assert the great fundamental principle that the only satisfactory system of education for Catholics is one wherein Catholic children are taught in Catholic schools by Catholic teachers under Catholic control.[7]

It is likely that the Protestant churches shared such sentiments in regard to the education of Protestant children.

What is most striking about the political changeover regarding the administration and management of the school system was the lack of change, and the continuity of the largely unquestioned structure of the inherited system. The first three ministers of the new state covering the period 1922 to 1948, are on record as favouring the inherited *status quo*. In 1922, Eoin Mac Neill formally stated that the role of the state was one of aiding and assisting agencies such as the churches in the provision of schooling.[8] Neither he nor his successors, John Marcus O'Sullivan (1926-32), Thomas Derrig (1932-48), had any difficulty regarding the control of schooling or problems with the existing interface of state and church in relation to education.[9] With regard to secondary schools, the Report of the new Department of Education for 1924-25 clearly enunciated the very limited powers of the state:

> The state at present inspects these schools regularly and exercises a certain amount of supervision through its powers to make grants to schools as a result of these inspections, but it neither founds secondary schools, nor finances the building

of them, nor appoints teachers or managers, nor exercises any power or veto over the appointment or dismissal of such teachers or the management of schools.[10]

Significantly, it sought no extension of these limited powers over four subsequent decades.

Where the state took more initiative was in the area of vocational/technical education with the Vocational Education Act of 1930, which set up thirty eight vocational education committees to operate a democratically controlled, non-denominational school system. In the lead-up to the Act a delegation from the Catholic hierarchy met the minister, who assured them in a written reply that this form of education did not involve 'general education' and was to be severely practical and vocational in its emphasis. It would not be allowed to infringe on the broader education provided in secondary schools. He also assured them that he had been most careful not to introduce a new principle of control in education, and to ensure that the Act did not run counter to established Catholic practice or the Maynooth decrees on such matters.[11] While the original Act did not contain precise provision for religious instruction, this was remedied by Memo V 40, a decade later, whereby Committees were directed to provide facilities for religious instruction and to incorporate it in the timetable. It was also the case that clergymen became chairpersons of the majority of the Vocational Education Committees. The Vocational Education Act had the effect of copperfastening a binary form of post-primary education, whereby the middle and upper classes attended secondary schools and aspired to public service employment or higher education, while many children of less well off parents attended vocational schools (or techs, as they were popularly called), with a view towards employment in a trade or applied occupation.

The centenary of Catholic Emancipation was celebrated with fervour in 1929, the year which also saw the publication of Pope Pius XI's encyclical, *On the Christian Education of Youth*. This set out an exclusivist view regarding Catholic schooling:

It is necessary that all the teaching and the whole organisation of the school, as well as the teachers, the syllabus, and the textbooks in every branch be regulated by one Christian spirit, under the direction and maternal supervision of the church ...

The encyclical also clearly set out the subsidiary nature of the state's role in education *vis-à-vis* the family and the church.[12] The document also condemned trends such as sex education and co-education, in the latter case echoing the Irish hierarchy statement to a government in 1926 that 'mixed education (that is co-education) in public schools is very undesirable, especially among older children'.[13] This encyclical was to be an important framework of reference for Irish clergy in subsequent years.

In an address to a Catholic education conference in Louvain in 1931, Rev. Professor T. Corcoran was in a position to present an exemplary overview of the position of Catholic schools in Ireland when he stated:

> The Catholic ownership of Catholic primary schools is secured in nearly all cases, and the Catholic character of all subjects of instruction is guaranteed by the presence of Catholic teachers, using books acceptable to Catholics ... The Catholic secondary schools are always the property of the pastoral clergy and of Religious Orders of men and women, only some six small schools are controlled by Catholic lay teachers.[14]

In the Irish constitution, adopted in 1937, Articles 41, 42 and 44 relating to educational rights of the family, the individual, religious denominations and the state are in alignment with Catholic moral and social teaching. The state acknowledges the family as the primary and natural educator of the child. In Article 42.4 it is stated, 'The State shall provide for free primary education and shall endeavour to supplement and give reasonable aid to private and corporate educational initiative ...' Article 44 assures that the state shall 'not discriminate between schools under the management of different religious denominations', and 44.5 and 44.6 assures religious denominations on the private property character of their schools. These constitutional guarantees were to be of great importance to the stabilisation of the *status quo*.

Following the foundation of the state in 1922, the previous boards of commissioners were abolished and power became very centralised in the Department of Education and its associated bureaucracy. Ownership and local control of the great majority of the schools rested with religious authorities. There was no forum for other stakeholders, nor did parents or teachers have a consultative status, except through teacher unions in the case of teachers. Calls to establish an advisory council on education were opposed, until the coalition government, elected in 1948, agreed to set up a Council of Education in 1950, as an advisory body. Twenty-five per cent of the Council were Catholic religious, as was its chairman. Minister Mulcahy, in his inauguration address, stressed the co-operative partnership which existed between church and state in relation to education policy. This was echoed by the chairman of the new council, Rev Canon O'Keefe, who stated: 'There lies beneath all our educational efforts a sane and balanced philosophy – an exact appreciation of what is and what is not the legitimate function of the state. On this there is almost universal agreement.'[15] The council's two reports, on the primary curriculum (1954) and the secondary curriculum (1962) were remarkable for their conservative endorsement of the *status quo*, suggesting only minor changes. They were symptomatic of an insular complacency which had affected Irish schooling at the time, but which was soon to be shattered.

A number of studies of Irish primary and secondary schooling during the first four decades of independence have been critical of its quality, equality, accountability and lack of innovation. Authors such as Akenson, Titley, Ó Buachalla and O'Donoghue have imputed significant blame to the nature of the influence of the Catholic Church in particular, and to the character of the relationship which was forged between church and state on schooling policy.[16] While recognising the significant contribution by religious men and women in expertise, time and resources, the authors view the climate which existed to have had many stultifying, narrowing influences which, in the long run, were not beneficial to either the church or the state. In his major study, *Church and State in Modern Ireland, 1923-70*, John H. Whyte concluded:

> Over most of the period since independence, the remarkable feature of educational policy in Ireland has been the reluctance of the state to touch on the entrenched positions of the church. This is not because the church's claims have been moderate; on the contrary, it has carved out for itself a more extensive control over education in Ireland than in any other country in the world. It is because the church has insisted on its claims with such force that the state has been extremely cautious in entering its domain.[17]

In his detailed study, *Education Policy in Twentieth Century Ireland*, Ó Buachalla concluded:

> Defence and consolidation were frequently the objectives of

policy in relation to the concrete issues which arose in the six decades since independence. The structural *status quo* and the dominant role of the church in the education system were to be defended; the position was to be consolidated by the removal of surviving structural features which were not favoured and the assimilation into favoured structures of any new institutions established.[18]

Ó Buachalla includes the Protestant churches when he states: 'Their (the churches') contributions to policy formation have been fundamental, extensive and consistent in their main themes; while primarily defensive of the *status quo* they have touched on most aspects of policy and provision.'[19] The *modus vivendi* between church and state on educational affairs prior to political independence, became a consolidated and cosy partnership following partition, in a system characterised by continuity and stability rather than by expansion or innovation. Therein may have laid a form of entrapment for the churches if they interpret their roles in a counter-cultural mode, with a focus on radical critique and empowerment of the marginalised. This is acknowledged in a recent publication by the Conference of Religious of Ireland (CORI), when it states:

> The early efforts of religious congregations were so successful that they had by the 1880s become part of a new establishment. As Corish (1985) suggests, the Catholic Church had become a 'kind of semi-state body'. Being part of a new establishment, particularly when the Catholic nation achieved state power, entailed a dramatic change in the *raison d'être* of religious in education. No longer were they running schools which were in some way counter-cultural; instead, their schools were now some of the principal <u>agents of socialisation</u> (original underlining) into the values and outlook of the new establishment.[20]

3. Sharing Control

The early sixties introduced an era of policy appraisal and change in Irish education which brought strains in the *entente cordiale* between church and state. When allied with other profound social changes, the following four decades were to witness a gradual, but distinctively changing configuration of the roles of state and church in school policy, control and provision.

Involvement with international agencies or events in the

early sixties proved to be a propulsion for change within the state Department of Education and within the Catholic Church regarding their attitudes to education. In 1962, the Department of Education embarked, with the support of the OECD, on a major statistical and analytical appraisal of the education system, resulting in the Investment in Education Report, published in 1966. The report highlighted glaring deficiencies in the education system. The report coincided with new pro-active, governmental policy on investing in education for the improved economic and social well-being of the nation. The Irish Catholic Church became exposed to the radical new thinking of Vatican II, which included significant new directions for education policy. It would take time for the full implications of changing attitudes to become fully manifest, but the signs were there early on that a new era was opening up.

Dr Hillery, who commissioned the Investment in Education Report, signalled a much more pro-active, directive role as minister and changed an image of the job put forward by his predecessor, Minister Mulcahy, as an oilman just knocking the pipes of the system to that of captain on the bridge. In 1963 he introduced the first state capital grants for secondary school buildings. He raised the status of the vocational schools and announced a new type of post-primary school – the comprehensive school. In 1970 this concept was elaborated into that of the community school. Minister Colley sought co-operation between local vocational and secondary schools in 1966 and that same year Minister O'Malley announced the 'free' post-primary education and transport schemes. Such initiatives gave rise to some resentments in church quarters at this more intrusive role of the state.[21] The new status for the vocational schools was seen as breaking the agreement with the hierarchy, and the comprehensive and community schools were viewed with suspicion and seen by some as inspired by alien influences. Civil servants who sought to explain the concept of the community school at regional public meetings met with a lot of hostility, some of it promoted by church interests. An impactful article in *Studies*, Autumn 1968, by the Assistant Secretary of the Department of Education, Seán O'Connor, gave rise to a great deal of controversy. In a section of the article on church and state in education he stated:

I lay stress on these things because I believe a change must be made, otherwise there will be an explosion, maybe sooner than later. No one wants to push the religious out of education; that would be disastrous, in my opinion. But I want them in as partners, not always as masters. I believe that there is need for dialogue at the highest level between church and state on the problems in education now surfacing ... The dialogue must be frank and range over a wide area.[22]

The tone of this public statement by a senior official of the Department was unprecedented and was resented by many, including the Executive of the Teaching Brothers' Association who characterised Mr O'Connor's views as corresponding to 'Nationalisation by stealth'.[23]

However, away from the public gaze in these years, the dialogue which Mr O'Connor sought was taking place, predominantly with the Catholic hierarchy. Ó Buachalla sums up the pragmatic achievements of the bishops as follows:

Perhaps the major contribution of the Catholic bishops to policy in that decade (sixties) lay not only in shaping the nature of the proposals coming forward but in securing their acceptance of the government policies by the Catholic managerial bodies, in the creation of an effective consultative infrastructure and in influencing the character of the comprehensive and community schools so that they approximated, as closely as possible, to the Catholic ideal in management, ownership and staffing.[24]

Some critics of the outcomes of these changes misinterpreted the state's intentions. For instance, Akenson states:

In return for massive dollops of money the church has surrendered no powers of any significance ... Far from being revolutionary, the new financial arrangements reinforced the existing divisions of power between church and state.[25]

The Department's aim was not to set up a state system but to shape a partnership system of schooling which would be efficient, economical, and curricularly flexible in keeping with the needs of an expanded clientele in a fast changing society. The process was successfully put in place which would greatly modernise the primary and post-primary systems over subsequent years.

Another impulsion towards modernisation based on partnership came from the documents relating to education from the Second Vatican Council. Among many important new emphases was the stress on the centrality of parents' roles in the school system and the role of the laity in education. This coincided with stirrings which were taking place among some parental groups seeking a more practical expression of their constitutional rights in education. In 1969, the Irish hierarchy issued a statement supporting parent-teacher associations. In 1973, Seán O'Connor again took issue with the managerial practice in national schools, whereby the full powers and responsibility of school management rested on a local clergyman. He urged the setting up of boards of management including parents and principal teachers. In 1975, boards of management were established in the great majority of national schools, with the patron appointing the chairperson and the majority of the membership. In the context of the historical record, this was a breakthrough development, and was subject to further change and more equal representation in later years. Shared management by trustees, parents, teachers and community representatives was slower to be applied to post-primary schools but, in the nineties, such a system applied in the great majority of such schools too.

An interesting 'bottom up' movement by parents for the establishment of multi-denominational schools also began in the early seventies. The first such school was established by a group of parents in Dalkey, Co Dublin. One of the group, Áine Hyland, has recorded that this was not an easy task: 'Overt opposition was difficult to identify but the opposition was there. Some administrators at both local and central levels seemed to have difficulty in accepting that a multi-denominational school could be a vital part of the National School system.'[26] However, difficulties were surmounted and, under the banner 'Educate Together', about twenty multi-denominational schools have been established through the actions of interested groups of parents. The parents' voice in schooling became much more co-ordinated through the establishment of the National Parents' Council in 1985, and the granting to it of consultative and negotiating rights with the Department of Education and Science. These various trends gave a more democratic character to educational debate and administration.

While the thinking of Irish clergy was being influenced by Vatican II documents and through missionaries' engagement with 'liberation theology', a new historic trend was also beginning to affect the Irish church, which would have many serious consequences. Following over a hundred and fifty year period of remarkable expansion in personnel, the Irish church was now experiencing a decline in numbers and in vocations to religious life. This trend has continued since, and has raised fundamental questions for the church's future role in education. A report in 1973, *The Future Involvement of the Religious in Education* (FIRE), sought to encourage a strategic response to this new phenomenon. It encouraged a retrenchment policy to schools in which the religious presence could be maintained at a significant level and a policy of sharing responsibility for the management of religious run schools with lay people. As an illustration of the decline of numbers of religious and priests, in 1965-66 they constituted 50 per cent of post-primary teachers, but by 1970-71 this was reduced to 34% and by 1995-96 the percentage had gone down to 6% of the total post-primary teaching force. Furthermore, the age pattern of those currently in service is very much in the post 50 age range. Such a decline in numbers in a short time period was itself a major factor in promoting strategic thinking about the nature of the future involvement of clerical personnel in schools.

The appropriateness of the highly centralised administrative structure of Irish education came publicly into question in each of the last three decades of the twentieth century, each time under a non-Fianna Fáil coalition government. In autumn 1973 the Department of Education opened discussions with educational interests on a policy of decentralisation involving regional authorities and county education committees. A large list of requests for statutory guarantees relating to their schools by the churches, as well as opposition from the vocational sector, combined to scupper the regionalisation plans, and the minister dropped the initiative.[27] Regionalisation plans emerged again under the coalition government led by Dr Garret FitzGerald, 1982-87. A Green Paper, *Partners in Education,* was published in 1985 which proposed the establishment of thirteen Local Education Councils. A very critical response to the Green Paper was issued by the Council of Managers of Catholic Secondary Schools (CMCSS), the Conference of Major Religious Superiors and the Episcopal Commission on Education. The Secondary School Council of Governors (Protestant) also issued a critical response. The vocational sector added further opposition. In the face of such opposition, the government did not proceed with the proposals.

When a Green Paper was issued by a Fianna Fáil government in 1992, Dr FitzGerald criticised it strongly for its exclusion of any proposal for a local or regional co-ordination body. In the general debate on the Green Paper there were other voices pushing for regionalisation. Reflective of changing thinking within the Catholic Church, its organisations no longer spoke with one voice. A notable development was the published document of the Conference of Major Religious Superiors (CMRS) in January 1993 arguing in favour of regionalisation of educational administration as being in line with contemporary needs. However, division existed in the ranks, with the CMCSS taking a contrary view. The CMRS held to its view and argued in favour of regionalisation at the National Education Convention in October 1993. At the request of the Convention, Minister Bhreathnach published a discussion document on regionalisation in April 1994, which was discussed at round table talks between the education partners in May/June 1994. The White Paper of 1995 included provision for ten Education Boards, and the Education Bill of January 1997 made provision for their structure and powers. In response to the Bill the Catholic hierarchy retained its traditional opposition to such agencies and warned that the Education Boards would exercise 'excessive control' over church-linked schools and that they would be an extra 'costly layer of bureaucracy'.[28] The Fianna Fáil opposition spokesperson, Mr Micheál Martin, strongly opposed the Education Boards. When he assumed office, following the general election in June of that year, 1997, he proceeded to drop all reference to such Boards and in his own Education Act of 1998, no provision was made for regional education authorities. However, it is likely that the decentralisation policy will emerge again in the future, and it would seem that many religious have changed their attitudes and would now favour such a move.

The provision of management boards for all schools and the composition of their membership re-emerged as a very live issue of debate during the nineties. The proposals of the Green Paper (1992) meant that school owners would have a minority of members on the boards. During the discussions at the National Education Convention (1993) the church bodies took a very hard line, warning of strong resistance to any attempt by the state to interfere with either the composition of boards or their functions. The Convention Report opted for the model of boards with equal representation of patrons, teachers and parents, and urgent co-option of individuals from the local community. In June 1994, Minister Bhreathnach published a position paper on the governance of schools, and in September held a two-day conference to discuss it. At this conference Bishop Thomas Flynn, chairman of the Episcopal Commission on Education, made the very astringent statement:

> We find within the documents on the governance of schools and on the Regional Education Councils the bricks of a secularist agenda and a bid to control the schools to such an extent as to undermine the principle of subsidiarity. The ideology behind some of these proposals is seen by some bishops as an attempt by the state to push the church out of education.[29]

As might be expected in the light of this attitude, agreement was not reached at this Conference. Yet, such a statement may be seen as something of a last hurrah of an older perspective. Facilitation talks under an independent mediator began shortly afterwards, but it was to take two years of negotiation before agreement was reached, in November 1996. The outcome was, as the Convention Report had suggested, equal representation for owners, parents, teachers and the community. The churches received statements guaranteeing the ethos of the schools. The concept of partnership in the management of schools was stitched in as the first section of Part IV of the Education Act of 1998.

Another significant change in the operation of schools in recent years, particularly voluntary secondary schools, has been the transition to lay principalships. The severe decline in personnel, the more onerous role of principalships and changing priorities within some religious congregations, have all contributed to this development.

In recent years many religious congregations have been engaging in reflective self-questioning and re-visiting the original charism of their founders for inspiration. Many conferences, seminars, position papers and booklets have contributed to this major process of reflection and planning. There has been quite a withdrawal from the frontline activity of schools towards a concentration on support structures for schools and a re-structuring of trusteeship with a view to securing values and ethos in the schools of the future. As a recent publication of the Christian Brothers puts it:

The decision to set up boards of management and to appoint lay principals can now be viewed as initiating an intermediary phase of lay/religious collaboration in CB (*sic*.) schools; the success of this experiment has now made possible the enaction of the ultimate transformative decision to share the trusteeship with lay people.[30]

The Conference of Religious of Ireland (CORI) has been a very influential agency in this process. Through its Education Commission it has sought to guide and to co-ordinate the process. In recent publications on the theme 'Religious Congregations in Irish Education – A Role for the Future?', CORI takes a longitudinal overview of the involvement of religious in Irish education. Against a time chart from the 18th to the 21st century it traces the patterns of engagement as follows: foundation > growth > decline in membership > rediscovery of charism > new beginnings.[31] CORI sets out 'to develop a new mission in education' and draws attention to two related challenges for religious:

First:

They need to engage with others in the task of developing new structures to take over the responsibilities for schools currently held by religious congregations. This task is now well under way, and is going into its implementation phase.

Secondly:

They need to identify new ways of being involved in education which will:

- enable urgent needs to be identified and responded to;
- give rise to the empowerment of poor and marginalised groups;
- represent a counter-cultural voice promoting an alternative vision of society, based on gospel values.[32]

CORI identifies three key elements of the projected new mission as engaging in trail-blazing initiatives, public debate and advocacy, and forming alliances. There is a radical dimension to CORI's discourse which is very different from the language and sentiments used by church representatives in the past:

However, it is being argued that virtually all of the analyses of society which have been undertaken from a gospel perspective have shown society's problems will not be solved by a process of continuous improvement, where existing strategies are extrapolated and 'more of the same' is prescribed.

What is needed is a radically different approach – one which is *discontinuous* with the past and involves a quantum leap into the future, or as some would have it, a paradigm shift.[33] (Author's italics).

A striking feature of contemporary Irish society is its growing multicultural character and increasing secularism. The majority of the Irish population remains at least nominally Catholic, and there are also long established Protestant denominations, a small Jewish community, a growing Islamic community, people of the Baha'i faith, Hindus, Buddhists, Sikhs and adherents of the Greek and Russian Orthodox churches. There are also increasing numbers of Irish people of humanist or secular beliefs. Over 90% of all primary schools are under Catholic management. The majority of non-Catholic schools are under Protestant management. There is one Jewish school and one Islamic school, both in Dublin. None of the other minority religions have access to their own state-supported schools. Currently, less than 1% of primary schools are multi-denominational in character. This means that many of those belonging to minority faiths, or of secular beliefs, are obliged to attend whatever local school admits them, regardless of religious affiliations.

This issue was examined at the National Education Convention in 1993, recognising that 'the pressure for the provision of other than denominational schooling is likely to grow and it is important for the state to have an informed policy on this developing situation'.[34] A good level of understanding of the issues involved was reached by Convention participants. The dilemma posed for some parents was recognised by the Conference of Major Religious Superiors (CMRS) whose representatives stated, 'We recognise, however, that issues of civil liberties remain because of genuine conscientious objections on the part of some families to the principle of the integration of religion with other aspects of the curriculum (in denominational schools).'[35] The National Education Convention recommended that the Department of Education convene a suitably qualified and representative working party to develop 'good practice' guidelines and, also, to explore the legal and constitutional issues involved.[36] While the state did accept a significant recommendation in this context that, for the future, primary school buildings would be publicly owned and leased out to school authorities, the Department of Education did not take a pro-active stance with regard to a working party on the problems posed in the provision of schooling for the needs of a fast-changing society, although it accepted the Convention's proposal in its White Paper of 1995.[37]

However, the problems have not gone away and are likely to become intensified. As in the past, denominational education is likely to be the predominant requirement of most citizens, but accommodations also need to be satisfactorily worked out for citizens desiring multi-denominational, inter-denominational and non-denominational education. Indeed, problems relating to how religion would be dealt with in an inter-denominational school became a major public issue of debate in the summer of 2002, resulting in the dismissal of a school principal and institution of legal proceedings. Arising from this, the teacher's union, the Irish National Teachers' Organisation, has called for a national forum on inter-denominational education and associated issues, and it has sought the support of the Department of Education and the churches for this initiative.[38] The state has a responsibility to take the initiative in clarifying relevant issues involved and in promoting good practice so that citizens may have the maximum possible opportunity of obtaining schooling for their children according to their consciences and preferences. The churches have an obligation to assist in this process and there are indications that there is a realisation of this. As Sr Teresa McCormack stated in a recent article:

> There is now a very strong consensus in Irish education that the most appropriate way of accommodating the growing pluralism in society is through the availability of a diversity of school types. There is a commitment on the part of government, arising from a corresponding concern in contemporary society, to try to ensure that, as far as possible, parents will be able to choose schools that reflect their religious, ethical or cultural values.[39]

This acceptance of a changing reality is strongly echoed by Dermot Lane's embracive viewpoint when he states:

> The Catholic Church, therefore, should welcome the development of other alternative forms of educational choice such as Gaelscoileanna, multi-denominational education and non-denominational education ... Such diversity of form and choice in education can only be good for Catholic education as it will act as a stimulus to develop what is distinctive

about its own identity and ethos. The absence of diversity in education in the past has not always served the best interests of Catholic education.[40]

Reflecting back over the years on state-church relations on education a great deal of the debate focused on issues such as legal rights, ownership, trusteeship, patronage, managerial control, rights of teacher appointment and dismissal, controlling the ethos of schools. The eminent Catholic theologian, Dermot Lane, suggests that some of this was linked to the concerns of the Counter-Reformation Church which, he states, 'was defensive, exclusivist and introverted'. He goes on to state that 'this church flourished in Ireland, and elsewhere, up to the mid-1960s'.[41] As can be noted above, the Catholic Church has taken many new initiatives and has adapted many older practices in keeping with the spirit of Vatican II and changing circumstances, including trusteeship, management of schools, appointment of lay principals, openness to pluralism in education. This trend, Lane would suggest, is linked to the evolving 'educational self-understanding of the church'. While respecting the educational rights and values of people of other denominations, and those of no denomination, the new Catholic perspective does not see this as constituting any dilution of the character of Catholic denominational schooling. However, it is being inspired by a new ethic, invigorated by the educational self-understanding which emerged from Vatican II, and subsequent reflection. Lane states that, 'The Catholic school of the future ought to be distinctive in its critical openness to the modern and post-modern world, prominent in promoting ecumenical activity, and active in the embrace of inter-faith dialogue.'[42] This perspective was also endorsed in a recent statement (September 2002) by Cardinal Connell. He stated:

> To be sure, Catholic religious education is concerned to communicate clearly the full meaning of Catholic identity and faith. However, I think it is also important to emphasise that Catholic identity and faith is of itself both ecumenical in relation to other Christian denominations and respectful of other religious traditions. Recent documents from the Catholic Church have clearly spelt out the ecumenical and inter-faith dimension of Catholic religious education.[43]

Only time will reveal how the new directions for religious involvement in education will evolve, but of one thing we can be certain, and that is that it will be very different from what it has been in the past. It is also noteworthy that following a period of great difficulty in relation to such developments as the decline of personnel and various scandals associated with clerics, the reflection and strategic thinking which have been engaged in have given a new sense of mission and a reinvigorated *esprit de corps* to many religious regarding their future involvement with education and society. On the other hand, one is not convinced that responsible office holders in the state have been engaged in qualitative depth of thought in developing policy to help all the citizens of a fast changing Ireland to achieve their schooling aspirations, from a religious perspective. Yet, we are in a transitional era and developments in recent decades, on accumulation, reflect a significant break from the past. With well-informed and courageous leadership, there are grounds for hope that future church-state relations in education will be both productive and well-based.

CHAPTER EIGHT

Catholic Influence on the Health Services 1830-2000

Ruth Barrington

Catholic hospitals and Catholic involvement in public hospitals

Ireland is probably unique in the extent to which the Catholic Church has influenced the development of health policy. This involvement began relatively late in the 1830s. It developed on the foundations laid in the eighteenth century by government support for new hospitals founded by philanthropic lay people of a Protestant ethos and the major government initiative of the 1830s that provided a minimum level of support for the poor in a network of workhouses across the country. Neither the lay hospitals nor the poor law was capable of responding to the needs of the burgeoning population of destitute people or the catastrophe of the Great Famine. From the 1830s, Catholic religious orders began to respond to what they identified as a major social need. Liberated by Catholic Emancipation, supported by a growing Catholic middle class and led by a number of well educated and able women, the Irish Sisters of Charity and the Mercy Order founded hospitals in Dublin (St Vincent's 1835, Mater Misericordiae 1861) Belfast (Mater) and Cork (Mercy 1857). The hospitals were established under the patronage of the bishop or archbishop of the diocese in which they were located. As patron, the bishop or archbishop was appointed chair of the board of governors, a role usually delegated.

It needs to be emphasised that what we call a hospital and what our nineteenth century ancestors called a hospital are very different things. A hospital in the nineteenth century was a refuge, a place where destitute people could live out the rest of their days or die from their injuries or diseases. Medical practitioners had attachments to the hospitals, for which services they were not paid. They made their income from the medical students who learned to practise their profession in the hospitals to which their teachers were attached and from attending paying patients who were always treated at home. Until the end of the nineteenth century, hospitals were far too dangerous places for the better off classes to frequent.

Added to the danger of infection was the low status of those who provided care in the hospitals. A hospital attendant was not seen as a respectable occupation for women, in a society obsessed with the 'respectability' of its womenfolk. The nature of nineteenth-century hospitals gives some idea of the courage and commitment required of the women who dedicated their lives to caring for the poor and sick as members of the pioneering religious orders. They could only engage in such a difficult task because their motives and way of life was beyond reproach by the standards of the day. They were not to know that hospitals would become the great powerhouses of healing and medical research of the twentieth century. However, by raising the standard of care in their institutions, they contributed in no small way to the emergence of the new hospital. It was the commitment of the religious orders that helped lay the foundations for the profession of nursing. Florence Nightingale, who did so much to professionalise nursing in both these islands, spent part of her training in St Vincent's Hospital. The religious orders made nursing a respectable and popular career for the daughters of generations of Irish families, even if many aspects of nursing formation outlived their usefulness.[1]

The emergence of Catholic hospitals was supported by the growing number of Catholic medical specialists who realised their potential for medical teaching. Sir Dominic Corrigan, one of the leading specialists of his day, was a strong supporter. The Mater and St Vincent's Hospital provided the hospital element of medical teaching when the Catholic University of Ireland was formed in 1854 and later for the medical faculty of University College Dublin.

The religious orders were not only involved in running their own hospitals. They also penetrated, against considerable resistance, the workhouses in an effort to raise the standards of care for the destitute inmates. Workhouses in the second half of the nineteenth century were repositories of much human suffering and misery. Little attempt was made to differentiate between the ill, the infirm, the intellectually disabled, the destitute elderly, orphans, unmarried mothers and others who had no role in society. The efforts of the nursing orders to get involved were opposed in many cases by the lay Boards of Guardians, who for different reasons did not want to see publicly funded institutions developing a Catholic ethos. In other cases, their involvement was tolerated because their services did not cost the local rate payers any money and they did much to improve the quality of care of the residents. With the democratisation of local government after 1898, the pace of involvement of the religious orders in workhouses quickened, at least in the southern part of the country. As with so many other aspects of church-state affairs in Ireland, this involvement appears to have happened on an informal, *ad hoc* basis, without much being written down about formal roles and responsibilities. Interestingly, the religious orders did not get involved in the extensive system of publicly funded mental hospitals, perhaps because those hospitals were more centrally controlled and funded than the workhouses. Those religious orders with an interest in the care of the mentally ill – the Daughters of Charity and the St John of God Order – founded their own hospitals.

Medical Benefit 1911
Apart from the establishment of charitable hospitals and the penetration of the workhouses, the religious orders and the Catholic hierarchy seem to have been little concerned with the development of social policy other than education, despite the appalling living standards of so many people in rural and urban areas in the last part of the nineteenth century. The first sign of engagement came in 1911 in response to the Liberal government's proposal to introduce unemployment insurance and medical benefit throughout the United Kingdom. Medical benefit would have funded general practitioner care for insured workers, care that they previously had to pay for or accessed through membership of friendly societies. The hierarchy, taking its cue from the propertied classes opposed to the increased costs that would fall on business and concerned about the cost to a native government of home rule, particularly since the introduction of old age pensions in 1908, opposed the introduction of unemployment insurance and medical benefit for the employed in Ireland. The Irish Party, with a courage not always shown by political parties after independence, stood up to the hierarchy and argued strongly for the extension of the radical social provisions to Ireland. They succeeded in securing unemployment insurance for Irish workers and would have secured medical benefit

but for the opposition of significant sections of the medical profession.[2] Medical benefit was introduced in Northern Ireland in
1929 but not in the South. Coverage for general practitioner care
remains a significant health issue in this part of the island to this
day.

Sweepstakes – funding for Voluntary Hospitals
The voluntary hospitals, both Catholic and Protestant, faced a
major financial challenge in the years following independence.
The role of the hospital had changed beyond recognition since
the middle of the nineteenth century. The control of infection,
the development of anaesthesiology, radiology and pathology
meant that hospitals were no longer refuges for the untreatable
but had become places for the diagnosis and treatment of a wide
range of diseases. The growing sophistication and specialisation
of medicine meant that it became increasingly expensive to run
a hospital. The value of the hospital endowment funds was reduced by inflation during the first World War and income from
charitable sources dwindled. Voluntary contributions and be-
quests, topped up by small grants from government, even
where supplemented by the unpaid efforts of religious nursing
sisters, were no longer adequate to fund a hospital. The hospitals relied increasingly on income from paying patients and
their commitment to treating the poor declined. The new government, determined to keep the burden of taxation low by running public affairs as economically and efficiently as possible,
was not sympathetic to the case of the hospitals. It refused to increase the value of parliamentary grants to the hospitals last
fixed in the 1850s.[3] This was the same government that reduced
the weekly value of the old age pension by one shilling.

A number of business people linked to the hospitals made
the case to government that a well run sweepstakes could provide the funds necessary to run the hospitals. Sweepstakes were
illegal at the time as there was a widespread view that they
could not be run without fraud. A number of hospitals ran *ad hoc*
lotteries and sweepstakes to raise money and a blind eye was
turned because of the good cause for which the money was
raised. Matters came to a head in 1929 when the National
Maternity Hospital, a lay hospital under the patronage of the
Catholic Archbishop of Dublin, threatened to close its doors if it
could not raise money. The government agreed to legalise a

sweepstake on horse racing for the purposes of supporting hospitals under the Public Hospitals Act, 1930. To benefit, a hospital had to reserve at least one quarter of their beds for non-paying patients. The venture was an outstanding financial success, with ninety per cent of the £1 million income raised in the first year coming from abroad. The hospitals received much more money than they expected and the manner in which the funds were divided up between the hospitals gave rise to adverse comment. In 1931, the government passed legislation to regulate the disbursement of the funds and to make one quarter of the funds available for the public county hospitals. The success of the Hospitals Sweepstakes ensured the survival to the second half of the twentieth century of a relatively large number of voluntary hospitals – 52 in 1933 – which otherwise might have closed or amalgamated during the 1930s. It probably also provided a supportive climate for the opening of additional Catholic voluntary hospitals such as Our Lady of Lourdes in Drogheda and Portiuncula in Ballinasloe.

Religious involvement in public services
An early priority of the government on independence was the rationalisation of the poor law system. The rationalisation had been recommended by a number of bodies, concerned at the primitive conditions and lack of specialised care in workhouses that still provided a refuge to all forms of destitution. The approach of the new government, however, was motivated more by the need to reduce expenditure on the poor law system than by humanitarian motives. Many workhouses were closed. The functions of the remaining workhouses were changed. Some were designated county hospitals, with a primary commitment to treat the acutely ill. Others became county homes with a mandate to care for the destitute elderly, the infirm, the intellectually disabled and unmarried mothers. Orphans were gradually transferred to orphanages run by religious orders or lay people with a Protestant ethos. Some of those with an intellectual disability were transferred to dedicated services also run by religious orders such as the service run by the Daughters of Charity on the Navan Road in Dublin. Religious orders stepped up their involvement in providing nursing in many of the county hospitals and homes. It was an involvement that met the interests of reluctant rate payers, the Christian commitment of the orders and the needs of the destitute ill and infirm.

The strength of the Catholic voluntary hospitals, involvement in county hospitals and homes and the development of specialised services were all made possible by the extraordinary strength of vocations to the religious orders in the first half of the twentieth century, a level of recruitment that not only met domestic needs but also provided manpower for missionary work in the colonies of the British Empire.

Growth of Catholic Social Thinking and Action
From the early 1930s, under the influence of papal encyclicals such as *Casti Connubi* (1930) and *Quadragesimo Anno* (1931), the government made explicit reference to its desire to govern the country according to Catholic principles. In 1933, the Minister for Local Government and Public Health, Seán T. Ó Ceallaigh in a speech in Geneva, announced that his government's programme of economic and political reform was based on the same principles as *Quadragesimo Anno*.[4]

Following representations from the hierarchy, the government passed the Criminal Law (Amendment) Act 1935 that banned the importation and sale of contraceptives. The desire to mould society according to Catholic principles increased as the generation of bishops appointed prior to independence passed away and were replaced by more socially active and politically ambitious prelates. John Charles McQuaid, Archbishop of Dublin, personified the new generation of bishops. He, like some of the other new bishops, set out to mould his diocese into his perception of a Catholic community. Profoundly suspicious of state involvement in the social sphere, he attempted through the Catholic Social Service Council, the founding of Our Lady's Hospital for Sick Children, the invitation to the Bon Secours Sisters to open a private hospital in Glasnevin and support for the established Catholic voluntary hospitals, to establish a Catholic health and social service that would be largely independent of the state and under the control of the diocese.[5] He opposed efforts to tackle social problems where the leadership was outside his control, as demonstrated by his opposition to the Anti-Tuberculosis League which had a strong Protestant involvement.[6] He was especially suspicious of the influence of medical practitioners trained in Trinity College, outside the influence of the constituent colleges of National University of Ireland where he and fellow bishops could influence the curriculum and the appointment of professors.

Health policy: A Crisis of Church and State
The determination of government in the late 1940s to respond to the popular demand for much improved health services provided the spark for a major show-down between the hierarchy and government. The major problems to be tackled were the control of tuberculosis, improved care for women before, during and after child birth, protection of the health of children and enabling people on moderate incomes to access increasingly costly medical care in hospitals without the fear of catastrophic costs. To tackle these problems the government proposed in a White Paper in 1947 the gradual development of a national health service in which treatment would be free to all at the point of use. The model proposed was not too dissimilar to that being planned in the United Kingdom, although there it was planned to launch the new service at the same time in 1948. The Health Act, 1947, which included provision for an improved health service for mothers and children, was the occasion for the first exchange of views between the hierarchy and the government over its plans for health reform. Lobbied by the medical profession and clearly influenced by their concerns about absorption in a state-run medical service and the possible takeover of the Catholic voluntary hospitals, the hierarchy opposed the Bill principally on the grounds that the state should not be interfering in matters that were best left to heads of families, the medical profession and the church to regulate. Their opposition was made known by way of a private letter to the Taoiseach.

There was a change of government shortly after the Health Act, 1947 was passed and a young and inexperienced Noel Browne replaced the experienced Jim Ryan as Minister for Health.[7] Browne pushed through an ambitious hospital building programme to provide sanatoria to treat tuberculosis and cancer and to provide public hospital accommodation. He funded this programme largely from funds accumulated by the Hospitals Sweepstakes, refusing to use these funds to pay the deficits of the voluntary hospitals, to the intense annoyance of the voluntary hospitals and their medical establishments, both Catholic and Protestant. He compounded his unpopularity with the medical establishment by unwise and insulting comments about their behaviour. The opposition to his policies came to a head in late 1950 when he announced his proposals for an improved health service for mothers and children. Reflecting the general mood of the day, he agreed that his proposals could not succeed without the support of the bishops, support that he thought he had secured. However, the hierarchy, under the influence of arguments refined by the medical profession, persuaded John A. Costello's government that it should not proceed with Browne's proposals. Browne resigned, but by ensuring that the correspondence between the hierarchy and the government was published, his resignation led to a major crisis of confidence in government and the republican ideals of the state.

Fianna Fáil was retuned to government in 1951 with a mandate to continue with health reform, including the introduction of a mother and child scheme. It was no accident that De Valera appointed the trusted Jim Ryan as Minister for Health. Ryan began work immediately on a mother and child scheme and a new health act that would give those on moderate income – the vast majority of the population – access to hospital and specialist care at little or no cost. His proposals were opposed by the medical profession which criticised them as an attack on the voluntary hospitals, favouring the growth of public hospitals and public consultants at the expense of consultants in the voluntary hospitals and undermining of professional control of medical teaching. The proposals provoked an unusual response from the hierarchy. Learning some lessons from their earlier intervention, the hierarchy this time sent a letter to the Taoiseach outlining their opposition to the Minister for Health's proposals, indicating that the letter would be published in the press the following day. The hierarchy's opposition to the health reforms had little to do with Catholic social or moral teaching and is only understandable as a defence of the interests of the powerful Catholic voluntary hospitals, their consultant staff and associated medical schools from further state encroachment. The Taoiseach and Dr Ryan moved quickly to persuade the hierarchy to withdraw their opposition and to engage in negotiations. Some minor concessions were made to the hierarchy on the mother and child scheme and the proposed widening of access to hospital and specialist care, but the core reforms were protected and subsequently implemented.

The experience of the establishment of the National Health Service (NHS) in Northern Ireland in 1948 provides an interesting comparison with the outcome of the triangular conflict in the South. There is no evidence that the Irish hierarchy (or the British

hierarchy for that matter) formerly opposed the introduction of
the NHS on the grounds of Catholic social or moral teaching.
The medical profession, sharply divided on religious grounds,
was less likely to find a natural ally in the Catholic bishops and
those that were opposed concentrated their efforts as part of the
wider opposition of the British Medical Association. Nor would
the hierarchy have expected the same deference to their views
from the Stormont government, even if they wished to oppose
the introduction of the NHS. They did, however, take the only
course of action open to them. They refused to allow the nationalisation of the Mater Hospital in Belfast and it continued without government support until an acceptable solution to its involvement in the NHS was agreed in 1973.[8]

Legacy of Conflict
While the Dublin government succeeded in achieving the core
of its health reforms by the mid-1950s, the implementation of the
Health Act 1953 did mark the end of the commitment to establish a national health service on the British model in this part of
the island. It did not stop, however, the increasing involvement
of government in funding and organising the increasingly complex and expensive health system. The triangular conflict of
state, church and medical profession of the 1940s and 1950s left
its mark in a number of ways on the health services to this day.
First, means tests were enshrined as a principle of access to
many health services, in contrast to the universal access offered
by the NHS north of the Border. Second, the defence of the medical profession of their private practice led to the tolerance by
government of an extraordinary degree of such practice, to the
extent that it is extremely difficult to distinguish where the
public element ends and the private element begins in the health
service. The contrast with Northem Ireland, where private practice is quite limited, is striking.

Third, was the need of government to develop innovative
structures to gain the co-operation of the independent hospitals
and their medical staff. A key issue was how to control the appointment of medical consultants to the hospitals, in the interest
of rational development of medical services and the best use of
public funds. The response was the establishment of Comhairle
na nOspidéal, a unique organisation in the pantheon of world
health systems, under the Health Act 1970. An Comhairle was

given the authority to approve every medical consultant post in publicly and independently-owned hospitals. (The hospital remained free to fill the post once approved by An Comhairle.) The membership of An Comhairle has always included strong representation of the independently-owned hospitals. Since its establishment, the decisions of An Combairle have resulted in a major rationalisation of medical specialties in the country. On the negative side, the highly centralised nature of the approval system has probably also contributed to the small numbers of consultant posts in the health system relative to other countries.

Fourth, the alliance between the Catholic Church and the medical profession, formed to protect their mutual interests in the 1940s, has survived, most obviously in the defence of Catholic ethical standards. The tortuous provision of access to family planning, including sterilisation, had much to do with the reluctance of the majority of the medical profession to deviate from the policy of the Catholic Church. The alliance was at its most political in the efforts to preclude the legalisation or practice of abortion under any circumstances in this part of the island. These efforts may have backfired at a constitutional level but the alliance has also made it politically impossible to define the circumstances in which legal abortions may take place in Irish hospitals. The body politic is relieved of having to deal with this issue because of the relatively easy availability of abortion in Britain, to which many Irish women resort each year. Finally, the influence of the alliance is to be seen in the continuing independence of the voluntary Catholic hospitals and to a lesser extent, other voluntary services run by Catholic religious orders from the kind of controls imposed on publicly-run services, even though more than ninety per cent of their funding comes from public sources. The voluntary hospitals, both Catholic and Protestant and the voluntary mental handicap services, for example, continued to receive their funding direct from the Department of Health up until the late-1990s, even though, legally, the health boards were responsible for administering all health services within their administrative areas.

Current Influence
Even if the legacy of the past remains strong in the way in which the health service is managed and organised, the influence of the Catholic Church in today's health service is only a shadow of its

former self. The first reason for the decline in influence is the reduction in the number of vocations to religious life, beginning in
the 1960s. Second, was the impact of the Second Vatican Council
which led many orders to reassess their contribution and re-
order their priorities. Third, was the increasing secularisation of
Irish life and the weakening of Catholic influence over government policy. Finally, there was the impact of a more organised
and comprehensive public health service than previously available, following the establishment of the health boards in 1970.

The first effects of the changes were felt by the nursing sisters
in public hospitals and homes who gradually withdrew from
these services from the 1970s, either voluntarily or when the
hospitals closed. Next were the orders that owned hospitals who
found that they no longer had the manpower to run them or that
younger sisters preferred to contribute in a different kind of way
to the charism of their orders. In the 1990s, Portiuncula Hospital,
Ballinasloe and Our Lady of Lourdes Hospital, Drogheda were
sold by their owners to the Western and North Eastern Health
Boards and became publicly owned hospitals. The transfer of
ownership was not without its difficulties, particularly in the
case of Our Lady of Lourdes Hospital where the health board
found it necessary to suspend medical consultants following its
assuming responsibility for the hospital. In the same decade the
religious orders withdrew almost entirely from the care of
orphaned or neglected children, a withdrawal accelerated by
revelations about the abuse of some children in their care over
the years. Least affected by the changes were the orders providing specialised care for those with an intellectual disability. By a
combination of rationalisation of services and greater involvement of lay staff, orders such as the St John of God, the Brothers
of Charity and the Daughters of Charity have continued to play
a leading role in the development of innovative services for
these people and their families. The Brothers of Charity have,
however, had to come to terms with a legacy of abuse by a small
number of brothers in the past.

What might be called the 'flagship' Catholic hospitals, St
Vincent's and the Mater Hospitals in Dublin and the Mercy
Hospital in Cork, remain in the ownership of their religious or-
ders. Since the professorial staff of the medical school of
University College Dublin is appointed to one or other of these
hospitals, the ethos of the hospitals continues to play a major

role in medical education in the largest medical school in the country. All three hospitals have received or are in receipt of major capital funding from government to enable them to provide a modern hospital infrastructure. All are also in receipt of the major part of their running costs from public funds, since the late 1990s via a health board or authority, with minimal interference in their governance or management. It is interesting that the issue of the relationship of the independently-owned hospitals to the health system has not been an issue in recent discussion of the need for change in the governance structures of the health system.

One wonders how long, in the light of the continuing decline in vocations, the orders will continue to remain active in the hospitals. Will they follow the route of some orders and sell the hospitals to the state or follow the example of some Catholic schools and formally hand the running of the hospitals to lay persons charged with protecting the Catholic ethos of the hospitals? The successful conclusion of negotiations by the Adelaide Society with the Minister for Health in the mid-1990s to ensure that governance of the new hospital at Tallaght, built to replace the Adelaide, Meath and National Children's Hospitals, reflected a Protestant ethos, suggests another course that might be followed to protect the particular ethos of those hospitals.

The Future
What is the role of a Catholic or, for that matter, a Protestant hospital, in the twenty-first century? The spokespersons for the Protestant minority in the negotiations over governance of the new hospital in Tallaght were clearly determined that at least one hospital in the state reflected their more liberal ethos. Catholic hospitals served an important purpose in the nineteenth and early twentieth century at a time when the Catholic majority felt they needed institutions to cater for their needs. A Catholic hospital, such as the Mater in Belfast, may still fulfill an important symbolic role in Belfast for the Catholic minority. Is the Catholic hospital of the future, however, to be defined by the services it does not provide, such as abortion, sterilisation and 'artificial' contraception or by more frequent use of extraordinary means to prolong life? Or is it to be known for standards of care and service that make it in some way different to other hospitals, the majority of whose staff and patients may also be

Catholic? Is it simply the ownership that will make a hospital 'Catholic'? With the rise in standards of care in public hospitals, has the Catholic hospital become a victim of its own success? To what extent is involvement in private hospitals compatible with the original commitment of the religious orders to the care of the poor? On a wider note, one can ask 'is a vital interest of the church served by owning and operating modern hospitals?' Does the emergence of a pluralist society paradoxically provide a rationale for maintaining hospitals with Catholic ethos? The value of hospitals with a distinctive Catholic ethos may depend on the extent to which one believes that they form an important part of the church's mission in society or the extent to which one feels that the church's presence in society could be better met by other forms of action.

There are fewer questions to be asked about the continuing involvement of the religious orders in the care of those with an intellectual disability. The majority of people with intellectual disabilities are receiving that care in services that have a Catholic ethos. A significant issue for those involved in this field is coming to terms with the evidence that a small number of religious brothers in the past abused clients, and ensuring that such abuse does not happen again. The charitable impulse that underpins the care of these highly dependent clients is, however, being challenged by the new emphasis on the human rights of people with disabilities. However, it is not clear at this stage that a rights-based philosophy will provide the motivation for the numbers of staff required to provide personal care on an ongoing basis to these clients. Integrating the benefits of a rights-based philosophy and the Christian ethic of caring will be a major challenge for these services and for government in the next decade.

As Ireland becomes a more pluralist society, both more secular on the one hand and home to more religions on the other, a number of questions arise about the relationship between a publicly-funded health system and religious ethos. There is nothing incompatible in principle about a secular government recognising the religious ethos of hospitals or schools, and funding those institutions, on whatever conditions may be needed to protect the public good. It does not seem reasonable that these conditions should, for example, require the hospital to carry out procedures that are incompatible with its religious ethos. If, however, these are services to which the public are entitled, government should ensure that people can avail of the services in another institution. Should government have to provide a health service that is compatible with every religious ethos, for example, provide a hospital where blood transfusion is never used since it is against the ethos of Jehovah's Witnesses? This seems to this author to go too far. However, the wishes of a Jehovah's Witness not to have a blood transfusion should be respected in all publicly-funded hospitals where the refusal of consent, as in the case of a parent refusing consent for the transfusion of a minor, is not incompatible with the law.

One of the striking features of many publicly owned-hospitals is the extent to which a Catholic ethos prevails, whether in the form of holy pictures and statues on wards, the naming of hospitals and wards after saints and the prevalence of Catholic prayers and sacraments. This is not surprising given the presence of so many religious sisters in public hospitals over the years and predominance of the Catholic faith among patients and staff. However, too many staff do not see an incompatibility between a publicly-managed hospital that should respect all religious traditions and the overwhelming presence of Catholic symbols. This complacency was challenged some years ago when an attendant in St James's Hospital, on religious grounds, refused the request of a nurse to carry a crucifix to a dying patient. Whatever about the merits of the particular case, the incident illustrated the need to take the issue of religious symbols and conscientious objections seriously. A more explicit policy of respect for all religious traditions in our public hospitals would demonstrate the separation of state from any particular faith and, at the same time, emphasise the particular ethos of Catholic hospitals.

CHAPTER NINE

Religion and Bio-Ethics in Ireland today

Maureen Junker-Kenny

It is hard for 'religion' to engage in debate on issues in biomedical ethics, if the surrounding culture shows a marked reluctance to accept these issues as worthy of attention for the agendas of politics and civil society. So the first matter for analysis is the lack of debate in Irish society on questions such as medical research performed on persons incapable of consent, genetic testing, the legislative framework for techniques of assisted procreation, the permissibility of reproductive and 'therapeutic' cloning, of embryonic versus adult stem cell research and assisted euthanasia (1). Yet, if there was to be such a critical process of argumentation in Ireland, what philosophical and theological choices exist? The recent debate between two schools of liberal social philosophy, John Rawls and Jürgen Habermas on the question of genetic intervention, provides orientation by identifying some of the alternative options ahead for policy makers, experts, and citizens (2). What could be resources (3) for more than a minimal consensus on the use and limits to be set for techniques that will have profound effects on our lifeworld? Besides the hopes invested in them to cure illnesses, they have the potential to cause irreversible changes to physical human nature, to alter unilaterally the relationship between generations, as well as established balances of rights, e.g., between employees and their companies. At a time when humanism is considered to be no less in crisis than Christian convictions,[1] I shall argue for an approach to Christian ethics that combines recognition of the autonomy of the human subject with the resources of Christian anthropology. The Christian view of the human person is still widely shared in Ireland, and the values of justice and compassion are acknowledged insofar as society is also measured by its willingness to care for those in need of support. Having shown how Christian ethics can partake in public debate about the future shape of our lifeworld by virtue of its communicability, I shall conclude with the dimensions it adds to this debate, due to its distinctiveness.

1. Bio-Ethics – an Irish non-debate?

Both with regard to the significance of the new genetic technologies and in comparison with the level of debate in Europe the lack of discussion in Ireland is remarkable (a). Why is this so (b), and what can ethical reflection achieve (c)?

a) Significance and comparison with Europe

The effect of the rate and depth of technological and structural changes on people's private lives has been called a 'de-privatisation of life forms' (Ludwig Siep).[2] Examples of such structural and technological changes that blur the distinction between public and private are the impact of individualisation on family life and community networks; the creation of novel food products and the struggle to protect consumer choice through food labelling; the effects of information overload and the virtualisation of life on the internet on ordinary citizens; changes in the parent-child relationship through genetic design; the link between private genetic testing and the right to be insured, and a relationship to nature, including the human body, that sees it as material ready to be subjected to our projects.

In view of the urgency of these questions, their absence from an otherwise thriving culture of debate in Ireland is all the more surprising. On the Continent and in Britain, issues in biomedical ethics have at different times been the No 1 news feature. When the European Convention on Human Rights and Biomedicine was finalised in 1997, the European newspapers were full of it. In Ireland, few people seem to know why some countries, Ireland being one of them, have not signed this document of the Council of Europe. In 2001, the German weekly *Die Zeit* commissioned a series of articles from different viewpoints on the moral status of the human embryo in the context of assisted reproduction and pre-implantation genetic testing. The present state of the national debate is regularly summarised in philosophical and theological journals, such as *Information Philosophie*. No such sustained debate exists in Ireland, and the way in which those human interest cases that make the news are discussed only confirms this analysis. Whatever events are reported from Britain, biomedical ones are scarce. While universities have invited speakers and hosted conferences on such themes, there is a lot of ground to make up, having arrived ten years late on the scene. At the political level, Ireland still belongs to the 'cowboy countries' without legislation despite the dire need for it in the age of cloning, and although a private member's bill was introduced in the Senate. The only regulations existing are medical guidelines that are binding merely for medical practitioners, not biologists or other scientists. In 1999, a Committee for Assisted Reproduction was set up initially without any ethicists by the Department of Health. Subsequently, after protest, two or three were included in subgroups. Yet the fact that the main body of more than twenty experts proceeds without any members specialised in the international ethical debate confirms the disregard for ethics. It also raises the suspicion that the goal is 'consensus management,'[3] not national legislation that has stood the test of the exchange of critical ethical arguments.

b) Reasons for the Irish abstinence
Not having grown up in Ireland, it is hard for me to imagine why politicians and journalists, medical and scientific experts, lawyers and business people are trying so hard to bypass ethical reflection on matters that will shape the future of everyone's immediate and larger worlds. No matter how much the double functionalising of morality for religion and of religion for morality in the past may be to blame for this disregard, it should be clear that the transformations of cultural standards that the life sciences contain within themselves are in need of public ethical debate. The executive and the legislative have to be joined by an 'ethicative' (Peter Liese, German MEP, at the European Ethics Summit, 'Sustaining Humanity beyond Humanism', Brussels, August 2002). I can see at least three reasons why the Ireland of the Celtic Tiger has been slow to interrupt the pace of progress with ethical reflection.
• Irish political reflection is still too much caught up in the battles of the past, e.g., of making contraception and divorce available in the state against the resistance of the Catholic hierarchy, to notice the more recent threats to the human flourishing and self-determination of women, children, and citizens in general that arise, e.g., from the commercialisation of the human body in bio-patenting, in some techniques of assisted reproduction, and genetic testing. While in the 1970s and 1980s the main dividing line ran between 'conservative' and 'liberal' positions, the debate elsewhere has moved on, and the lines of alliance have been redrawn. The structurally conservative may support

the *laissez-faire* liberals, just as the value-conservative may join forces with the egalitarian liberals. This differentiation and re-alignment expressed itself, e.g., in the joint support in Germany between feminists, the Greens and the churches for the Embryo Protection Act in 1990. Would such a coalition be thinkable in Ireland?

• In Irish experience, 'ethics' seems to be identified not with self-obligation by reason to respect and promote the equal dignity of the other, but with diktats of unquestionable conclusions. The deductive method of classical natural law as used by the Vatican lends itself to such a view. The lack of differentiation, evident, e.g., in banning *in vitro* fertilisation even for married couples, the failure to take the level of education reached by the faithful seri-ously, the resistance to honouring the achievements of women at work outside the family, as well as the general neglect of fos-tering the reflection of church members on matters of faith and ethics, has not only led to their low expectations with regard to ethical orientation by religious authority but to a discrediting of ethical demands themselves.

• The weakening of belief in moral standards came at a pro-pitious time for Ireland. The heyday of the Celtic Tiger brought with it the assured conviction of the goodness of wealth, worlds apart from the dark ages of a morally strict and materially poor Ireland. In this new climate, attractiveness for foreign invest-ment is the unquestioned way of gaining the future. It is not the time for the moral proofreading of biotechnological research projects and production. Is any percentage of the €635 million accorded to Science Foundation Ireland (from 2.5 billion provided in the National Development Plan for research in general) ear-marked for ethical research?

In conclusion, a public disinclination to engage in 'divisive issues' is not good news for ethics. It leads to the privatisation of public matters, and is typical of non-committal *laissez-faire* plur-alism.[4] If Ireland wants to strive towards an ethical identity of its own, it has to work out its position between the different camps in Europe, through a critical reassessment of its own and other traditions. Otherwise, economic self-interests and strategic con-cerns will be allowed to carry the day.

c) Resources and goals for ethical reflection
Does not the call for ethical standards from outside science un-

derestimate the inherently ethical motivation and standards within science itself? Without engaging further in this debate,[5] I want to offer two observations. If the norms of accuracy, honesty, and motivation to help are constitutive of science, there should be no conflict but only welcome co-operation with the discipline of ethics. Yet in the process of debating the desirability and sustainability of changes made possible by science and technology, professional ethicists are needed to introduce 'the moral point of view', which is distinct both from statistical evidence of polls on what people find acceptable, and from the art of political compromise which is needed for implementing policies. It is only recently that moral philosophy has caught up with the tradition of treating questions of applied or domain-specific ethics that theology was used to considering under the heading of 'casuistry'. The 'rehabilitation of practical philosophy' in the last three decades in Europe and the boom of technology-linked ethics have only just reached Ireland. The lack of philosophical conversation partners in Ireland in the disciplines of ethics and applied ethics is regrettable since the individual social, human and natural sciences such as sociology, biology, genetics, and medicine can provide relevant empirical information but neither an integrating horizon for their differing perspectives nor the discipline of practical philosophical argumentation in which points are argued out. This is what philosophical and theological ethics have to offer to these debates, while being informed themselves by the empirical findings of the individual sciences.

The second observation is that scientific findings are not just matters of fact, but of interpretation. Nowhere is this clearer than in genetics, where the importance of genetic heritage, of uniqueness and of diversity can be played up or down according to the ethical conclusions one wants to support. The role of genetic factors in illnesses is played up where hopes to find therapies for illnesses are at stake. The genetic base for the uniqueness and individuality of persons is played down at the beginning of life, since it would make experimentation on early embryos questionable. It is also played down in reproductive cloning where suddenly the 'environmental' factors become all-important to allow for some degree of difference to the original. This is used as one of the arguments why cloning would not affect the clone's autonomy. The whole purpose and justification of IVF was to allow infertile couples to have children genetically their own. Yet, the role of genes can equally be declared as only half important when it comes to the split parentage made possible through this technique (sperm and egg donors, mitochondrial DNA from surrogate mothers, anonymity of donors despite the drive to molecular preventative medicine). In view of such contradictions, there seems to be an urgent need for the exchange of ethical arguments on which of these techniques are in keeping with human dignity, with the justified interests of all individuals affected, and with human flourishing within the community.

The role of ethics, however, is complicated by the fact that only some of the questions raised by new genetic technologies concern matters of autonomy and justice, i.e., questions of the 'right'. Here, with regard to the duties and rights citizens owe to each other and are entitled to be granted, it has been reasonable to expect that a consensus on 'the moral point of view' could be reached. But the examples mentioned above comprise issues of the 'good' as well as of the 'right,' i.e., evaluations, lifestyle options, ideals of a flourishing life that remain subjective and that no consensus has been expected on since Kant because they were deemed to be private and dependent on the different worldviews people held. Now the typically modern distinction between public and private has been bypassed by technological change and the public expenditure for it that both enables and restricts private choice.

How shall conflicts of values, e.g., between adults' reproductive freedom and children's rights, be dealt with? What models of consensus are there?

• The minimal consensus of the lowest common denominator in which the conflicts are hidden in seemingly shared normative concepts such as 'dignity' and 'autonomy'?

• A Rawlsian 'overlapping consensus,' to which people from different convictions are supposed to agree?

• A consensus on the basis of a maximum of human rights for all affected, including those who cannot voice their interests?

If only the third model is deemed sufficient to be true to our self-image in a pluralism based on respect for the other, then the question of shared ethical and religious values as the basis of such a consensus arises again. Before the origin of such values is discussed in part 3, it will be interesting to see what types of consensus Rawls and Habermas advocate in their treatment of genetic intervention.

2. Human flourishing and justice through genetic design?

I want to examine how and why the two most often-quoted Neo-Kantian liberal-egalitarian schools of social philosophy, of John Rawls and Jürgen Habermas, come to radically opposite answers with regard to the admissibility of genetic intervention. Norman Daniels and Alan Buchanan from the Rawls School are 'beyond humanism' in that they are ready to 'dispense with' the concept of human nature since the *opportunity* of genetic intervention (which they demand as a matter of justice) is going make it obsolete.[7] J. Habermas on the contrary sees the *threat* of genetic intervention as a compelling reason to complement his proceduralist discourse ethics with a 'species ethic' in which it needs to be 'embedded.'

I shall first sketch how the demand for genetic repair and enhancement is developed as a consequence of Rawls' Theory of Justice. Secondly, I shall treat Habermas' significant modification and enlargement of his communicative ethics approach. A comparison of their key terms will then show the roots of their disagreement, and conclusions from the controversy for the Irish context will be drawn.

a) Genetic intervention – precondition and means of justice (Rawls School)

It is in direct consequence of the second of the two principles of justice (that inequalities can only be allowed if they benefit the most disadvantaged),[8] that genetic intervention is justified and demanded. Buchanan and Daniels regard it as the necessary next step after compensating for structural social disadvantage. It has been asked whether such compensations, here for bad luck in the genes lottery, are indeed part of the principles of justice, or whether they are owed to a concrete history of values.[9] Is the idea that justice entails compensation really a freestanding product of reason, or is it the result of the European emphasis on the values of justice and compassion, which are owed to the prophetic tradition in Judaism, and the importance of deeds of mercy in Christianity?[10]

Yet whatever the roots of the idea of compensation, historical, particular, and at least partly religious, or reason-borne, universal, and secular, Buchanan's and Daniels' point is that 'fair equality of opportunity' also refers to access to the chance of improving one's *natural* assets:[11]

'Two major conclusions should guide public policy choices in the age of genetic intervention: There is a principled presumption that genetic intervention to prevent or to ameliorate serious limitations on opportunities due to disease is a requirement of justice. And justice may require regulating the conditions of access to genetic enhancements to prevent exacerbations of existing unjust inequalities.'[12]

Let's take stock:

1. Irreversible germ line intervention into the next and all subsequent generations is introduced as an uncontroversial measure of social politics, indeed, as a matter of justice.

2. The distinction between genetic repair (presumably in the case of monogenetic severe diseases) and enhancement is made, but immediately surpassed. The size of the circle of people included in the provision of genetic intervention fluctuates. First, it seems restricted to people suffering from a 'serious' genetically caused disease. Then, it is enlarged to cover also enhancements. There is a lack of clarity about the indications for germ line intervention.[13]

Social and physical-genetic disadvantage are put on the same level. Yet the identification of what constitutes a genetic 'disadvantage' presupposes a non-existent consensus on concepts of illness and health, on whether normality is more than statistical frequency and whether diversity is the norm. Equally, measures to tackle such 'disadvantage', could it be defined, are not as uncontroversial as providing early-start programmes for children in disadvantaged neighbourhoods: Pre-implantation genetic diagnosis is still forbidden in most European countries, and ideas of the elective breeding of desirable traits caused a storm in the German media when they were proposed by the philosopher Peter Sloterdijk in 1999.[14] Corresponding to their failure to note the significant differences between social and genetic disadvantage, as well as remedies for either, is their lack of distinction between parents influencing their children through their education, and through determining their genetic make-up.

The only limit they pose to parents' efforts to procure 'the best life possible' for their child through genetic intervention is their acknowledgement of the child's right to an open future. However, this right is not a categorical one, but a constraint that can be dealt with as a matter of gradation. Parents are asked not to foreclose a wide range of life plan possibilities by too narrow a specialisation, e.g., in sports, at the expense of other possible genetically enhanceable interests.[15]

The decisive moral criterion is their definition of justice, which remains a distributive one even if it now also includes the physical presuppositions for competing for positions and resources within society. But what is the criterion for justice? As Buchanan concedes in his 'conclusions', justice no longer has to be tied back to a concept of human nature. Our 'deepest assumptions of theorising about justice' are 'challenged' by the promises of genetic intervention:

> that justice only requires compensating for natural inequalities rather than attacking them directly; that the basic problem of distributive justice is how to distribute goods among persons whose identities are given independently of the act of distribution; that a theory of justice must be based on human nature, and that we can adjudicate among rival theories of distributive justice by seeing which is most consonant with human nature; and that moral progress consists largely of growing awareness of our common humanity, and with it an increasing compliance with universal principles of justice rooted in a single, common humanity.[16]

These are significant normative presuppositions to be sacrificed to the age of genetic design, especially the concepts of a shared human nature and a single, common humanity. It is also in this respect that Habermas goes in quite the opposite direction, demanding the 'moralisation of human nature' in a 'species ethic'.

Without a concept of human nature, one cannot even raise the objection Ludwig Siep puts forward from philosophical anthropology: Is the idea of optimising anybody's genes to suit their possible life project a plan that makes anthropological sense? L. Siep points out the artificiality of the concept of human flourishing contained in the wish to design a life plan and then to harness the suitable genes. Humans are marked by their problem-solving capacities; we come to discover who we are by mastering the challenges that we encounter, as often despite our genes and inclinations as because of them.[17]

Cautionary notes are sounded by the Rawls School, but they are limited to 'the foreseeable future' and based on the recognition of 'value pluralism', but not of human dignity; in any case, they do not affect the principal attitude of welcoming the chance of tailoring one's children's genes to one's ideals and demanding equal access to such techniques (to be applied, presumably, at the pre-implantation stage). They admit that standards of inter-action in family life may be just as important as the inherited genes:

> We bequeath to future generations not just our genes but also our patterns of family life and our sense of what matters when deciding whether and how to have a child, just as we bequeath our commitment to reproductive freedom. To the extent that this heritage is valuable, it may offset some draw-backs denominated in genes, deficits in transmitted genes relative to what a more determinedly eugenic society might offer its descendants.[18] (336)

Yet their appreciation of historically achieved standards does not show the sense of possible conflict between the choosers and the recipients of modified genes that is decisive for Habermas. The major objection to this justice project is therefore its unre-constructed paternalism, or *'Zwangsbeglückung'*,[19] a forced sub-mission to another person's idea of happiness. This is the central argument of J. Habermas' most recent book, which was written prior to *From Chance to Choice* but comments on some of its posi-tions in added footnotes.

b) Species ethic against the threat of unilateral domination through genetic intervention (Habermas)

Habermas's opposite view is equally based on the principle of his ethics, namely, that constitutive for argumentation is the mutual recognition as equals. This rules out measures that defy reci-procity.

> Eugenic interventions that are meant to enhance certain quali-ties for someone harm ethical freedom insofar as they fixate the affected person to rejected, but irreversible intentions of a third person and thus deny her to understand herself naturally (*un-befangen*) as the undivided author of her own life ... The convic-tion that all persons have the same normative status and owe each other reciprocal-symmetrical recognition presupposes a fundamental interchangeability of human relationships.[20]

Genetic intervention is ruled out because it does not only decide on the existence of a child, but on its specificity (*Sosein*), its part-icular desired traits. Educational determinations can be counter-acted and revised by the child. Her genetic design and that of her descendants, however, have to be borne forever in an interminable loss of symmetry. The critique of instrumental reason and its use as a tool of domination, as well as the struggle for emancipation, which have been core concerns of the critical social theory of the Frankfurt School, take on a new impetus in the context of unilateral genetic design. The interesting turn, however, is that now Habermas is ready to place discourse ethics in the larger framework of a 'species ethic'. Before investigating what the 'moralisation of human nature' in this framework entails, two other questions need to be clarified:

i) Is this a consequentialist argumentation, as D. Birnbacher judges, against the slippery slope of undermining the foundations of discursive morality,[21] or a categorical one, based on the deontological 'ought' of mutual respect? I read it as the latter, based on a transcendental reflection on the conditions of the possibility of discourse. If there is to be discourse, its participants must be free to exchange roles and to requite or reject initiatives. Descendants whose genome has been altered irreversibly have been divested of this condition of symmetrical communication.

ii) Is autonomy threatened as much as equality?[22] Couldn't children grow up to be autonomous despite their genetic design, which only affects their physical make-up, not their moral capacity? This point has been made to defend reproductive cloning, which would then not violate human dignity since it is based on autonomy, not on genetic uniqueness. But the argument also comes from the opposite side. Instead of completely separating moral capacity and human embodiment, the second version blurs all distinction between them. Could autonomy not even be advanced by engineering features such as control of emotions and ego strength?[23] To this, the counter question would be, how can it be strength of the I if it is genetically programmed? The most pertinent problem, however, arises from the addition of the new framework:

What is the status, function, and content of the proposed 'species ethics' in which discourse ethics is to be 'embedded'?

• Is it to put the individual in relation with the species?

• Is the proceduralist approach now seen as insufficient, as seriously lacking criteria for deciding on matters of universalisable interests?

• Is it taking recourse to anthropologically immanent norms, which need to be respected if the radical equality presupposed in discourse is to be achieved?

Two obvious norms immanent in anthropology would be the imperative to remain *one* human species instead of genetically designing different species from its ancestor, the present 'natural' human race; a second norm from 'moralising human nature' is to ensure that the interaction between generations remains reversible, and to exclude parents' intervention into their children's natural genetic make-up.[24]

While the debate about the implications of the enlargement of discourse ethics goes on, one conclusion that can already be drawn is that Habermas no longer regards questions of the 'good life' as merely 'evaluative', private, and unfit for rational discussion. He is now open to include into rational dialogue 'the premises and consequences of a life form'. Is he ready to go as far as Siep in demanding that 'orders of goods are to be decided in the light of a hermeneutically enlightened self-understanding'?[25] While it is clear that this cannot happen on a universal but only on a local scale, and that it will not produce binding decisions on what is right or wrong, it is the realisation of what S. Benhabib suggested ten years earlier:[26] that dialogue on visions of the good life does not fall outside the sphere of rationality, even if no universally valid conclusions as in the sphere of the 'right' (e.g. to forbid slavery and torture) can be drawn. If one interprets Habermas' call for a 'species ethic' to include anthropologically relevant features that are normative for a humane life form, then the brief for 'rational discourse' has been enlarged substantially.

c) Key concepts

In view of their diametrically opposed evaluations, it is insightful to go back to the key terms of each theory. Rawls derives his two principles of justice from a fictitious social contract made in the 'original position'. A contract theory, however, is the classical liberal model of justifying law, based on balancing different interests. It succeeds in offering a justification for legality but not for morality since it does not reach the problem of obligation, of the 'ought' we are bound to as moral beings. It is not surprising that his concept of autonomy has been found to lack 'a distinction central to Kant, of law and virtue (morality).'[27] Rawls thus reduces morality to law, and moral debate to the negotiation of interests between those who can voice their interests.

The second source of ambiguity on whether his theory reaches the level of ethics is the introduction of game theory as a method of rational choice from behind the 'veil of ignorance' in the 'original position'. Even if it does not fully amount to an explicit foundation of his principles of justice on self-interest, it puts them in the light of a functionalist *'do ut des'* calculation. P. Ricoeur's and O. Höffe's critiques coincide in pointing out both the circular or tautological character of the 'veil of ignorance' device, and his distance from ethical argumentation:[28]

> When Rawls construes justice as derived from self-interest, he seems to miss Kant's concept of justice which contains as an idea of pure practical reason the negation of self-interest and the recognition of ... a general interest ... Since the methodical status of game theory is not clarified sufficiently and Kant's methodical insights (above all the distinction of the rational from the empirical, and of law from virtue) are not grasped clearly enough, Rawls' *Theory of Justice* remains marked by ambiguities.[29]

It corresponds to this low-key approach to ethics that the justification for setting 'at least some limits on genetic or other interventions with children' in Buchanan *et al* is not human dignity, but 'autonomy' understood in a certain way, namely that 'our society accepts a very strong commitment to individualism or individual self-determination or autonomy.'

Leaving the question aside of whether there are two competing models of foundation, reflective equilibrium, and contract,[30] a further observation is that the 'coherentist' type of justification (in the sense of accepting the systematic coherence with other convictions as enough of a justification)[31] which avoids any 'foundationalist' assumptions, is close to the idea of 'overlapping consensus'. With no first principles to go by, the existing consensus of what is held in public opinion is the starting point. This gives the approach a more communitarian basis than it thinks it has, although the shared field of commonly held assessments does not have the Hegelian weight of *Sittlichkeit* (existing morality) attached to it. 'Ethics' consists in mediating between different legitimate interests in a pluralistic society,[32] which comes closer to politics and to the 'consensus management' that D. Mieth identifies as the opposite of ethics. Thus, the 'truth' of a consensus is measured by its pragmatic capacity to be accepted and implemented. Although the idea of an 'overlapping consensus' contains the recognition of different 'comprehensive views' supporting it, it tends towards a minimal consensus in the interest of 'stability.' It requires us to suppress those elements of our comprehensive views that are at odds with the lowest common denominator. The worldviews and religious convictions remain as privatised and unfit for communication and debate as our ideas of a good life. Even if this idea figures as one of the two 'moral capacities', together with the 'sense of justice' which continues the concept of a *sensus communis*,[33] the ways in which the goal of a flourishing life is pursued remain arbitrary. It is an extension of individual self-determination with no link to anthropology. As in his use of Kantian concepts, Rawls fails to engage with the normative horizon on which the classic idea of the 'good life' has to be understood and to make the connection to the social, political, theoretical, and reason-oriented nature of the human person that is Aristotle's universalist claim.[34]

Habermas' logic is different: He recognises the obligation, the phenomenon of 'ought', even if he does not justify it. But the sense that we ought to respect the other is established as the condition of the possibility of proper communication. Mutual recognition as autonomous, truthful, sincere, responsible subjects is constitutive for argumentation. Despite the controversy on whether this recognition applies only in discourse or in all communication, his transcendental pragmatic approach is utterly different from legal bargaining and the negotiation of interests. For Habermas, discourse is oriented toward the consensus of everyone affected, not only those present and able to voice their interests; whether an existing consensus is a true one can only be verified in the future. He maintains the critical Kantian element of the non-negotiability of human dignity. In contrast, Rawls and his school tend to collapse the distinction between the empirical and the rational in three instances: in their identification of autonomy with self-interested individualism, in their acceptance of the existing overlapping consensus as true, and in their premature closure of debate on the right and the good in the interest of stability. In each case, the empirical wins, and the critical element which Habermas's transcendental pragmatic approach retains is lost.

d) Conclusions for Irish bio-ethical debates
The controversy between the Rawls School and the Frankfurt School may help Ireland's quest for identity in Europe, discern-

ing where to look for ethical bearings – in Boston or Berlin, London or Strasbourg? While the European Parliament in January 1998 urged a ban on both reproductive and non-repro-ductive ('therapeutic') cloning, recent reports that US scientists are moving to Britain since President Bush restricted embryonic stem cell research to existing lines move the increasing gap be-tween the research practices permitted and justified in different democracies even closer to Ireland's neighbourhood. In addi-tion, the Irish state will have to decide in a year or two what to do with the embryos that have been frozen in assisted reproduc-tion units in Ireland for a number of years, postponing the deci-sion on the fate of the unclaimed ones to another day. With no prior Dáil discussion on their status and on the consequences of this practice for questions such as embryo research, what will the fact that it has not been challenged be interpreted to mean?[35]

The compromise formulations offered in international and European documents cannot paper over the deep divisions in interpreting what, e.g. 'human dignity', the foundation of human rights, signifies and to whom it is attributed, e.g. only to conscious 'persons', or to all 'human beings'. The only way for-ward is sustained public debate. Yet it has already become clear how widely the conceptions of rationality, autonomy, justice, and the significance of human nature can differ even within lib-eral social philosophy. Can the belief that each human being is created in the image of God, inscribed in God's hand, justified as he or she is, offer the resources of meaning needed not to justify, but to sustain human dignity as a 'primary good'[36] against the understanding of autonomy as life plan options? 'Options' is the language of the stock market, here turned into investing into the most profit-promising genes, in order to improve performance in a competitive society. Christianity links the deontological call for justice to the teleological quest for meaning[37] and offers an encompassing horizon of hope also in situations of suffering. Beyond integralist ambitions and sectarian withdrawal from a vicious world, it could spell out how the comprehensive world views silenced in the project of an overlapping consensus are morally relevant to a pluralism based on recognition and cri-tique: as heuristic frameworks, horizons of meaning, sources of motivation, and ways of relativising the moral (and physical) striving for perfection by the promise of redemption.[38]

3. Towards a Christian voice in bio-ethical debates that is both communicable and distinctive

The way forward for ethical debate in Ireland is to get beyond two oppositional attitudes: the first, of having moral precepts imposed on citizens *qua* church members, ignoring the debate within Catholic moral theology and presenting the positions taken by the Vatican as if its authority was absolute. Apart from its failure to recognise the pluralistic and interdisciplinary setting of ethics, this approach betrays a deficient understanding of church and of the relationship in which the ecclesial *magisterium* stands to the sense of the faithful, scripture, tradition, and theology.[39] The second widespread attitude which has arisen from resistance to the first, is to see the decisive moral quality in being 'non-judgmental'; this leads to the *laissez-faire* liberalism characterised before which only benefits the economic powers pressing for liberalisation in the interests of the scientific-technological-economic complex, the major factor for growth in advanced societies. This power network is at times also criticised by scientists, e.g. when it comes to handing on genetic test data to insurers and when patenting legislation turns potential cures into lucrative monopolies against the interests of patients in whose name research was initially justified.

The approach to Christian ethics I have been following because of its ability to combine distinctiveness and communicability with other disciplines and with non-believers, stresses both the autonomy of morality, and the importance of the Christian context.[40] 'Autonomy of morality' means that the moral obligation to unconditional recognition of the other is justified on the basis of human freedom, and does not need belief in God to be valid (even if it may need hope in God to be sustained). Once the foundation of morality on human freedom has been recognised, the task for Christian ethics emerges to seek dialogue with secular approaches. The communicability of Christian ethics lies in its adaptability to existing discourses in philosophy and the human sciences. This includes the ability to move between the different conceptual frameworks of various disciplines, to analyse and mediate between their different presuppositions and integrate their insights into an ethical judgement. But beyond the interdisciplinary task, which it shares with philosophy, 'adaptability' or 'translatability' means that Christian ethics uses the language of the public sphere to ex-

press its convictions. The reason for dismissing genetic intervention is not that this would mean to 'play God', i.e. to allow the
creature to take the place of the creator, but that it endangers
human autonomy and equality. Likewise, the belief that every
human being is made in the image of God is not used as if it was
an argument for every discourse participant, but is translated
into its secular equivalent, human dignity. Using the language
of reason allows Christian insights to be presented also to non-
believers in a way that can be of service to them.

However, if so much respect is shown for the pluralist conditions of moral discourse in civil society, then the question arises,
in what does the *distinctiveness* of Christian contributions consist? What has Christian ethics got to offer to interdisciplinary
and public debate? What is the difference, in this case, between a
foundation on neo-Kantian discourse ethics and on a Christian
ethical approach?

I want to start with the image Alfons Auer, one of the
founders of the autonomous approach within Christian ethics,
uses: One can explain all the functional parts of a ship, all the
things that make it sail, when it is in dry dock – which is what
discourse ethics does. But will the ship swim? And what will
keep it afloat? One may find the difference between dry dock
and being afloat only minimal, if all that matters is the ship. And
the image of the sea may be found too amorphous to designate
the ragged reeks and steep inclines of the Christian faith. The
reason why the water image strikes me as more fitting than
mountain metaphors is that it provides an answer to one of the
most urgent issues in social, cultural and political theory: the
question about the origin of values, or about the conditions of
the possibility of morality.

a) Values and their origin
The contemporary boom of ethics can mean two things: either,
we have never been more moral, or we are in the deepest moral
crisis. The fact that one has to flag the need for moral evaluation
can be taken as a sign that there are problems. And the more one
clamours for morality, the farther it vanishes.

If it is true that 'prior to the crisis of norms we are dealing
with a crisis of values',[41] the question becomes pressing, how do
we get 'values'? From where are they generated? What makes
them resonate in people's self-understanding?

It is with regard to this problem that ethicists and politicians have to admit their profound powerlessness. The fact remains that society has to *deliver* values, and then debate on norms and goals has something to go on. But from what sources do societies produce values?

J. Habermas, for one, is acutely aware of the dialectic between the individual art of living, and societal development. This is why the gap that remains between 'facticity' and 'validity' is such a problem.[42] One may be able to demonstrate the validity of the principle of human dignity a hundred times by reason, but if there are no 'life forms' in which individuals are at home, where it finds resonance, then such principles are in danger of dissolving into thin air. Habermas, like any other ethicist, is aware that he can only *appeal* to lived values, but that he cannot *create* them. Having come to realise over forty years of emancipatory writing that there is after all, only the 'weak power of reason', he turns to the force of law to shore up the crumbling walls of civil society.

However, in his Peace Prize speech of 2001, he deals with the concrete convictions and values lived by religious believers that are in danger of being suppressed by secularisation. Alarmingly for some, he calls our society 'post-secular' not because it is so religious but because it is becoming aware of what is missing when faith in God declines: When faith in the resurrection is no longer shared, there is nothing to substitute for it: 'The lost hope of resurrection leaves a palpable void.'[43]

Habermas acknowledges that the key concepts of his ethics – mutual recognition, consensus – need resonance within 'life forms' to be operative. He sees, too, that secularisation also impoverishes a culture, especially of hope. Hans Joas, another member of the Frankfurt School, states clearly that 'values cannot be produced rationally or disseminated through indoctrination'. They are created in 'processes of self-formation and self-transcendence';[44] it is in experiences of faith and love that the commitment to values arises from the affective-emotional and the imaginative sides of the human person.

b) Christian life forms as heuristic context of norms
Normative concepts need more than principled argumentations to sustain them; they are supported by values that arise from lived convictions. The contribution of Christian 'life forms', or

communities to core concepts of Western constitutions becomes especially clear with regard to the idea of unconditional recognition and to the readiness or the refusal to define what it is to be human.

• *The idea of unconditional recognition:*

It is the summit of Kant's and Fichte's autonomous ethics; but does it remain a heroic moral effort, especially in asymmetrical relations where recognition is not requited, if it does not receive resonance from being supported, granted, and completed by God?

• *The definability or undefinability of being human*

Habermas's critique of attempts to determine in advance the specific nature of a future child can be seen as including a more principal refusal: to define what is or should be human. From a religious perspective, this voluntary, chosen passivity is part of one's understanding of being created by God. Does the will to accept the human powerlessness to define the human being, the consent to leave this question open, need belief in God as the creator as the alternative to humans creating and defining what counts as human? Or can such renunciation to the power of definition be sustained on its own on humanistic grounds? Is it necessary to experience life as a gift from God to resist the temptation to define and dominate, patent and commercialise? It is at least a powerful motive to sustain and renew resistance against replacing the openness and mystery of what it is to be human with technologically devised man-made standards.

c) Morality relativised by redemption

Finally, it may be news, especially for the Irish experience of the near-identification of Christianity with a repressive morality, that a Christian faith context not only adds resonance to but also profoundly relativises the Kantian ethics of obligation. Its last word on the human person is not her capacity for moral perfection but her need for redemption.[45] It is crucial for ethics not to be construed just as the discipline of ought and action, but also as the art of human flourishing and receptive fulfilment; not only of must-do, but can-do, the fragments of which will be completed by God. This is why the task of Christian ethics is not to construct a hypermorality, but to strike the right balance between a sense of urgency in responding to human suffering, and what P. Ricoeur calls, 'the playfulness of grace'.[46]

CHAPTER TEN

Christian Critique of Economic Policy and Practice

Sean Healy SMA *and Brigid Reynolds* SM

1: A QUESTION OF PERSPECTIVE

The Republic of Ireland has been changing dramatically in recent years. Its economic boom, euphemistically called the Celtic Tiger economy, has been making headlines worldwide. The changes are evident in the increasing levels of economic growth, employment growth, unemployment decline and significant current budget surpluses over a number of years. The population has been growing. Traditional emigration patterns have been replaced by net immigration. Dependency ratios are falling. Standards of living have been rising for most of those in employment. Income *per capita* is rising dramatically. The national debt as a proportion of GNP has been falling dramatically. Ireland is seen at both EU level and by the OECD as a success story in terms of the conventional macroeconomic indicators.

On a more visible level, we witness dramatic changes every day in terms of a massive growth in consumption indicators. The sale of new cars, foreign holidays and other consumer items has grown at an unprecedented rate since the mid-nineties. The private housing sector is booming. New shops, restaurants, night clubs and pubs are opening every week and attracting a foreign as well as a local clientele. Dublin has become the favourite European capital city for many in search of weekend entertainment.

This picture, however, does not tell the entire story of what has been happening to Irish society over the past fifteen years. There is another aspect of this story that must also be recognised and acknowledged. Side by side with the 'new Ireland' of the Celtic Tiger is another Ireland characterised in terms of a widening rich/poor gap, long-term unemployment, run-down inner-city housing estates, hidden rural poverty, early school leaving, lone parenthood, homelessness, growing aggression and violence. There are long, in some cases growing, waiting lists for medical care and public housing. Ireland has a two-tier education system as well as the highest level of adult illiteracy among all European Union countries. There is little evidence of the Irish economic 'miracle' in many of the deprived sectors of the Irish economy. The fruits of economic transformation have not benefited all members of Irish society. The 'rising tide' of the Irish economy has failed to lift all boats.

There is still considerable poverty and social inequality in Irish society. While employment has grown dramatically, the divisions in Irish society have widened and the proportion of people living on income equivalent to less than 50 per cent of average household disposable income (i.e. less than about €155 a week for a single person in 2002) is not falling. It is clear that economic growth can widen divisions in society and create greater levels of income inequality. In the absence of government intervention the benefits of economic growth will not 'trickle down' to the vulnerable and disadvantaged groups in society. While failing to tackle poverty on an adequate scale, government policies are also failing to address issues of income distribution and social equity.

These issues have not been seriously debated in Irish society to date. The government has introduced a substantial range of anti-poverty strategies that target disadvantaged groups. However, it has failed to seriously address the structural causes of poverty in Irish society, which have been exacerbated by the recent economic 'miracle'. A minimalist approach to the eradication of 'absolute' or 'consistent' poverty', which ignores issues of equality and distributive justice, will not produce a fair society.

Today many people ask questions such as: If Ireland of the Celtic Tiger is so good why do we meet so many anxious faces on our streets? Why are so many people experiencing stress in meeting their commitments, be they financial, social, family, etc? Why do so many parents have a struggle to find the resources necessary to keep their children in school? Why are so many people homeless or living in overcrowded accommodation? Why is there so much fear and anxiety in our communities? As the pace of change escalates, those who have the economic and social resources acquire the equipment necessary to ride the crest of the present boom while a large minority live in fear of being submerged. Those on the crest of the boom have anxieties about staying there. This anxiety fuels the tendency to accumulate more and more to the point where, in practice, they adopt the slogan that 'greed is good'. Meanwhile those who struggle to 'hang on' are feeling their grip loosening and the prospect of being part of this society becoming more remote.

This reflection brings to the fore the issue of values. People find their fears are easier to admit than their values. Ireland seems to accept a two-tier society in fact, while deriding it in principle. This dualism in our values allows us to continue with the *status quo*. In practice this means that it is okay to exclude between a quarter and a third of the population from the mainstream of life of Irish society while large resources and opportunities are channelled towards other groups in society. This dualism operates at the levels of individual people, communities and sectors.

CORI Justice Commission

One of the groups concerned about the growing divisions in Irish society was the Leadership of Religious Congregations. In 1981 they established CORI Justice Commission to promote justice in society. The Commission studied the direction of Irish society, the decisions that were shaping the society, and the arenas in which these decisions were made. It set itself the task of trying to influence these decisions. Two of the key arenas are the National Budget and the National Social Partnership process that has produced a number of national programmes.

Since 1987 these three yearly national programmes have had a major impact on the development of Irish society. The social partners have agreed these programmes. Three pillars negotiated and agreed the first three programmes with government, namely, the business community, the trade unions and the farming organisations. At that time CORI Justice Commission pointed out that a large section of society was not represented in this process but was affected by the decisions made. A number of groups from the voluntary and community sector including CORI Justice Commission were invited to be social partners in 1996.

A question of Christian values

Our concerns in this socio-economic reality are deeply rooted in Christian values. Christianity subscribes to the values of both human dignity and the centrality of the community. The person is seen as growing and developing in a context that includes other people and the environment. Justice is understood in terms of relationships. The Christian scriptures understand justice as a harmony that comes from fidelity to right relationships with God, people and the environment. *A just society is one that is structured in such a way as to promote these right relationships so that human rights are respected, human dignity is protected, human development is facilitated and the environment is respected and protected.*

As our societies have grown in sophistication the need for appropriate structures has become more urgent. While the aspiration that everyone should enjoy the good life, and the good will to make it available to all, is an essential ingredient in a just society, the good life will not happen without the deliberate establishment of structures to facilitate its development. In the past charity, in the sense of alms-giving by some individuals on an arbitrary and *ad hoc* basis, was seen as sufficient to ensure that everyone could cross the threshold of human dignity. Calling on the work of social historians it could be argued that charity in this sense was never an appropriate method for dealing with poverty. Certainly it is not a suitable methodology for dealing with the problems of today. As world disasters consistently show, charity and the heroic efforts of voluntary agencies cannot solve these problems on a long-term basis. Appropriate structures are required to ensure that every person has access to the resources needed to live life with dignity.

Few people would disagree that the resources of the planet are for the use of the people, not just the present generation but also the generations still to come. In Old Testament times, these resources were closely tied to land and water. A complex system of laws about the Sabbatical and Jubilee years (Lev 25:1-22, Deut 15:1-18) was devised to ensure, on the one hand, that no person could be disinherited, and on the other, that land and debts could not be accumulated or the land exploited.

Interdependence, mutuality, solidarity, connectedness are words which are used loosely today to express a consciousness which is very Christian. All of creation is seen as a unit which is dynamic, each part is related to every other part, depends on it in some way and can also affect it. When we focus on the human family this means that each person depends on others initially for life itself and subsequently for the resources and relationships needed to grow and develop. To ensure that the connectedness of the web of life is maintained, each person is meant to reach out to support others in ways that are appropriate for their growth and in harmony with the rest of creation. This thinking respects the integrity of the person while recognising that the person can only achieve his or her potential in right relationships with others and the environment. All of this implies the need for appropriate structures and infrastructures.

CORI Justice Commission is guided in its reflection on the reality that is Ireland and the wider world today by Catholic Social Thought (CST). Over the years CST has sought major changes in the socio-economic order. In previous centuries there was huge commitment to action in areas such as education and healthcare. Over the past thirty to forty years there has been a growing realisation that the churches need to seek deeper changes in socio-economic realities if the reign of God is to be advanced. There is also a growing recognition that talk alone is simply not enough. Neither is it sufficient to proclaim injustices and expect other people to go and transform reality. We were reminded by the Synod of Bishops in 1971 that every Christian is called to be involved in transformation. Those in leadership have particular responsibilities to chart the way forward.

Catholic Social Thought has a range of themes that provide a coherent focus for action. These include:
- Dignity of the human person
- Human rights and duties
- Social nature of the person
- The common good
- Relationship, subsidiarity and socialisation
- Solidarity
- Option for the poor.

The Justice Commission has believed from its inception that ongoing action was crucially important if change was to come and if the Justice Commission was to be credible. These themes have provided a framework to underpin its action. Talking about solidarity is not enough. It is crucial that action is taken to generate the necessary change to build solidarity. The Commission understands that building the reign of God involves doing what we can to move the present reality from where it is towards the gospel vision of a just society. This provides the Commission with a number of issues to be addressed on an ongoing basis. These include:

- Identifying what the present reality really is
- Developing some awareness of what alternatives to the present situation are viable or possible
- Discovering which of these are closest to the gospel vision
- Taking action to move towards these alternatives
- Recycling the process on an ongoing basis.

In practice the CORI Justice Commission divides its work under four major headings:

- Public Policy
- Enabling and Empowering
- Spirituality
- Advocacy and Communication.

In all of this the Commission recognises and acknowledges that it does not have all the answers. Rather, it is always struggling to get more accurate answers to the questions it asks and trying to seek out and develop better alternatives to what is already available. It constantly offers its analysis and vision and proposals for action to the wider society for comment and critique. It seeks an ongoing dialogue on these issues with the wider society as well as with those who share its faith. The following sections provide a short outline of key aspects of the Commission's approach in these areas.

2: ESSENTIAL COMPONENTS OF
CHRISTIAN CRITIQUE OF ECONOMIC POLICY AND PRACTICE

Reflecting on the experience of the Justice Commission in its various projects and efforts to influence the shape of society, we suggest the following seven requirements for church to be a credible actor in the economic, political, cultural and social spheres. This is not meant to be an exhaustive list but these seem to us to be especially relevant given our experience in the social partnership and related contexts of Ireland at the start of the twenty-first century. The seven we suggest are:

- Social analysis
- Dialogue – the issue of conversation
- Being bilingual
- Vision-building
- On-going action
- Being prophetic and resisting the temptation to be absorbed by the *status quo*
- Realising credibility comes through involvement.

Social Analysis

For the most part there is no one, clear, obvious, unambiguous reading of reality. However, the Justice Commission seeks to underpin its work by detailed and objective as possible social analysis. In doing this work of social analysis we follow a relatively standard approach. Whether we are addressing an issue such as social exclusion, a geographical area such as Ireland or a problem such as drug addiction, we seek to develop a comprehensive, integrated understanding by addressing the reality's following components:

- Economic structures: what resources exist in this reality and how they are organised?
- Political structures: what power resides in this reality and how is decision-making organised?
- Cultural structures: what the core meaning in this reality is and how it is organised and transmitted.
- Social structures: arising from the economic, political and cultural structures, how are relationships organised?
- If appropriate the different levels of these structures are analysed (e.g. local, regional, national, international).
- The history of whatever we are analysing is also looked at and built into the analysis.

Dialogue – the issue of conversation

Dialogue is a crucial component of the Justice Commission's work. The understanding of a social partner also demands that we dialogue. It demands that we dialogue with our own membership and constituency, with the wider society and with the policy-making process.

In this context 'conversation' becomes an important issue. According to David Tracy (1987:19):

Conversation is a game with some hard rules: say only what you mean; say it as accurately as you can; listen to and respect what the other says, however different or other; be willing to correct or defend your opinions if challenged by the conversation partner; be willing to argue if necessary, to confront if demanded, to endure necessary conflict, to change your mind if the evidence suggests it.

In this context 'conversation' is a deeper engagement than might often be associated with that term. O'Connell (2001:7) states that:

Conversation is not just sharing in another's folklore, food or art. These sorts of meetings can be important as a prelude to conversation. Conversation is more to do with the type of encounter that enlarges one's sense of connection and responsibility. It ... transforms the participants and energises them to work towards what is good for all in society. Where there is a constructive, enlarging engagement with the other, there is a greater commitment to the common good.

Sharon Parks and her co-authors (Parks *et al*: 1996:70) state that 'the single most important pattern we have found in the lives of people committed to the common good is what we have come to call *a constructive engagement with the other.*' This highlights the importance of conversation in this process. The Commission has recognised this and sought to develop conversations in a variety of areas as we have seen already. Sometimes they are called conversation and sometimes not. The issue of conversation is central to church's involvement as a real actor in these arenas.

The issue of developing communities of discourse which produce a basis for generating change is also relevant here. Wuthnow (1989) has expanded on this in his work. He notes remarkable similarities in the social conditions surrounding three of the greatest challenges to the *status quo* in the development of modern society, i.e. the Protestant Reformation, the Enlightenment and the rise of Marxist socialism. He argues that each episode of cultural ferment occurred during a period of rapid economic growth that fed new resources to central governments at the same time as it uncoupled traditional alignments between the states and factions of their ruling elites. These conditions were receptive to powerful new ideas and also facilitated greatly increased public discourse about social and individual responsibilities. The parallels with today are striking and highlight, again, the importance of 'conversation' that forms the foundation of any community of discourse.

Being bilingual
Dialogue involves the Justice Commission in two different 'conversations' going on all the time. These dialogues or conversations are with:
- Those who share our faith, and
- The wider society.

Both of these have two sub-groups with whom the Commission

seeks to conduct an ongoing 'conversation'. In both convers-
ations the subgroups with whom dialogue is sought are:
- People who are committed/involved and interested
- People who are less committed/involved or interested

The methods and approaches used vary in the two main dialogues. They also vary in the two sub-dialogues being conducted
on an ongoing basis.

The Justice Commission believes very strongly that both
main dialogues must go on at the same time. In both conversations reality is being constructed. There is a perspective
brought to bear in reading reality by those who approach it with
the eyes of faith which is different to the perspective of one who
does not approach it in that way. It is the same reality, however,
that is being approached, no matter what one's perspective on,
or reading of, that reality.

The conversation the Commission conducts with the wider
society is deeply informed by the conversation it conducts with
those who share our faith. The stance taken in the wider society
stems from the conclusions being reached in the faith conversation. Choices have to be made constantly concerning what issues to pursue in the wider reality, what position to take on
these issues, what actions are to be sought, etc. Always, the
Commission's decisions in these areas are informed by its conversation with those who share our faith.

To engage meaningfully in either conversation, social analysis
is crucial. The Commission approaches it with a faith-based perspective. That, however, does not mean that the work of social
analysis needs to be any less thorough. As we have seen already
the Commission follows a particular model of social analysis
which it finds useful in its work. This work is always 'work in
progress'.

The dialogue is a two-way affair, however. This means that
the realities of the wider society are constantly challenging and
influencing the faith-conversation. Often, there are aspects of
the wider reality that the faith-conversation has not recognised
or has sought to avoid. If the dialogue is to be real and transformative, it must be two-way and must involve a real engagement.
It must also include a willingness to change one's mind if the
evidence suggests this is what is required.

The language spoken in the first of these conversations is different from that spoken in the second. This, in effect, means that

the Commission has to be bi-lingual in its work. One language is spoken in the dialogue with those who share our faith. A different language, sometimes very different, is spoken in the dialogue with the wider society. In these two conversations there are different assumptions, different core meanings, different perceptions of the world.

The dialogue with the wider society is critically important because those with whom we dialogue are actively involved, they make decisions that have major impacts on people's lives and on the wider world generally. However, if we fail to maintain a second conversation, i.e. with those with whom we share faith, then we are very likely to accept uncritically as our own the analysis, the perceptions etc. of the dominant culture in the wider world. In fact, we believe that the conversation with those with whom we share faith is the critically important one of these two conversations.

Church education should therefore be bilingual. Christians should have the capacity to engage in both of these dialogues, speak the appropriate language in both of these conversations.

We believe the language used in the conversation with those who share our faith would not be effective in the conversation with the wider world. In fact it is likely to be irrelevant. The failure to appreciate this fact, and the consequent need for bilingualism, lies at the root of many failed interventions by church in wider society debates in Ireland over recent years.

Vision-building
The Book of Proverbs tells us that 'without a vision the people perish'. We believe this to be as true today as it was in Old Testament times. The dominant vision being offered at the moment sees wealth, employment and production growing steadily into the foreseeable future. This is seen as producing a world in which everyone has a stake and where the good life can be accessed by all. It assumes that everyone, in a world population twice as large as it is today, can reasonably aspire to and achieve the high-consumption lifestyle enjoyed by the world's affluent minority at present. This is seen as progress.

We believe this conventional economic vision of the future is unattainable. Environmental degradation, encroaching deserts, unemployment, starvation, widening gaps between rich and poor, exclusion from participation in either decision-making or development of society: these are the global realities confronting decision-makers today. Social inequality, endemic deprivation and environmental stress accompany economic globalisation. Millions of people in richer parts of the world recognise these problems and are seriously concerned about the plight of the billions of people on all continents whose lived experience is one of constant exclusion from the resources and the power that shapes this world.

The Justice Commission believes that if we are to be serious about the reign of God then we must be serious about this issue of vision-building. We need to be willing to envisage alternatives that are attainable. This is especially important in the Irish context, as much of Ireland's development is dependent on the wider world providing a positive environment.

Planning our future is not just the work of sociologists or economists. It is very much also the work of theologians and philosophers. Historically, the best theologians were those who fashioned a more profound vision and a more vibrant motivation for action for the Christians of their own era and context. It is crucially important therefore, if one is to be a credible actor in the economic, political, cultural and social context, to be involved in vision-building.

On-going action
Following on this work of seeking out alternative futures, the Commission seeks to design action that could lead towards reaching that alternative future. This results in the Commission being involved in a range of activities that must be addressed if the 'vision' issue is to be treated seriously by others who are sceptical, threatened or comfortable with the *status quo*. In practice this has involved the Commission in a wide range of activities ranging from piloting programmes to researching issues to advocating policy positions.

Reflection on what is happening, and constantly recycling the process of analysis, dialogue, vision-building and action, is crucially important. Hopefully some of the wider world reality is being changed, as a result of our involvement. However, we ourselves are also being changed. Our experience of the wider reality is brought to bear on our faith reflection just as our faith reflection is brought to bear on the wider reality. We try to ensure that this produces constant development in and between both conversations with which the Commission engages. This is critically important if there is to be any real learning from experience over time. This learning is inserted into the policy process to contribute to more enlightened action.

Being prophetic and resisting the temptation to be absorbed by the status quo

The more one is involved in the wider reality the greater the danger that one will be absorbed by the *status quo*. Instead of proclaiming the good news of Jesus Christ and working for a world that is closer to its core message, there is a likelihood that one may accept the dominant core meaning underpinning the *status quo*. Brueggemann (1978) has put it succinctly when he argues that it is crucial that we always seek 'to nurture, nourish and evoke a consciousness and perception alternative to the consciousness and perception of the dominant culture around us'. This is the prophetic task. This is the call to members of religious institutes today.

This involves critiquing the dominant consciousness and working to dismantle it. But it goes beyond this. It also seeks to energise people and communities. In this context the issue of an alternative vision is central. According to Brueggemann, 'The key word is "alternative" and every prophetic minister and prophetic community must engage in a struggle with that notion.'

The dominant culture that underpins the *status quo* is uncritical. More than this, it finds it very difficult to tolerate serious and fundamental criticism and goes to great lengths to stop such critique. At the same time the dominant culture becomes a wearied culture, unable to be energised by alternative ideas or visions. We acknowledge that few people relish critique! The challenge to the prophetic dimension is to hold these aspects together. Either by itself is not faithful to the Christian tradition. For us, this is the point at which compassion is central. Without compassion the activity lacks a central component of the Judeo-Christian understanding of what it means to be prophetic. As far back as Moses we see a dismantling of the politics of oppression and exploitation and its replacement with a politics of justice and compassion. In the Exodus experience this politics was not just focused on developing a new religion or new religious ideas or a vision of freedom. It was clearly focused on the emergence of a new social community, a community with a history that had to devise laws, a form of governance and order, norms of right and wrong and sanctions of accountability.

Central to this is the notion of the freedom of God. If the God we worship is a static God of order who simply protects the interests of those with resources and power then oppression will follow. On the other hand, if the God we worship is free to hear the cry of the poor, free of control by those with resources and power, then that will emerge in what we do and what we are. It will show itself in the work of justice and compassion. It is necessary to focus on the politics and social change dimension and on the God dimension. Both dimensions are essential if we are to be prophetic.

Realising credibility comes through involvement

Finally, it must be recognised that credibility never comes by 'speaking from on high'. Involvement is essential for credibility to be present. In part, at least, this mirrors one of the characteristics of social partners we identified earlier. Being a voice is not enough. One must also be an actor. If one is to be credible in the economic, political, cultural and social context then it is crucial that one be involved in a real way and not just pronouncing from 'on high'.

The Justice Commission always offers its analysis, critique, vision, alternative ideas, activities etc. as contributions to the public debate on the specific issues addressed. It seeks responses to its positions. It is always conscious that it has no claim on having all the answers or that what it offers is coming directly, or indirectly, from God! Rather it realises that dialogue and conversation with the wider reality are crucial aspects of seeking the truth. It is also aware that it must be open to change in response to what emerges in the dialogue. Too often positions emanating from church bodies are presented in an unintelligible language and/or depend for their credibility on claims that they are emanating, even if indirectly, from God. This is not a credible position for an actor in these arenas in the twenty-first century. The scriptures and our Christian tradition provide us with a rich heritage from which to draw inspiration and direction in our engagement in the political, economic, cultural and social issues of our time.

'The future of humanity lies in the hands of those who are strong enough to provide coming generations with reasons for living and hoping' (*Gaudium et Spes* 31).

CHAPTER ELEVEN

Human Rights have no Borders:
Justice for the Stranger at Home and Abroad

Joan Roddy, Jerome Connolly and Maura Leen

At a crossroads where prosperity meets diversity

One of the most noticeable features of Irish society in recent years has been the arrival of growing numbers of asylum seekers and immigrants. The scale of these arrivals represents a completely new phenomenon in the history of modern Ireland as it moves from being a country of emigration to one of immigration. This demographic opening up and growing diversity of race and religion is a step of great importance in the journey of the Irish church. After a long experience of sending missionaries abroad, the church is now challenged to welcome and include growing numbers of people from other ethnic, racial, linguistic and religious backgrounds in the community of the faithful in Ireland. This presents an opportunity for the church to rediscover itself as part of a universal community of believers and of human beings. The sudden growth in immigration and flows of asylum seekers has prompted a range of responses from the Christian churches. Their variety and relevance is witness to a greater awareness that the arrival of immigrants and asylum seekers demands a response in faith not only pastorally but at the level of reflection, teaching and critical analysis.

Until the early 1990s Ireland, unlike almost all other EU states, had no experience of receiving asylum seekers and immigrants to any significant degree. In 1992 the number of those seeking asylum in the Republic was only 39. While the figure began to increase from this point, during the next three years less than 1,000 additional asylum seekers had arrived. By 1997 the annual number of new arrivals had risen to just under 3,900, representing a hundred-fold increase on the 1992 figure. It was about then that the reality of asylum seekers and refugees began to impress itself both on the government and Irish society at large. This figure continued to rise after 1997, reaching a high point of 11,600 in 2002. To put this in perspective, it is worth noting that in 2001 the total number of people worldwide of concern to the Office of the UN High Commission on Refugees numbered 21 million, of whom 12 million were refugees, with the majority of others being asylum seekers and internally displaced people.

Only a small percentage of those who come to Ireland, around 10%, are accorded full refugee status or the right to remain on humanitarian or other grounds. Even this low percentage is likely to decrease following the January 2003 Supreme Court ruling that non-EEA (European Economic Area) nationals no longer have a right to residency in Ireland on the grounds of being parents of Irish children. Despite the high rate of refusals, few failed asylum seekers have been deported. Apart from an unknown number who have subsequently left of their own accord, other asylum applicants remain perfectly legally in the country. Even those served with a deportation order remain legally in Ireland until the order is actually executed, which so far has not been the case with the majority of orders served. However, those subject to a deportation order endure a precarious, vulnerable and uncertain existence.

While public and media attention has tended to focus on the inflow of asylum seekers, it has generally failed to recognise the equal and in many aspects even greater significance of the concurrent stream of legal immigrants into the country, motivated by economic reasons. The mid 1990s onwards coincided with a period of record economic growth in Ireland leading companies and parts of the public sector to actively recruit foreign staff. These immigrants included highly qualified personnel, working in such fields as information technology, medicine and nursing, and less skilled workers in manufacturing, construction and tourism. Work permits were introduced for the first time only in 1996, when a total of 3,780 were issued. In the year 2000, work visas were introduced, and in 2002 the total number of work permits and work visas issued to non-EU immigrants exceeded 41,000. To this must be added the inward flow of immigrants from other EU states, which totalled over 90,000 between 1996 and 2002. Thus the numbers of economic migrants arriving in Ireland from other EU states and from outside the EU between 1996 and 2002 exceeded asylum applicants by more than three times. The recent slowdown in Ireland's economic growth performance, coupled with the lack of ratification by the government of the 1990 International Convention on the Rights of All

Migrant Workers and Members of their Families, poses the threat that these migrants are vulnerable to facing poor or declining living standards and working conditions.

The Religious Impact of New Arrivals and the Church's Response
Increased immigration means that Muslims number around 15,000 persons and may now form the third largest religious community in the Republic, after Catholics and members of the Church of Ireland. The Orthodox (Romanian and Russian) presence has also grown appreciably and there is now for the first time a presence of African Evangelical Christian communities with an estimated membership of some 10,000 people.[1] This unprecedented movement of people is impacting on existing religious communities as well as on many other areas.

It soon became evident that the presence of asylum seekers would demand a response at several levels from host communities. Their arrival is a call to the Christian community to expand its definition of neighbour, to revise its understanding of church, to reflect on what it means to belong to the family of God where all people are sisters and brothers of Christ, and to recognise that the earth's resources belong to all and are for the benefit of all.

Church responses on the ground can be grouped into those which are organisational, those which entail ecumenical co-operation, those focused on education and formation in values and attitudes, and advocacy and public policy critiques.

• Organisational
From the early 1990s the Irish Refugee Council took the lead in providing a service for asylum seekers and in seeking to influence policy. Religious congregations played an important role in the early stages of the Council by sustaining it through difficult times with financial and other support. As the pace of arrivals quickened in the latter part of the 1990s the Irish Commission for Justice and Peace (ICJP) and Trócaire, as bodies of the Irish Catholic Bishops' Conference, began to engage with the policy challenges posed by the growing numbers of asylum seekers. In December 1997 the two agencies published a booklet[2] setting out a systematic framework for a long-term pastoral and policy response by the church. After situating the Irish experience in a global context the booklet outlined the centrality of hospitality

towards the stranger to the Christian tradition and the fact that Christians share with all people a fundamental belief in our common humanity. After emphasising that a response to the plight of asylum seekers and refugees required the creation of a worldwide culture of peace and human rights, the document also sketched out the elements of a sustainable and morally defensible admissions system at national level.

In response to the growing need for a fuller involvement at an institutional level by the Catholic Church on asylum issues, a proposal was made by the Irish Commission for Justice and Peace, Trócaire and the Council for Social Welfare to the Bishops' Conference in 1998. From this followed the decision of the Conference in March 1999 to set up a Refugee Project dedicated to giving a pastoral response to the growing number of refugees and asylum seekers in Ireland. This project is mandated to advise the bishops on policy issues and pastoral responses. At the same time many religious congregations were identifying the needs of asylum seekers as a priority, and a variety of services were set up, initially in Dublin but soon extended country-wide.[3] These were rapidly followed by many local and regional initiatives, in the great majority of which local Christian churches were actively involved. Very quickly services expanded to include local refugee support groups, English language and other classes for adults, social activities to provide meeting points for new arrivals and the local population, assistance with refugee application procedures, and advocacy with relevant statutory bodies. The Protestant Churches, although numerically far smaller, reacted energetically and usually in a very inclusive manner, involving asylum seekers in their parish communities from the beginning, thus enabling them to adapt and integrate.

• Ecumenical co-operation

A positive feature of the churches' response has been the spirit of co-operation and practical ecumenism evident from an early stage. In September 1999, at the initiative of the Catholic Bishops' Refugee Project, an all-Ireland nexus of church-related groups and individuals was established in the shape of the Churches' Asylum Network (CAN). CAN has expanded to include representation from seven Christian churches and the Baha'i community in Ireland and regularly brings together representatives from the majority of Catholic dioceses, religious orders, and many church-related refugee support groups.

• Education and formation in values and attitudes
While the task of deepening the faith response to the arrival of asylum seekers, refugees and immigrants in significant numbers is a continuing one, a number of initiatives have already been taken. ICJP and the Irish Council of Churches in Belfast commissioned a study guide entitled *What the Bible Says About the Stranger* from a scripture scholar, Fr Kieran O'Mahony OSA.[4] In 2001 the ICJP held a special conference to stimulate a more informed and committed Catholic response to racism in the light of the new situation posed by the growing presence in Irish society of people from different cultural, religious and ethnic backgrounds. Arising from the Conference a set of *Guidelines Against Racism* has been prepared for circulation amongst the Catholic community at parish, family, work and school level. *Sanctuary*, the bi-monthly newsletter of the Refugee Project, provides some statistical data on the asylum community in Ireland and gives an update and critique, from a Christian perspective, on asylum and refugee policy development at both national and EU level.

• Advocacy and Public Policy Critiques
In December 1999 ICJP published *First Notes Towards An Irish Immigration Policy*, which outlined a comprehensive human rights framework for a national immigration policy, which would be morally justifiable and economically and politically sustainable. Yet, to date, no comprehensive immigration policy has been put in place, even though a policy has been promised and consultations have taken place. In government statements on the regulation of immigration flows to Ireland, there is little recognition of asylum seekers as a separate category nor are there provisos ('saving clauses') which take account of the obligations to which the Irish state has signed up under the 1951 Geneva Convention on Refugees.

The Committee on Asylum Seekers and Refugees of the Bishops' Conference, to which the Refugee Project reports, has been active in publicly critiquing public policy on asylum issues from a social justice and human rights perspective. The first statement of the Committee appeared in December 1999 as a message for Christmas 1999 and for the Jubilee year 2000. It called for 'a passionate concern for the quality of life and human relationships, not only for those born here but for those arriving here fleeing persecution or seeking for a better quality of life'.

Highlighting the need for a transparent and sustainable national immigration policy, the bishops emphasised the importance of ensuring that the integrity of the legal and humanitarian concept of asylum be safeguarded. Between April 2000 and June 2001, the Bishops' Committee issued four separate statements.[5] All addressed policy and procedural shortcomings in relation to asylum seekers and illustrated how on several fronts Ireland is falling short in terms of complying with its international obligations in this regard. In recalling the human rights of asylum seekers, the bishops reminded the Christian community in particular of the obligation to create a welcoming, inclusive society, and of the Christian imperative of care and compassion for all the marginalised and vulnerable in our society, whether these were born here or had arrived as asylum seekers or immigrants.

Although many different sections of Irish society, including the media, various politicians, a wide spectrum of non-governmental organisations (NGOs), different Christian churches, academics and Trade Unions, aligned themselves with these Bishops' Committee critiques, the government, up to now, has by and large failed to take the necessary measures to address the urgent issues raised. Although the asylum processing system has become more efficient in terms of the average time required to process applications, many asylum applications still take years rather than months to determine. At the same time the vast majority of asylum seekers do not have the right to work. The denial of this right coupled with the shift to direct provision in specific accommodation centres for asylum seekers severely reduces the possibilities for their integration into Irish society. Even for those who are subsequently granted refugee status, the government has yet to put in place an integration policy and strategy, and to date has not followed up its own paper entitled 'Integration – a two-way process' published in December 1999.

There are a significant number of people who, after several years in the country, and having exhausted all the channels, have not been granted any form of right to residency, and who therefore remain here without any rights or status. Increasingly, there are indications that people who wish to travel to Ireland to seek asylum are being prevented from doing so by immigration officials located either at points of departure within the EU or at entry ports in Ireland. That asylum seekers are very unlikely to have all the travel documents required by such officials is inter-

nationally recognised, both in the Geneva Convention on
Refugees and by the UN High Commission on Refugees.

To be fair, the Irish government has not, in general, been
stinting in the financial resources which it has allocated to the
accommodation and welfare of asylum seekers. In many ways it
has done better than most other EU states and this is a major
positive aspect of our national response, even if there is now a
noticeable drift towards increasingly restrictive policies and
procedures in all that relates to asylum seekers. At the same
time, the adequacy of financial and administrative provision for
those who arrive here is unfortunately offset by the growing
evidence that a key plank of Irish asylum policy is to use administrative means to prevent as many would-be asylum seekers as
possible from reaching here in the first place, by the policy of so-
called 'pre-emptive exclusion'. This is largely directed towards
preventing inadequately documented persons from embarking
on carriers to Ireland, regardless of whether or not they have
well-founded grounds for seeking asylum.

Welcoming the Stranger: The Core Biblical Call

The nature and scope of its long-term pastoral and theological
response to the growing numbers of immigrants and asylum
seekers coming here may well be a more important defining response for the Irish church than some of the issues which have
occupied it in recent times. Taking a proactive role to promote
justice is not a choice but a requirement. Growing interculturalism and the increasingly diverse racial and ethnic mix of peoples
in Ireland pose challenges relating to the appropriate type and
scope of witness and evangelisation and do so with a new sense
of urgency. Is there a real difference between mission abroad
and the overall evangelising mission of the church? If it is taken
for granted in the so-called mission field that indigenisation and
cultural adaptation is extremely important, how far should the
home church be prepared to adapt itself to the newly arrived
cultural, racial and linguistic groups, and how far should it continue to insist that the onus of adaptation is on the new arrivals?

The present moment in Ireland calls for a clear Christian
proclamation of welcome to the stranger, opposition to xeno-
phobia and condemnation of racism. It calls for a wider definition of sharing and solidarity. Racism strikes at a core Christian
value, the equal dignity of each person, and so has to be con-

demned as essentially unChristian. The church cannot be true to itself if it lets particularisms triumph. In the event of a rising popular or media backlash of racism, anti-immigrant and anti-Islamic feeling, the church must be prepared to give an unequivocal counter-witness. Interfaith dialogue is increasingly required and interfaith co-operation and interaction at grass roots level is even more important.

The Catholic Church in Ireland and worldwide must also stand fast against any erosion of civil and political rights for opportunist reasons, and against any appropriation of more power by individual states and groups of states, who justify questionable expansion of their powers in this direction by the call to oppose terrorism. At the same time the church must promote those aspects of multilateralism and global governance which advance international human rights standards and human well-being. In fact what the arrival of asylum seekers in Ireland, and in Europe as a whole, primarily calls for is a greater and more effective commitment to international human rights law/standards, international peace making, peace keeping, and conflict resolution. There is an opportunity and a challenge to an alert Irish church to give prophetic witness by developing the same type of action-advocacy-education in these areas as it has done, and is doing, in regard to material help to developing countries

Making connections in seeking one just world
Agencies such as Trócaire and ICJP are both keenly aware of the causes and consequences of refugee flows. Trócaire was established in 1973 as the official international development agency of the Catholic Bishops' Conference of Ireland. Since then it has supported over 6,000 projects in 60 countries and has allocated 20% of its core income[6] to development education in Ireland. Many Trócaire partners have been victims of human rights violations, and some have been forced into exile.[7] At Trócaire's 25th anniversary conference on 'People, Power and Participation', held in February 1998, some spoke of having returned home to build up a culture of peace and human rights and to end the culture of impunity, which forced them to flee in the first place. The recent establishment of an International Criminal Court is a fitting tribute to their work and personal courage. One former exile, Guatemalan Lawyer, Frank La Rue, speaking at the 25th anniversary conference, pointed out that a child dying of a pre-

ventable disease like measles is just as tragic as a child dying of a bullet wound in the 36-year Guatemalan civil war, which ended in 1996.[8]

The vision behind Trócaire stretches back to the shared experience of Irishness as being a global one – in part this is tied up with Irish people's experience of exile and in development terms it is influenced by the work of Irish missionaries overseas.[9] From the outset Trócaire had a dual mandate: 'Abroad it will give whatever help lies within its resources to the areas of greatest need among the developing countries. At home, it will try to make us all more aware of the needs of those countries and our duties towards them. These duties are no longer a matter of charity but of simple justice.'[10]

At the core of Trócaire's work is a belief that 'Poverty remains the starkest violation of human rights. Poverty and violence are the enemy of human development, and poverty itself is a form of violence.'[11] At the start of the twenty-first century gross poverty amid plenty challenges us all. Yet the policy responses to this inequality are often perverse. For instance, EU agricultural subsidies mean that the subsidy for each cow in the Union, at about 2.5 euro per day, exceeds the daily income of about half the world's population.[12] At the same time the assets of the world's top three billionaires exceed the combined national incomes of the 49 least developed countries and their 600 million people. Thus, as Trócaire marks its 30th anniversary, its original mandate to tackle the root causes of poverty and injustice remains as relevant as ever. Inspired by Catholic Social Teaching it is called upon to 'challenge those unjust structures, which accentuate the situation of wealth for some and poverty for the rest'.[13]

In responding to these challenges Trócaire's work has become truly international. It undertakes advocacy on issues such as debt and trade at home as well as abroad through international networks such as CIDSE and Caritas Internationalis.[14] The Catholic Church is itself a global actor and can use its institutional strength to push for change. It has a responsibility to work with others to put forward alternative policy proposals to those which are currently being applied. This requires another vision of what is valuable, another perception of what is possible, and another recognition of what is required. Church agencies such as Trócaire must demand that the policies of governments and institutions at various levels serve the 'common good', benefiting all citizens, including minorities and the dispossessed.

The values guiding Trócaire and ICJP's work centre around the dignity of the person, solidarity, the preferential option for the poor, and participation of all in the development process. Thus, in critiquing current forms of globalisation and the role of international institutions such as the International Monetary Fund (IMF) and the World Trade Organisation (WTO), agencies such as Trócaire ask whether the policies which these bodies are promoting are advancing or denying human dignity and human wellbeing, particularly among the poorest and most vulnerable groups, and how accountable are these organisations for their actions? While church agencies may be viewed as leading from the front in terms of advocating for social justice, their real strength lies is supporting grassroots advocacy from below. Nowhere has this been more evident than in relation to the contribution by the Catholic and other churches to the international Jubilee 2000 movement for the cancellation of unpayable debts.

Since Trócaire's establishment, just one month after Ireland joined the then Common Market, the variety and scope of international relationships of which Ireland is a part, and helps shape, has grown more complex. Ireland was recently ranked number one for the second year running in an index of globalisation.[15] The most common meaning given to globalisation is that it refers to increased levels of integration or interdependence among countries, for instance in relation to trade, capital, technology and communications. However, one way in which the world is less globalised compared to the turn of the twentieth century lies in the increasing array of restrictions on migration and labour flows. The main reason for Ireland's holding on to the top position on the globalisation index is the huge significance of international trade and investment flows to its national income. However, the factors which make up the ranking for the index of globalisation are mixed, thus recognising the multifaceted nature of globalisation. For example, one criterion used, which shows Ireland's historic commitment to peacekeeping, is that it is one of a relatively small grouping of states which directly contribute to more than half of the UN's active peacekeeping missions.

As Ireland takes up the EU presidency in January 2004, the government is all too aware of growing public disquiet around certain aspects of globalisation and international relations, and realises that international policy issues are increasingly becom-

ing more a part of national political debates. International bodies cannot be effective in tackling global ills including the vast
levels of poverty and inequality in the world if these institutions
are not seen to be accountable. Yet the decision of the European
Council in June 2002 to abolish the Development Council, which
brought together international development ministers from various member states, means that the only ministerial forum wholly dedicated to development policy issues no longer exists. This
decision may well weaken the development impetus within the
EU, as it seems unlikely that international development issues
will be awarded significant space under the agenda of the
Union's General Affairs Council.

The decision by the Irish government in September 2000,
which had all-party support, to reach the UN 0.7% aid to GNP
target by 2007, is evidence of the influence of the development
community, including Trócaire. Yet despite ongoing growth in
the aid programme, which is particularly targeted at a number
of African least developed countries, the government did not
meet its interim aid target of 0.45 per cent of GNP in 2002.[16] At
the same time, in the context of an expanding overseas aid programme, it remains crucially important that agencies such as
Trócaire keep a spotlight not only on what Ireland gives to the
developing world but also on what Ireland and other developed
countries take. The lack of coherence between the trade, agricultural and development co-operation policies of the EU is a case
in point. Despite the Union's emphasis on the centrality of
poverty reduction it still maintains significant market barriers to
developing country produce and the Union's dumping of sub-
sidised agricultural exports has undermined fragile developing
country economies and the livelihoods of those dependent on
agriculture. Taking a different example, while Ireland is one of
the major contributors to UN peacekeeping, as well as a major
contributor to and on the boards of several UN agencies, there is
a need to constantly monitor and, as necessary, challenge the
Irish government on how it is working to promote international
security and adherence to international law.[17] This challenge has
taken on immense proportions in relation to the ongoing crisis
in the Middle East.

The global context for Trócaire's work has also changed over
time. On the one hand, tremendous progress has been achieved
in terms of life expectancy and literacy. On the other hand, the

1990s saw genocide in both Rwanda and Bosnia. The global economy has become more integrated yet it is also highly fragmented. The bulk of international investment flows and trade moves between developed nations, with the remainder going to a limited number of developing counties. At the same time progress in relation to human development is being undermined by the devastation wrought by HIV/AIDS, the creation of a vaccine for which economist Jeffrey Sachs has termed a weapon of mass salvation.

Religious fundamentalism has also been on the rise. This has become a source of conflict and global insecurity. One commentator noted that far from seeing a decline in religion we are seeing its powerful re-emergence in a grotesquely distorted modern form.[18] Rather that allowing such a scenario to hold sway, churches must work together to bring the values of solidarity, the dignity of the human being and justice to the fore. Interfaith dialogue has an even more central role to play in promoting peace and security, whether one looks at the situation in Northern Ireland or in many other parts of the world. Some falsely use religion and culture to justify violence and non-adherence to international human rights norms, yet cultural and religious specificity can serve to enrich rather than to undermine our understanding of, and adherence to, the principles and standards of human rights. Although in some countries where Trócaire works, notably in many parts of Asia, the Catholic Church is a minority church, while elsewhere it is a majority church, the Catholic Church's role has been important in both contexts. One cannot understand the politics of Central America in the 1980s without understanding the role played by the Catholic Church. When East Timor was annexed by Indonesia and its people oppressed for a quarter of a century, the Catholic Church was one of the few voices, and sometimes the only voice, which could speak out. In Mindanao in the southern Philippines, Christian and Muslim leaders are working together to build new paths to peace. Thus many religious leaders are acting as exemplars of good practice in peacebuilding and conflict resolution.[19] The challenge is to scale up such work rather than allow a misguided and dangerous view of religious intolerance to hold sway.

Politically, a significant development, which has taken place alongside globalisation, has been the push towards democratisation. This includes a heightened emphasis on good governance and respect for human rights. Since its foundation Trócaire has prioritised programmes which focus on the empowerment of marginalised groups in order to increase their participation in the development process. This approach to participation has manifested itself through a variety of programme areas, for instance through leadership training, community development and justice and peace work. It is now widely recognised by official donors and international institutions alike that meaningful participation is both a cornerstone of the development process and a key ingredient in ensuring outcomes that are poverty reducing and sustainable. At Trócaire's 25th anniversary conference Dr Barney Pityana pointed out that 'The implementation of economic, social and cultural rights requires democratic participation of society at all levels, an informed civil society, a democratic government and state institutions which monitor and inspire human rights action. The call for a new millennium therefore is clearly for an investment in people who can take charge of their own destiny.'[20]

For Trócaire, genuine participation means not only taking part but also having influence over the decisions which are made, their implementation and evaluation. It also requires that institutions or duty-bearers are fully accountable for their actions, be these national or international bodies. This respect for the involvement of civil society can also be seen as a contemporary expression of another principle of Catholic Social Teaching, subsidiarity, the requirement that decisions should be made at the level of those who can best determine the needs, interests and priorities of those who will be affected.

At home, Trócaire's work and partnerships in the field of development education continue to promote active citizenship, based on a critical understanding of and interest in Ireland's stance in international relations as this affects developing countries, whether through the integration of development issues within the schools' curricula or working with trade unions. Such education helps in promoting better understanding of the human rights abuses which give rise to asylum seekers coming to Ireland, and thus links closely with the work of ICJP. Looking ahead, Trócaire is committed to enhancing its role as an effective pro-poor advocacy institution through empowering particular social groups, including most marginalised groups such as bonded labourers, in order to define obstacles or problems, to design and implement programmes to address those problems and ultimately to participate in determining outcomes. Trócaire is also committed to working simultaneously on this justice agenda at multiple legal and institutional levels (local, national, regional, and global), and to utilising its international solidarity networks to advance this work.[21] Such actions are vital, as in the end significant progress in support of international development will only happen when societies in both developed and developing countries, and key political leaders and decision-takers therein, believe that structural change to tackle global inequalities is necessary.

The Human Rights Challenge of the 21st Century: Implementation
The language of human rights has become commonplace, yet the implementation of human rights standards remains patchy. Catholic Church actors and other civil society movements are increasingly holding states and international actors to account in meeting such standards. At home refugee and asylum policy is a litmus test of the state's commitment to international human rights standards. Internationally, we live in a world concerned with a narrow concept of security, yet the terror associated with hunger, displacement and poverty, and the violence against marginalised groups which these entail, is in danger of being overlooked in a situation where military responses to terror hold sway.

By linking their domestic and international policy agendas, agencies such as Trócaire and ICJP can raise awareness that human rights are indivisible and interdependent. Just as ICJP has been active in terms of promoting the incorporation of economic and social rights into the Irish constitution,[22] and in monitoring successive governments' performance in relation to human rights standards, Trócaire has been promoting an integrated approach to human rights in areas such as international debt and global governance.

At home and abroad the key challenge for agencies such as Trócaire and ICJP lies in helping to build inclusive and equitable societies. At an international level, if globalisation is to be accompanied by fair rules and regulatory institutions, political pressure must be brought to bear on world leaders. In their analysis and policy advocacy around economic globalisation and other issues, church agencies will need to be rigorous in their analysis and research, and in their commitment to engaging in strategic dialogue with policymakers over the long haul. Otherwise we risk taking the path, against which John Paul II has cautioned, towards 'A type of development which does not respect and promote human rights is not worthy of mankind.'

Perhaps the vision underpinning Catholic social teaching and the work of church agencies such as Trócaire and ICJP is best captured by the principle of solidarity, wherein we recognise our interconnectedness, in both ethical and empirical terms, through the personal and institutional activities that make up the fabric of human existence. Thus, in looking ahead, agencies such as Trócaire and ICJP realise that it is through international co-ordination and collaboration that they can best enhance the possibility that decision-makers in national governments and international institutions become responsive to the needs and voices of the poor.

Moreover, the message of the church about solidarity and sharing across frontiers takes on a new impulse in face of Ireland's national wealth. Morally the surge in Ireland's income per head (from roughly 60% of the EU average ten years ago to around 130% today) brings with it greater international responsibilities. At the same time the arrival of refugees and asylum seekers can show us how to be true Christians and enable us to understand and live our faith. As Irish society embarks on this new century, as part of a global community, we must ask of ourselves what kind of Ireland we want to see and what kind of world we want to live in. A key challenge in Ireland and abroad will be to build a world where human rights are fully respected, and where interculturalism and inclusion are recognised and practised.

The framework of international human rights law, whether the 1951 Convention on Refugees or the 1989 Convention on the Rights of the Child, are all part of a broad set of international treaties aimed at preventing abuses of human rights and enhancing adherence to commonly shared human rights standards. Linked to this, Ireland should, at the very least, become a signatory to the International Convention on the Rights of All Migrant Workers and Members of their Families, so as to initiate a national debate regarding its ratification and incorporation into Irish law. A world suffused by the Christian commitment to the dignity of each and every person would be one where no one would be forced into exile. It would also be a world where in both developing and developed countries all people would have all the rights to which they are entitled by virtue of their common humanity. That is not just an ideal to which we should aspire – it is in all our interests.

CHAPTER TWELVE

Irish Christians
and the Struggle for a Just Society

Dermot A. Lane

Garret FitzGerald entered active politics in 1964. One of the many factors motivating his decision was a personal interest in promoting social justice.[1] In that same year he contributed a paper to the Declan Costello Group in which he proposed the introduction of a wealth tax with a view to improving the distribution of resources in Ireland. This paper, along with others, fed into the Just Society policy drawn up by Declan Costello of Fine Gael in 1965. A good example of Garret's concern for social justice can be found in a paper presented at a Conference of the Irish Theological Association in Clongowes Wood College in 1977 entitled 'Political Structures and Personal Development'.[2] In that paper he discussed the need for a more 'equitable spread of material wealth', the duty of politicians to represent 'the interest of weaker sections of the community in the face of big battalions', and the need to balance the quest for human freedom with the equally important task of promoting economic and social justice.[3] Commenting on that particular period of Irish history, Austin Flannery OP singles out Garret FitzGerald and Declan Costello as politicians who 'showed themselves more responsive to changing church teaching on justice than did many of the Irish clergy'.[4] The pursuit of social justice could be described as one of the driving forces within Garret FitzGerald's distinguished career in politics and journalism over the last thirty-eight years.

It is appropriate, therefore, that a paper should be devoted to the subject of 'Irish Christians and the Struggle for Social Justice' in a collection to honour Dr Garret FitzGerald. In the text that follows we will chart in broad strokes the teaching of the Catholic Church on justice from the 1960s onwards, the reception of that teaching by Irish Christians, and conclude with a critique of current approaches to justice followed by some proposals for the work of justice in the future.

The last forty years have been a period of extraordinary cultural change in Ireland, not only in politics but also in the church. Ireland is certainly better off now from an economic point of view than ever before in its history. But what about the area of social justice? How have Christians in Ireland responded to the task of promoting justice in education, social policy and the distribution of national resources? What role has the Catholic Church played as agent and prophet in promoting justice? Is justice a priority in political and ecclesial life in Ireland at the beginning of the twenty-first century? Or is the language of justice simply an opportune piece of empty rhetoric? These are some of the questions that will be addressed in the course of this paper.

The Impact of Vatican II on the Struggle for Justice
In the period prior to the Second Vatican Council (1962-65) the teaching of the Catholic Church on justice was informed by appeals to the natural law and non-biblical, neo-scholastic theology. This natural law approach to justice changed quite significantly at Vatican II and this change is most apparent when one compares the original schemata prepared for the Council and the finally approved documents. Before outlining what happened at Vatican II in relation to justice, it may be helpful to summarise some of the important theological shifts which made possible a new approach to justice.

Probably the most important development of Vatican II was a change in outlook and this can be summed up in terms of a new openness to the world. The church began to see itself as that reality which exists *in* the world *for* the world. This new attitude is captured in a series of shifts that could be described in terms of a movement from *anathema* to dialogue, from isolation to solidarity, from opposition to conversation, and from being a subculture within society to entering into a real dialogue with modernity.[5] A new way of doing theology begins to come into being which embraces for the first time the importance of human experience,[6] acknowledges the emergence of a historical consciousness,[7] and recognises the reality of pluralism.[8]

Vatican II, for those who read the internal history of the council, was a qualified success over the old monolithic neo-scholastic approach to theology. There is a clear shift from a deductive-scholastic theology to an inductive-personalist theology. For example the Constitution on Revelation sees revelation no longer simply as a series of propositional statements about God but as an account of God's personal self communication to the world in history, especially in the life, death and resurrection of Jesus.[9] Further, the council sought to overcome the dualism that existed heretofore between nature and grace that was so strong in the neo-scholastic manuals of theology. In addition, the mission of the church was perceived in more unified terms as embracing a religious dimension as well as a temporal aspect in terms of renewing the secular order.[10] Consequently the role of the church in the world is to scrutinise the signs of the times and interpret them in the light of the gospel.[11] It is within this larger theological context that we can better appreciate what happened at Vatican II in the area of justice.

The Second Vatican Council gave a significant impetus to the search for justice. By far the most influential document of the council on justice was the *Pastoral Constitution on the Church in the Modern World* which has some twenty-four references to the subject of justice. The council grounds its teaching on justice in the dignity of every human being, in the social character of human nature, and in the right of every human being to participate in society.[12] Further, these aspects of justice are based on the Bible in contrast to the natural law, so that now the emphasis is on the person created in the image of God, redeemed 'in Christ', and called to create right relationships between humans and God.

1971: A significant year for Church Teaching on Justice
In the aftermath of Vatican II justice became a prominent theme in theology. 1971 saw the publication of two important church documents which touched directly on justice issues. On the one hand there was the publication of *Social Problems* (*Octogesimo adveniens*) written by Pope Paul VI to commemorate the eightieth anniversary of *Rerum novarum* (1891). This document acknowledges: 'it is difficult ... to utter a unified message and put forward a solution which has universal validity. Such is not our ambition, nor is it our mission.' Instead the document says that 'it is up to the Christian communities to analyse with objectivity the situation that is proper to their own country, to shed on it the light of the gospel's unalterable words, and to draw principles of reflection, norms of judgement and directives for action from the social teaching of the church. This social teaching has been

worked out in the course of history.' *Octogesimo adveniens* also notes: 'It is up to these Christian communities ... to discern the options and commitments which are called for in order to bring about the social, political, and economic changes ... needed.'[13]

A number of points are worth noting here in these quotations: it is not Paul VI's intention to suggest that a single universal message exists which awaits application, that the local community has an important role to play in discovering its social responsibility for the work of justice, and that the social teachings of the church are historically constituted.[14]

In the same letter Paul VI goes on to invoke 'the forward-looking imagination both to perceive within the present disregarded possibilities hidden within it and to direct itself towards a fresh future.'[15] This appeal to the imagination as a resource for promoting the work of justice is striking in a papal letter and is something we will return to later.

Equally significant was the Synod of Bishops gathered in Rome to address questions of justice in the world in 1971. That synod made two outstanding prophetic statements on justice which continue to challenge the church today. One the one hand it asserted that:

> Action on behalf of justice and participation in the transformation of the world appear to us as a constitutive dimension of the preaching of the gospel, or in other words, of the church's mission for the redemption of the human race and its liberation from every oppressive situation.[16]

On the other hand, the synod states that the church has a 'specific responsibility ... of giving witness... of the need for love and justice ... contained in the gospel ... a witness to be carried out in church institutions themselves'.[17] And then, as if to spell out the meaning of this, the synod states:

> The church recognises that anyone who ventures to speak to people about justice must first be just in their eyes.[18]

A few years later in 1974 Pedro Arrupe SJ summoned Jesuits from all over the world to address questions about justice within the mission of the Society of Jesus. This gathering, known as the Thirty-Second General Congregation, declared that: 'the promotion of justice is not one apostolic area among others ... (but) should be the concern ... of all ... apostolic endeavours' (and) 'the integrating factor of all ministries',[19] a decision that had an enormous impact on the work of Jesuits around the world.

The Emergence of Liberation Theology
While these developments were taking place in the life of the
teaching church, liberation theology was coming into being in
the Third World in the light of the new horizons opened up by
Vatican II. The birth of liberation theology was assisted by a
meeting in 1968 of the Latin American Episcopal Conference
(CELAM) in Medellin which discerned that 'the present moment' is one of 'alienation and poverty' that 'awakens among
large sectors ... attitudes of protest and desire for liberation, development and social justice'.[20] Out of this historical context
came liberation theology which, in the words of one of its founding figures, is described as 'a critical reflection on Christian
praxis in the light of the Word'.[21] As such liberation theology
'does not replace the other functions of theologies, such as wisdom and rational reflection' but rather presupposes them.[22]
Liberation theology, often described as the most influential development in theology of the twentieth century, 'is not so much
a new theme for reflection as a new way to do theology'.[23] This
new way of doing theology took off in the Third World and is increasingly appreciated in the First World. Liberation theology
places justice at the centre of its agenda and therefore begins not
with wonder but with indignation at the injustices of the world.
Within this indignation a preference is given to the plight of the
poor and primacy is accorded to the praxis of liberation in the
name of the gospel. Liberation theology in the long run seeks to
liberate not only the oppressed but also the oppressor.

In 1979 John Paul II took over from Paul VI and John Paul I,
and continued to develop links between justice and the proclamation of the gospel. John Paul II wrote several social encyclicals:
On Human Work (*Laborem exercens*, 1981), *The Church and Social
Concern* (*Sollicitudo rei socialis*, 1987) and *On the hundreth anniversary of Rerum novarum* (*Centesimus annus*, 1991). While these
social encyclicals are in some respects built around Vatican II,
they also signal a return to a non-historical deductive methodology and seek to work out universal principles of justice for application within the local Christian community.

Reception of the Teaching of the Church on Justice in Ireland
It is against the background of these developments at Vatican II
that we must now look at the struggle for justice among
Christians in Ireland in the second half of the twentieth century.

In spite of initial hesitations, the vision of Vatican II, especially in reference to justice, did take off with considerable success and many positive results, even if it is by no means clear whether the successes were consciously co-ordinated or contingent developments.

1969 saw the establishment by the Irish bishops of the Irish Commission for Justice and Peace. Over the years right up to 2002, this Commission under the very capable leadership of Jerome Connolly spearheaded many reports highlighting injustices within Irish society, signalling the importance of social and economic rights that ought to be inserted into the Irish constitution, affirming the rights of prisoners and refugees.

In 1970 the bishops also founded the Council for Social Welfare which deals with social questions, organises conferences and publishes documents. As such it acts as an advisory body to the Catholic bishops of Ireland.

In 1973 Trócaire – the Catholic Agency for Development – was launched by the Irish bishops with a short pastoral letter. Since then Trócaire has become a highly successful international aid agency, with an annual budget of €30,000,000 through voluntary subscriptions, with over 500 projects in some 50 countries worldwide, with a staff of 100 lay people. 70% of its resources goes towards development projects, 20% towards development education in Ireland and 10% to emergency relief work. The generous support of the work of Trócaire by donations from the people of Ireland on an annual basis, especially during Trócaire's Lenten campaign, is a measure of its success. The work of Trócaire was pioneered energetically by Brian McKeown, its first director and is now continued creatively by Justin Kilcullen, its second director.

In 1981 the Conference and Major Religious Superiors, now known as the Conference of Religious of Ireland(CORI), founded a Justice Desk which is run by Father Sean Healy and Sister Brigid Reynolds. The goal of CORI is to be a voice for the Religious of Ireland on justice issues. Over the years the CORI Justice Desk has consistently and quite prophetically challenged the existence of unjust structures in Irish society through a process of social analysis and Christian reflection. At the same time the CORI Justice Desk has engaged in advocacy work on behalf of the poor in Ireland and each year it contributes a professional critique of the annual budget from the prespective of the poor. In recent years the CORI Justice Desk has also become an important voice within the Community and Voluntary sector alongside Trade Unions and farmers in negotiations with government in the drawing up an annual budget through a process of social partnership. In this way the CORI Justice Desk seeks to influence public policy in Ireland and has succeeded perhaps more than any other church body in doing this.

Other groups actively engaged in promoting justice in Irish society include the Jesuit Centre for Faith and Justice, the Vincentian Partnership for Justice, the Society of St Vincent de Paul, and Crosscare of the Dublin diocese.

The work of justice by these different organisations has been complemented by other voices in Irish life. These include prophetic utterances over the years by individuals like Michael Sweetman, SJ, Peter McVerry, SJ, and Stanislaus Kennedy, RSC; the distinctive witness for justice by Irish missionaries such as Niall O'Brien, Shay Cullen and John O'Brien; the development of critical theologies of justice by Irish theologians like Denis Carroll, Séan McDonagh and Donal Dorr; and Irish campaigners for justice in the Third World such as Bono of U2 fame and Bob Geldolf who have made an impact on the international community.

Mention must also be made of contributions made by the former President of Ireland, Mary Robinson, who during her term of office and since then as United Nations Commissioner of Human Rights, has been an important voice for justice. Likewise President Mary McAleese has spoken out on behalf of the poor, drawn attention to needs of the people of Uganda and Kenya, and more recently gave the annual Trócaire lecture in Maynooth (2002).

Add to these voices a series of pastoral letters published by the Irish Bishops Conference which include *The Work of Justice*, 1977, *Work is the Key: Towards an Economy that Needs Everybody*, 1992, and *Prosperity with a Purpose: Christian Faith and Values in Time of Rapid Growth*, 1999. These letters were the fruit of consultations with various groups and the letter on work involved a series of 'listening days' with unemployed persons.

Critique of the Struggle for Justice in Ireland
When all of these bodies are grouped together they add up to a significant justice presence within Irish society and the Christian

community. The practical effect of this justice presence within church and society is something that would be very difficult to measure. At the very least it must be said to the credit of these justice groups that there is a deep awareness within Irish society of the need to bridge the gap between rich and poor as a matter of strict justice and to work towards a more equitable distribution of the nation's resources, especially at a time of economic growth.

There are, however, a number of anomalies that must be noted. These include the absence of any consistent process of public self-assessment and evaluation among church based advocates of justice – the CORI Justice Desk being an exception to this observation. There is, furthermore, an unevenness between generous individual almsgiving on the one hand and the relative neglect of social reform and structural change within church and society in the name of justice. There is also a conspicuous absence of co-ordination and networking among these different justice driven bodies. Clearly there is a need for a forum on justice that would bring together these different groupings as a unified force within Christian communities, Irish society and political life. If there had been a justice forum the so-called Celtic Tiger would not have been allowed to gallop at such a pace with so much indifference to social inequalities. Individual voices, such as the bishops in their pastoral on *Prosperity with a Purpose* and the CORI Justice desk, are insufficient when faced with the might of the free market.

These anomalies arise out of the existence of different approaches and theologies of justice within the church and indeed outside the church. At present there is a top down non-historical methodology espoused by the teachings of the church under John Paul II on the one hand, and the bottom up historical methodology initiated by Vatican II, Paul VI and more explicitly developed in a variety of liberation theologies. These two different approaches can and should be seen as complementary to and necessary for each other – and not set in stark opposition to each other as is so often the case at present in the life of the church. These contrasting approaches to justice reflect, however, a deeper theological tension at present within the life of the Catholic Church.

Two competing views of Christianity

At present there are two different conceptions of Christianity vying with each other. There is the self-understanding of the church as *a community of interpretation* dedicated to guarding a body of truths handed down from revelation and tradition. This body of truths is often referred to as the deposit of faith, though there is some confusion as to what constitutes the deposit of faith as distinct from secondary cultural accretions to the faith. This understanding of Christianity sees faith primarily as an intellectual assent to a body of truths given in revelation.

In contrast there is also an understanding of Christianity which sees the church as *a community of praxis*, dedicated to the continuation of the ministry of Jesus in the world today in the name of the coming reign of God. This community of Christian praxis is committed to a critical reflection on its own praxis in the light of the word of God, tradition and the teaching of the church. This understanding of Christianity sees faith embracing a praxis of justice and liberation that effects an ongoing process of personal conversion and social transformation. Within this self-understanding of faith, personal experience and the praxis of liberation in the name of the gospel are regarded as sources of theological knowledge and truth. According to this point of view, revelation is understood as the personal self-communication of God in history, with particular reference to the normative character of the life, death and resurrection of Jesus for understanding revelation today.

These two understandings of Christianity, the one theory based and the other praxis grounded, need to be brought together as mutually complementary and self-correcting. At present there is a serious separation of theory and praxis within the life of the church. The current standoff between a non-historical deductive approach and a historically conscious inductivist methodology in matters of faith and justice is a source of tension in the church today. This divorce between praxis and interpretation is damaging the credibility of the church in a variety of areas which range from social justice to liturgy, from ministry to the exercise of authority, and from Christian identity to the meaning of religious pluralism.

An echo of this tension between the church as a community of interpretation and a community of praxis can be heard in recent exchanges between Joseph Ratzinger and Walter Kasper over the relationship between the universal and the local church. The differences between these two theologians comes down to a differences of approach: 'One side (Ratzinger) tends to take as its starting point the Platonic view of the primacy of ideas, and finds the universal in them. The other (Kasper) tends to an Aristotelian view that the universal is realised in actual reality.'[24]

In overcoming the divorce between interpretation and praxis, it must be noted that the historical origins of Christianity go back to the liberating praxis of Jesus and that, therefore, a strong case exists for privileging praxis over interpretation at least as a point of departure. This will require a recognition of praxis as a point of departure that opens up the meaning of Christianity. The meaning of Christianity is not available externally for detached inspection prior to praxis but rather within the praxis of Christian faith. This praxis-point of departure is initiated by impulses coming from those contrast-experiences in life which highlight the difference between what is and what could be. There is a growing volume of indignation at the way the world's resources are so unjustly distributed between the rich and the poor, between the overproduction of the first world and the underproduction of the third world. Likewise there is an increasing awareness that current levels of first-world consumption are no longer sustainable from a justice or an ecological point of view.

Another expression of this turn to praxis can be seen in the newfound sense of social responsibility for the future of the world. This new social responsibility arises from a growing awareness that the way we are is not divinely pre-ordained but rather the outcome of man-made political decisions that can be un-made and re-made. The key to this awareness is the existence of a new way of experiencing the co-presence of God in the world. God is no longer experienced as 'a power over' human beings but rather 'a power with' people. God is co-experienced as a gracious presence that empowers people to do what otherwise they would not be able to do. An important theological shift is taking place from experiencing God as One who controls to One who inspires, from One who dominates to One who liberates, from One who intervenes from time to time to One who is already always there ahead of us. It is ultimately this new experience of God, based on the Bible and not metaphysics, which is the source of the Christian praxis of liberation.

The need for a new Imagination

These proposals to adopt praxis as a point of departure, and the
need to effect a dialectical relationship between praxis and interpretation, are not sufficient in themselves. Such moves will not
succeed unless they are accompanied by new imagination, a
point intimated by Paul VI in *Octogesimo adveniens*. Both the
praxis and theory of Christian faith at this time are in crisis – not
so much in themselves but in terms of their supporting imaginative frameworks. What John Henry Newman said of faith can
be said with particular force to the praxis and theory of
Christianity today:

It is not reason that is against us but imagination.[25]

This negative observation on imagination by the early Newman
is turned around by the later Newman into a positive appreciation of the power of imagination to animate faith. The crisis in
Christianity today is less a crisis of ideas and more a crisis of the
imagination.

Imagination is intrinsic to every human act of knowing. We
rely all the time on the use of imagination in understanding people, events and experiences – even though we may not always
advert to its use. Imagination is that part of the human mind
which bridges the gap between images of sense data and human
understanding, that effects a synthesis between what initially
may appear to be polar opposites, and is able to represent alternatives to the present understanding of the self in the world.
Further, the imagination is that unique capacity of the mind that
completes what is unfinished, fulfils what is partial, and heals
what is broken. In brief, imagination is that aspect of the human
spirit which breaks boundaries, advances knowledge, and ex-
pands horizons. At present, too much theory and praxis of
Christianity has assumed a life of its own, having become separated from its original revelatory experience, and is no longer
capable of serving the impulses of the contemporary religious
imagination.

In other words, the imaginative paradigm upholding Christianity is under pressure from a variety of sources, some of which
are internal and others external to Christian faith. Internal pressures on the imaginative support-structure of Christianity arise
from the turn to experience and praxis as sources of theological
knowledge, the rise of historical consciousness and its application to understanding the present, the reality of pluralism and

the challenge this poses for the identity of Christian faith. External pressures on the imaginative framework of Christianity include the new scientific cosmologies, the demise of teleology and the endless flux of post-modern culture. Up to now the imaginative structure surrounding Christianity was based on a series of assumptions that can no longer bear the pressures coming from these sources. These assumptions include an underlying presence of exclusivity, uniformity and essentialism which make up the imaginative framework supporting Christian faith.

Just as early Christianity made an imaginative jump from a Jewish self-understanding into new Hellenistic forms of self-understanding, so today Christianity at the beginning of the twenty-first century needs to move from being a predominately Euro-centric reality to becoming a polycentric, multicultural ecclesial reality. This new imaginative framework will have to be able to express and hold in existence the reality of a Christian faith that is at least inclusive, historically self-conscious, and pluralistic.

The wisdom saying of Jesus, first employed in his attempt to change the legal stubbornness of the Pharisees, applies with particular force to the new situation that Christianity finds itself in at present:

> People do not pour new wine into old wineskins. No, they pour new wine into new wineskins, and in that way both are preserved.[26]

The need for a new imagination in relation to the praxis and theory of justice is not just a bid to co-opt a category that is back into vogue once again in artistic, scientific and theological circles. Instead this call for a new imagination in this particular context is informed by the realisation that it is above all else the faculty of imagination that fuels praxis. The creative capacity of imagination to offer alternative views of life is precisely that which activates a new praxis of justice in the church and society. Imagination is one of the most potent sources of the praxis of justice.

The Praxis of Justice fired by Memory and Imagination
This call for a new imaginative framework will most surely be misunderstood unless it is accompanied by a further step. That further step is the importance of highlighting the link between

tradition and imagination, between history and the future. This
new, creative imagination will construct itself out of the past
and not in disregard of history or tradition. A close, dynamic relationship exists between historical memory and the creative
imagination. This relationship between the past and the future,
between history and the new, is caught strikingly by the observation of the Irish poet Patrick Kavanagh:

On the stem

Of memory imaginations blossom[27]

Memory and imagination are closely related and interconnected.
Memory, according to Walter Benjamin, is like an energy-filled
molecule from the past seeking to connect creatively with the
present. This exercise of memory enables us to realise that the
way we are is not the way we have to be, that in truth there is
very little that is preordained about the present, and that therefore both the past and present can be changed in the future
through the interaction of memory and imagination. Those who
ignore the past, especially past injustices, are bound to repeat
them in the present. Memory provokes imagination in the present and imagination enables memory to realise its promise in
the present for the sake of the future.

These three steps, namely the critical integration of praxis
and interpretation, the prioritising of praxis over interpretation
as a point of departure, and the linking up of memory with
imagination, taken together have the capacity to give new life to
the struggle for justice among Irish Christians in the present and
the future.

In conclusion I want to illustrate how the recovery of memory
and the invocation of imagination can give new direction to the
praxis and interpretation of justice in the future. Christian faith
seeks to keep alive the memory of the praxis of Jesus in society in
the name of the coming reign of God. The historical praxis of
Jesus had a direct bearing on the political and religious situation
of his day: good news to the poor, relief to captives, recovery of
sight to the blind and freedom to the oppressed.[28] One way in
which the historical Jesus sought to embody this vision of the
reign of God was through the creation of a new table fellowship
among those who were socially excluded, politically marginalised, and religiously outcast. The meal-ministry of Jesus,
prominent in the gospels, provoked a negative reaction from the
Pharisees who accused him of being 'a glutton and a drunkard, a

friend of tax collectors and sinners' (Mt 11:19). This new praxis of table fellowship initiated by Jesus in his ministry was formalised at the Last Supper and prophetically re-enacted by the washing of the feet and followed with the command: Do this in memory of me. The praxis of the celebration of the Eucharist in the church today has lost its organic connection with the meal-ministry of Jesus and the washing of the feet. With the help of a new imagination, building on the memory of the table fellowship initiated by the historical Jesus and instituted at the Last Supper and explained by the prophetic action of the washing of the feet, the way we celebrate the Eucharist could be transformed to recover its connection with the work of justice.

Worship without attention to the work of justice flies in the face of the prophetic utterances of Hebrew prophets against this praxis (e.g. Amos 5:21-25, Is 1:13ff). The work of justice without the celebration of the Eucharist is in danger of running out of hope, while the celebration of the Eucharist without justice runs the risk of becoming an empty ritual. Neglect of this close relationship between the work of justice and the celebration of the eucharist accounts in part for the presence of so much apathy and the absence of hope within liturgical assemblies.

If this neglected link between the work of justice and the celebration of the Eucharist can be re-established then we have a new context for re-opening discussions about eucharistic hospitality among Christians. Further, in this regard it is important to bear in mind that for many Christians the Eucharist is the sacrament of the feast and foretaste of the reign of God. Surely those who bring good news to the poor, release to captives, sight to the blind, and freedom to the oppressed in the name of the reign of God have a greater claim on the Eucharist than those who are indifferent to the socially excluded.

To sum up, the link between justice and liturgy is strong in both the Hebrew and Christian scriptures. If this link is not cultivated then both the work of justice and the celebration of the Eucharist will limp. The urgent task facing Irish Christians today in the struggle for social justice is to retrieve the biblical unity between justice and liturgy.

CHAPTER THIRTEEN

Churches, Governments and the Media: Confronting their own and each other's responsibilities

John Horgan

Any analysis of the interactions of church, state and media in modern Ireland – and, in particular, of the degree to which they acted (or failed to act) as invigilators of each other and of themselves in the business of creating a more just society – has to take as its starting point two central observations.

One is that the most pervasive ideology in modern (i.e. post-1922) Irish society was, in its initial stages and for a considerable period thereafter, one of self-satisfaction or, at least, embattled self-justification. With the severance of the British connection, there was, at least in influential official circles, a sense of completeness, buttressed by the profoundly, and often passionately, held belief that all significant threats to the well-being of Irish society were external in origin. In this context, the creation of a more just society was seen as a lower priority than defending the society we had, unfairnesses and all. This sense that the remedying of injustice was at best a task postponed was reinforced, in turn, both by the apparent willingness of the vast mass of the population to accept the *status quo* (with the evident exception of the masses who had departed involuntarily as emigrants, and whose voices were therefore conveniently absent from political discourse) and by the apparent stridency of those calling for radical action on social and economic injustice. It can be argued that there was a constituency for the social justice agenda, even at this early stage: Noel Browne, although he was undoubtedly something of a cuckoo in the Clann na Poblachta nest, identified this constituency almost in spite of himself with his single-minded vision of the elimination of TB and the creation of a decent public health service: it was a constituency which continued to elect him as a public representative for many years thereafter, despite the dogged contemporary opposition of the church and despite his heterogenous views on other issues. Elsewhere, the rhetoric (much more than the activities) of tiny groups such as the Communist Party of Ireland and Saor Éire, faced with such a monolithic and conservative culture, became so extreme that it simultaneously invited disbelief and prompted a harsh political and security response. It is instructive to remember that even in the late 1950s Browne was making anti-communist speeches and warning his followers against the danger that their ranks might be infiltrated by Marxists. At the same time, the US Embassy in Dublin was eagerly filing reports to the State Department in Washington (where they were filed under 'B' for Bolshevik) detailing every possible bit of tittle-tattle it could glean about communist tendencies in the Irish trade union movement.

The second is that – again for most of this period – the injustices highlighted by each of these institutions were for the most part self-referential. The state's greatest sense of injustice was reserved for the 'unjust' partition of the island, and the injustices visited in consequence upon northern nationalists. The latter injustices had the distinct advantage of being irremediable by any Irish government action, so that they served as a kind of communitarian glue for domestic ideology without requiring the development of any practical strategies. The (Catholic) church was really in a position of such power that it did not have a great deal to complain about, apart from the government's growing unwillingness to heed its diktats on the extension of the licensing laws. One possible exception to this was – however mixed the motives that might have inspired it – its frequent criticism of the social evil of emigration. This criticism was, however, and no doubt understandably by the standards of the time, innocent of any analysis of the social and economic policies which produced the phenomenon which the bishops denounced. Everybody was guilty, so nobody was guilty. The media, for their part, were equally limited, if occasionally less cautious. Radio Éireann could not and did not complain about anything because it was a government department. *The Irish Times* mounted its horse occasionally and rode off in all directions in defence of that variegated creation, the liberal ethic, most conveniently summed up in its denunciations of the appalling contemporary literary censorship. *The Irish Independent* was loud in its denunciations of the injustices experienced by Catholics behind the iron curtain; the *Irish Press* equally so in its defence of republicans in the new state and their presumed grievances.

Above all, they tended not to complain much about each other, or examine their own consciences too closely. It was a competitive world, in which each institution saw itself as a tribune of the people, and preferred to ignore the others, for the most part, rather than draw attention to them as potential rivals. A rare exception was Dr Cornelius Lucey, later Bishop of Cork, who wrote a thoughtful article on the freedom of the press in 1937. Included in his denunciations of media practices which he found offensive was the surprising suggestion that a libel law 'which tends to kill criticism of public officials, slum-landlords etc., except the criticism be clearly in the public interest, ought to be repealed. It is too much to expect any private individual, who has damaging revelations to make, to know beforehand whether these revelations will do good or not.'[1] The more orthodox view was expressed by Bishop Michael Browne of Galway, who told his colleague Archbishop McQuaid of Dublin in the mid-1950s that he did not read *The Irish Times*, *'ad tranquillitatem animae'*.[2]

The bureaucratisation – not to say ossification – of all three institutions was probably an inevitable consequence of the early years of self-defensive statehood. It was, if anything, intensified by the fact that Fianna Fáil were in power as a single-party government for 35 of the 41 years between 1932 and 1973. The same factor can, in turn, help to explain the sense of challenge and change which informed activities in all three spheres in the late 1960s and early 1970s, when Fianna Fáil were coming to the end of their second uninterrupted 16-year spell in government. There were other factors involved, of course: the Vatican Council, the disturbances among university students in Paris and other European cities, the advent of television, developments in relation to Northern Ireland, and enhanced economic growth, to name but a few. The political factor was probably among the most significant, however, not least because it was intensified by the failure of the opposition parties to present the electorate with a viable alternative government for much of those sixteen years. In an atmosphere in which the orthodox political opposition seemed ineffectual or self-regarding, other forces moved to fill what was perceived as a vacuum.

It is probably true to say that the media moved first, largely under the influence of numbers of young people who had moved straight into the newly-autonomous sphere of television straight from university. The politicians were, initially, only dimly aware that in creating the national broadcasting service and separating it from direct state control they had, in effect, cut a stick with which to beat themselves. The first decade of RTÉ's existence is replete with examples of range-finding on both sides, as broadcasters sought to extend the limits of permissible activity, and politicians sought to rein them in. Interestingly, one of the earliest flashpoints also involved the church. This was when the normally innocuous 'Outlook' programme on RTÉ television, normally a short and frequently somewhat saccharine few minutes of homiletics at the end of the day's broadcasting schedule, was devoted to brief but pithy commentaries by clergy on social matters, notably on the poor standards of urban housing for working class people. This was in itself partly a response to contemporary political pressures: clerics like Fr Michael Sweetman SJ, and political organisations such as the Dublin Housing Action Committee (itself in large part a front for the recrudescent social activism of Sinn Féin, later to lead to a split in the organisation) were seizing the headlines and presenting government with a problem it had not encountered for about three decades. Housing was taken up as a theme by 'Outlook' in a week in which it was presented by Fr Austin Flannery OP. The minister responsible for housing, Kevin Boland, reacted angrily to this – as he saw it – intrusion upon the territory of politics by unqualified commentators, and stigmatised Fr Flannery as a 'so-called cleric'. Fr Flannery had compounded the crime of using a religious programme for commentary on social policy by inviting a communist, Michael O'Riordan, to participate in one of the programmes. (The effect of Boland's name-calling was somewhat undermined when the *Evening Herald* published photographs of Mr Boland and Fr Flannery with the captions inadvertently transposed.) Certainly television was more risk-taking in this area, even if the tabloid nature of the medium resulted in occasional excesses: the newspapers followed suit more cautiously. *The Irish Times* broke new ground in recruiting a journalist, Michael Viney – whose British nationality was probably more of a help than a hindrance – to write well-researched series of articles on a carefully-chosen selection of social topics which to a large extent mirrored the preoccupations of that paper's readership: illegitimacy, mixed marriages, adoption among them. By the mid-1960s, all three Dublin morning newspapers had woken up to the ecclesial revolution that was taking place in Rome (again, RTÉ had been to the fore here since 1962) and all were subjecting the church to a new and informed critique. This was, for the most part, centred on the perceived slowness of Irish Catholicism to measure up to the norms established by Vatican II, and for this reason effectively lacked any dimension related to social justice. The closest this critique came to the justice agenda was in relation to the church's control of the majority of second-level schools, in that the opposition of some church leaders (and more particularly of some religious congregations) to the government's community schools initiative in the 1970s was occasionally portrayed as anti-social and elitist.

The church, for its part, seemed to be in semi-dormant mode, concerned more to manage its internal process of post-Vatican change than to interact in any meaningful way with the civil society in which it still held such a strong role. Cardinal Conway – fascinated by modern technology – frequently used a metaphor from space travel to explain his policy. If the space capsule returning from orbit, he used to say, re-entered the atsmosphere at too shallow an angle, it would bounce off again and be lost in space; at too steep an angle, it would burn up; at exactly the right angle, everyone on board would be safe. This involved (publicly) restraining what he and other clerical leaders would have seen as an unbridled appetite for change, fomented by the media, and (privately) restraining where possible those of his fellow-bishops who felt that the proponents of change had to be put firmly in their place or even publicly denounced.

One of his fellow-bishops undoubtedly went too far, but not in a direction envisaged by the Cardinal as he honed his metaphors. This was Dr Michael Harty, Bishop of Killaloe. In the late 1960s, when there was a growing, if still largely subterranean public consciousness that the fruits of economic growth were not being fairly distributed, and even that a powerful political and business elite was abusing its power and privilege for unjust financial gain, Dr Harty made a thoughtful speech suggesting that public standards were not what they might be. There was a brief flurry of media publicity, and a deafening silence from other bishops and priests. The issue died. A year or so later, I met Dr Harty for the first time since his speech and complimented him on it: his reaction – he said that it had been a bitter experience and he had no plans to repeat it – left me in little doubt that the private reaction to his comments, doubtless from clerical as well as from political circles, had been deeply wounding.

With the benefit of hindsight, however, it can be argued that there were at least two occasions in the 1960s when important initiatives by the state with strong social justice implications were either ignored by both the media and the church, or allowed to lie fallow until sufficient non-media pressure had built up from social and other pressure groups to restore them to the public stage. The first was the publication of the Report of the Commission on Itinerancy in 1966; the second was the Report of the Committee on Reformatory and Industrial Schools (the Kennedy Report), based on research carried out in the late 1960s but published finally in 1970. Each, in its own way, was a guardedly expressed but none the less damning indictment of neglect, discrimination and worse visited by many of society's agencies on some of the weakest and most vulnerable members of society. Each evoked a brief flurry of interest in the mainstream media, which was followed by a prolonged period of silence. It is difficult to guess at other reasons for these *lacunae*, but two might be suggested. The first is to underline the fact that those who worked in the media at this time tended to be middle-class, and tended to be male. It was not until the late 1960s that distaff journalism began to make its presence felt, and even here the extent to which distaff journalism abandoned fashion and cookery only for contraception and divorce was itself an indication that the new gender balance had not been accompanied by any radically different social perspective. Travellers, or children locked up in institutions, remained for the most part out of sight and therefore out of mind, along with other vulnerable groups. The preoccupations of the media remained, for the most part, the preoccupations of the middle class.

A second possible reason is more overtly political. The irruption of Northern Ireland as a new, or at any rate new-ish, factor in Irish political life after 1968 siphoned much political, journalistic and social radicalism away from issues related to class and diverted it into the maelstrom of nationalist conflict. There were real and substantial issues involved in that conflict, and indeed there still are; but its perceived implications rapidly expanded until they blotted out many other parts of the social landscape to which church and media (let alone the state) might otherwise have paid more attention.

This is not to say that the northern conflict is irrelevant to the theme of these reflections. There were many injustices in the North. The birth of the Civil Rights movement, and the near-chaos into which Northern Ireland subsequently descended, had a major role in highlighting many of the macro-injustices which had been visited on the minority nationalist population for many years, and indeed helped to bring about substantial legal changes. In all of this process, the state, the church and the media, for all that their attitudes were often articulated in some-what atavistic terminology, were vitally important in bringing about these changes. It is indeed doubtful that many of the changes would have occurred at all, or would have occurred when they did, without the stimulus of international television coverage.

However, even as the macro-injustices were being ad-dressed, and partially solved, there arose out of the conflict an important number of micro-injustices, which failed to receive the necessary attention from church, state or media. I have part-icularly in mind here the treatment of suspects by the authorities in Northern Ireland, and the role of the judicial system in both Northern Ireland and Britain. The one major initiative by the Irish state in this area was bringing a case against the British government in Strasbourg for its interrogation methods – a case in which a modified verdict was handed down against the British government. This was, however, a small enough victory to chalk up against some of the more obvious failures.

I have two specific examples in mind. One was a statement by Fr Denis Faul of Dungannon, who expressed, in his normal, pungent, fashion, the view that the Northern Ireland judiciary was on occasion given to behaving in a sectarian manner. It was a general accusation, and indeed in the circumstances could hardly have been other. But it evoked a rapid response from Cardinal Conway, who dissociated himself from the criticism and censured Fr Faul. Unusually – for I think I disagreed with Fr Faul about almost everything else on the sun – I wrote privately to the Cardinal to say that I felt that his response had been unjust to Fr Faul. Some time later, on the fringe of a press conference after a hierarchy meeting at Maynooth, the cardinal brought the matter up with me to say that, although he felt there was some weight in Fr Faul's accusation, he himself had had no option (i.e. politically speaking) but to issue the statement that he did.

The second example, however, is altogether more serious. Even with the benefit of hindsight, it is difficult now to excuse the lengthy official silence, and the silence by media and church, in relation to the long-running campaign carried out by Fr Raymond Murray and others in relation to the Birmingham Six, and the related campaign in relation to the Guilford Four. There was an explanation, of sorts. The early 1970s were marked, in a particularly dramatic way, by the rapid and frequently random extension of violence in Northern Ireland. That violence, when perpetrated by the provisional IRA, frequently resulted in horrible civilian deaths (the development of the 'proxy car bomb' was an act of black genius in this regard) and in the growing alienation of large sections of the population in the Republic, not just from the IRA, but from irredentist nationalism *tout court*. Here again I can speak from personal experience. As a member of the Seanad, and later of the Dáil, I was in receipt of countless missives from those who alleged that a gross miscarriage of justice had been perpetrated in both these cases. As the IRA campaign in the North intensified, as civilian and other casualties mounted, and as it seemed increasingly likely that this ungovernable conflict would spill south across the Border, the temptation to avoid endorsing a cause that was also supported by some of the forces one distrusted and even feared became irresistible. The press releases kept on coming. If they were lucky they ended up in a filing cabinet, generally not even acknowledged. As frequently they ended up in the bin. There are questions not just of morality but of political courage here, and I think most of us failed to answer them adequately.

If some of the Northern issues of justice could be pushed to the margins by the overall political situation, the very intensity of that situation continued to obscure, in the Republic, the continuation of systemic and deep injustice (I am speaking in particular of the position of children in the reformatory and industrial school system) despite the fact that these injustices had been exposed by a body set up by the state itself. Not even the somewhat bureaucratic language of the Kennedy Report can be advanced as an excuse. I quote almost at random: 'Offenders occupy single cells ... for approximately fourteen hours per day ... Facilities were altogether insufficient and primitive ... In most cases the nuns running these institutions have neither the training nor the resources to enable them to rehabilitate these girls ... Some of the children detained (...) should never have been com-

mitted to these institutions in the first place ... This position
(Marlborough House) is deplorable and must be altered without
delay.'

If this report had been published in 2001, would it have been
ignored by the media? Could it have been? It is undeniable that,
had the Kennedy Report been published in any year from about
1984 onwards, the issues it raised would have been the subject of
prolonged media speculation and investigation. It is also
important, however, to avoid the danger of drawing possibly
ahistorical comparisons between different periods. In the early
1970s, the reports of government-appointed bodies were treated
as just that: in the absence of any organised response by professional pressure groups (e.g. women's organisations, social workers), potential issues just fizzled out and, in the case of Kennedy,
pressure groups like these were still some years away from formation. It is also possible to suggest, by way of explanation if
not necessarily by way of excuse, that even if the media had
been interested in exploring some of the issues raised in
Kennedy, the need to put names (even the names of institutions)
to specific accusations would have been regarded by news exec-
utives as so extraordinarily hazardous (from a legal point of
view) as to preclude detailed investigation.

In 1970, however, that continued injustice was also facilitated
by the fact that state and church alike had a vested interest in not
exposing it. The existence and maintenance of these institutions
(although undoubtedly some of those who worked in them
were highly motivated and did their best) had become a part,
and quite possibly in some circumstances an economically significant part, of the church's infrastructure. The state, on the
other hand, was securing institutional services at bargain-base-
ment rates: there were virtually no recommendations of the
Kennedy Report which did not have financial implications:
taken together, they represented a potential increase in public
spending which must have rendered civil servants, and their
political masters, so apprehensive that almost nothing (apart
from the closure of Marlborough House) was achieved. It is
tempting to suppose, although impossible to prove, that part of
the ferocity with which the media visited these issues in the
dying years of the twentieth century was related to a subliminal
sense of guilt that the signposts of 1970 had been ignored or
forgotten.

In the years that followed, social workers and others who were aware of at least part of what was going on worked, with little enough help from the media, to push this topic onto the political agenda. It was to be another three decades before what had evidently been common knowledge among members of the Kennedy Committee, in particular, became part of general public and media discourse.

There were some exceptions. First *Hibernia*, and then *Magill*, at least in its formative years, displayed something of a new kind of journalism, one which was not afraid to hold institutions (including now also the media themselves) to a greater degree of accountability than the political system itself seemed able to exercise. But overall the relationships between the institutions seemed to be becoming characterised by tetchiness and by a general sense that each was the object of unfair attention by one or even both of the others. Writing in 1981, Bishop Brendan Comiskey complained that 'The RTÉ television and radio journalist ... is likely to view any spokesperson for the government or the Catholic Church as handing out propaganda, something in favour of the government or the Catholic Church. The journalist then sees his or her task as that of bringing a note of "objectivity" into the proceedings.'[3]

The date is of interest. There is a hint here, in the language, of fight-back. Dr Comiskey was one of the most able and articulate members of the hierarchy, who enjoyed a relationship with some members of the media that could almost be described as 'matey'. I can recall inviting him out to the National Institute of Higher Education (as DCU was then known) to talk about church and media to an averagely anti-clerical, sceptical, even cynical class of post-graduate journalism students. None of them even landed a glove on him. Since the end of Vatican II, not a few Irish bishops and priests had undoubtedly felt themselves unjustly treated by or in the media (although there may well have been an element of blaming the messenger in this: much of the criticism was coming not from media commentators, but from within their own ranks). If there was to be a fight-back, this was the time to start it.

Within three years, however, a number of events – probably beginning with the discovery of Ann Lovett's body at the Marian grotto in Granard, Co Longford, in January 1984 – combined to effect a distinct shift not only in power relationships but in the perceived roles of the key institutions involved. Up to then, the church had been – although it was a role characterised by a growing sense of defensiveness – the self-appointed moral guardian of the community. From then onwards, the media, increasingly, became the moral policemen of the church, as Tom Inglis put it. If this trend had ever been in doubt, it was copperfastened by the Fr Brendan Smyth case in 1994, with its additional overtones of alleged state collusion in covering up the horrific case in which Smith was involved.

It is beyond peradventure that the church's response to this and what seemed like an ever-growing list of clerical sex abuse scandals was marked, initially and for quite some time thereafter, by evasion, dissimulation and a no doubt desperate, silent hope that the whole thing would blow over. The media's role in this can hardly be understated, but even here there are aspects of it that merit closer examination. There is a popular impression abroad, for example, that it is not until an Irish social issue is highlighted by external (usually British) media, that anything is done about it. Careful scrutiny of Irish media archives suggest that this is not always necessarily the case. RTÉ, for example, was broadcasting both radio and television programmes on the problem of child abuse from the mid-1980s onwards, even if their producers, like the country at large, were for the most part ignorant of its extent and its seriousness. Many clips from these earlier programmes found their way into exposés by UK television companies of Irish practices – exposés which were greeted by a storm of public and media attention that had unaccountably been absent when the earlier, Irish-produced programmes were shown. This points strongly to the provincialism of much moral protest in Ireland: issues, especially in the areas of justice, become moral issues only when they are pointed out or publicised by external agencies. Our own prophets, few though they be, remain unhonoured.

Today, relationships between church, state and media have come to resemble an eternal triangle of mutual recrimination. The ongoing horrors of the North, the economic crises of the mid-1970s, and the political volatility of the electorate have combined to intensify, if anything, the symbiotic relationship between the three. But to what extent is the media's new-found role as moral policeman of the church an accurate representation of a very complex reality?

In relation to child abuse in particular the question is frequently posed: what does the church's initially hesitant and unwilling response, amounting in some cases to what can only be described as a cover-up, say about its Constantinian approach to institutional self-defence at whatever human cost? But there are other questions that could equally well be posed. To what extent, for example, is the media's eager pursuit of the church on this issue motivated more by a desire to criticise the church than by a desire to right the wrong done to some of our most vulnerable citizens? The lack of any focused or research-based media attention to the much larger problem of the non-institutional abuse of children within their own families is, perhaps, a straw in the wind here. But that is a much more complex problem, in which the perpetrators cannot be so easily identified or so readily demonised, and the solution of which remains desperately hard to grasp. And to what extent does the silence of the state – which bears a huge share of the responsibility for what has occurred – speak more loudly of a discreet relief that it is still not being seen as an agency with any real responsibility for putting things right (an expensive business with few clear or politically-advantageous outcomes in sight)? Even in an age which has largely abandoned the practice of confession, a collective examination of conscience might be in order.

Religion and Politics
at the turn of the millennium

Garret FitzGerald

Introduction

I am somewhat embarrassed by Jim Mackey's and Enda McDonagh's initiative in hanging this book on the peg of a recent birthday of mine. Despite anything Jim Mackey has said in his Introduction in an attempt to justify this approach, the fact is that my knowledge of theological matters is limited, and is mainly confined to ethical and moral issues in the sphere of public affairs.

At the same time I am naturally pleased to have provided the occasion for these reflections on religion and politics at the turn of the millennium. And I am, of course, delighted to have been accorded the opportunity to read and reflect upon the ideas contained in the other thirteen chapters of this book. Each of the authors in her or his own way has sparked off reflections of my own.

I start with Jim Mackey's own contribution in Chapter 1 which, because of its historical approach, I found particularly thought-provoking.

The enduring impact that Constantine and the late Roman Empire had upon the evolution of the Christian Church is, of course, a well-worn theme, but Jim Mackey ties this in to a more extended historical perspective. He sees the evolution of the church as having reflected a concern to improve society by repeatedly adjusting to a succession of different aspects of that society, within which it has at different periods found itself.

In his view, this process explains first of all the origin of the priesthood, which he sees as having happened around the end of the second century. At that time, he says, Christians, expanding into a society with a cultic priesthood, wisely decided to select, educate, and 'ordain' particular people to preside over local Christian communities, and eventually even called these people priests. But instead of a priesthood-of-the-laity, confined to the convening of Christians for the eucharist and to leadership in the exercise of that function, what was thus introduced subsequently developed into a cultic priesthood.

In Jim Mackey's view, Christians were also right to have later modelled the leadership of what had by then become an expanding community along the lines of the government of the Roman Empire. And he also accepts that it was wise of leading church thinkers to have sought to express the fullness of Christian truth in terms of Greek neo-Platonist philosophy.

In all this, he says, there was no unavoidable or invasive falsehood to the founder, or to the faith that formed around the founder and his life and death. But, later, he says, 'falsifications' crept in, which became the root of the eventual 'self-destructive decline of the Roman Catholic Church'.

I am inclined to feel that Jim Mackey may have been a little too tolerant of that early process of acculturation to the Roman world. For, within an institution manned by fallible human beings, was it not inevitable that, once church leaders had gone so far in seeking to adapt themselves to so many aspects of the culture and institutions of the world around them, 'falsifications' would take hold?

Moreover, once this process had gone as far as it did in the closing stages and immediate aftermath of the Roman imperial period, was it not inevitable that in the monarchical and feudal society that started to emerge later in that first millennium through the fusion of Germanic tribes with the debris of the Roman Empire in Western Europe, the church as it had by then developed would adopt the 'feudal customs' to which Jim Mackey later refers – with popes anointing emperors, and bishops becoming feudal lords, expecting people to kneel and kiss their hands, a custom that has survived unto our own time?

Underlying all this lies the essential dilemma of how the Christian faith can be preserved without an authority structure that would have the capacity to maintain and protect it, but the over-use of which can generate amongst its ministers a fear of disciplinary action in relation to matters that are not central to the Christian faith. Such fear can eventually lead to dissimulation and hypocrisy amongst some of its ministers.

That ever-present dilemma has in very recent times been high-lighted most vividly by the *Humanae Vitae* controversy. Many priests, subject to hierarchical authority, have been constrained to hide or dissimulate their views on this subject, views that appear to reflect the *sensus fidelium* more accurately than the church authorities have done – most especially those priests who may have an aspiration to lead Christian communities as bishops. In turn bishops who find the *Humanae Vitae* arguments unconvincing have felt constrained to maintain a silence on this subject that does not fit well with their role of giving witness to the truth as they know it. The quality of church leadership has been deeply eroded by this unhappy situation, and the confidence of the laity in the honesty and truthfulness of their clergy has been undermined.

Jim Mackey goes on to point out that two other problems have also recently greatly weakened the moral authority of the Roman Catholic Church: the institutional church's handling of the paedophilia issue, and the refusal to address the issue of the role of women in the church.

Human weaknesses amongst ministers of the church are understood by the laity – who are conscious of their own moral frailty. But, precisely because they are Christians, what members of the church simply cannot under any circumstances accept is the adoption by church leaders of double standards and cover-ups in respect of criminal activity, most especially where this involves abuse of children. That aspect of institutionalism is at flagrant, polar, variance with Christian witness to the truth. And nothing is or can be more fatal to religion than hypocrisy amongst those whose role is to proclaim and give such witness.

Jim Mackey is of course right to say that the refusal to address the role of women in the church has also weakened its moral authority – most of all amongst women, whose commitment to the church has in the past always been very strong. The argument that, simply because in the patriarchal society of Christ's time his apostles were all men, consequently women should for ever be excluded from the priesthood, does little justice to the spirit of his teaching.

Moreover, the fact is that women are notably more spiritual and more caring than men, so that their exclusion from priesthood at this stage of human history is simply perverse. Behind this stance may lie an at least sub-conscious recognition by the present elderly male leadership of the church that once this ban is removed, women may within a couple of generations come largely to replace men in this vocation – as they have done in other caring professions such as primary teaching, nursing, and recently medicine.

Enda McDonagh, in referring to Irish episcopal leaders, uses a phrase from Tom Inglis's *Moral Monopoly*: viz. 'a social (quasi-political) power'. But is that still the case today? One does not get the impression any longer of a self-confident hierarchy flaunting its power. Quite the contrary. Even before the Irish bishops blundered into, and through, the paedophilia controversy, there were signs that they were already feeling unsure of themselves, because of pressure on other fronts, both from liberal opinion but also, less publicly, from the extreme Catholic right.

For I feel there may be truth in the stories about complaints having been made to Rome by some right-wing lay Catholics about an alleged failure by Irish bishops to support more extreme lay positions. The refusal of the hierarchy to meet the government in 1983 to discuss what had transpired to be the defective wording of a constitutional amendment on abortion did not suggest to me as Taoiseach that they were brimming with self-confidence. I felt it showed, rather, a fear that such a direct dialogue would face them with the fact that there was a compelling case for a change in the wording, one that they could not honestly resist, but acceptance of which might have got them into trouble with the lay Catholic right – and thus with Rome. Better to avoid such a potentially troublesome dialogue, they seem to have felt.

Whilst there are today individual bishops in Ireland who certainly retain their moral authority because of their openness, it is difficult to avoid the impression that at least since the late 1960s the criteria employed in selecting bishops has worked against the emergence of an Irish hierarchy of high intellectual capacity, capable of offering effective moral leadership to the Catholic clergy and laity of our island.

Enda McDonagh suggests that 'a clean break with the Christendom mentality is necessary'. He envisages 'an end to clericalism, to the caste system of bishops, priests and religious, with their power and privileges'. They should rather be 'integrated into the believing community'.

And he continues: 'This, of course, suggests that (bishops) be chosen as in the past by the believing community they are to serve, while confirmed in the unity of the whole church by local bishops and by the church's traditional symbol of universal unity, the Bishop of Rome.'

To some this may sound revolutionary but in fact it is the traditional view of the church, a return to which was vigorously fought for by the papacy a thousand years ago. For, well before the end of the first millennium, many bishops as well as being spiritual leaders had become rulers of territories as feudal vassals of monarchs – a duality of episcopal roles which finally disappeared only with the reconstruction of Europe after the French Revolution. In the eleventh century the church demanded that the choosing of bishops revert from monarchs to the people of each diocese, who in an earlier period had always exercised this function – for a thousand years ago the church was insistent on ecclesiastical democracy. Why not once again in the third millennium as in the first?

A return to the church's traditional stance on the appointment of bishops could be the key to a profound reform of its hierarchical structure – for under present conditions such a reform seems likely to come only from below. Even a very strong reforming pope – if such were to emerge from a future conclave – could not hope to reform the top-heavy bureaucratic structures of the Vatican on his own. But just such a bold decision – perhaps at a new council – to revert to the traditional method of episcopal appointment could pave the way for an eventual radical reform of these structures, as bishops thus appointed responded to the voice of the people of God.

Vatican II showed how much can be achieved by a council of the church, and even the subsequent effective reversal of the reforms of that council by the curia offers useful lessons to a future council as to the steps it would need to take in order to avoid its conclusions suffering a similar fate.

A quite different point made by Enda McDonagh is that the term 'natural law', which had been thought to transcend religious affiliations and to embrace the whole range of human morality and rights – the 'common good' – has suffered an eclipse in Ireland, partly due to the Catholic Church's claim to be the primary, perhaps even sole, interpreter of this universal natural law. He does not develop this theme, but it is certainly the case that the past abuse of this concept by the institutional church has done great damage to the acceptability to the lay public of the natural law concept of the common good.

The widespread rejection of this concept in recent times has served to weaken the fabric of society. For, unless there is acceptance of some basic common ground within society, it cannot function in a manner beneficial to human beings.

Perhaps the use of the term 'law' in this context has been a source of confusion. But what I take 'natural law' to mean is securing conditions that favour the successful survival of the human race, and the good order, health and happiness of human beings in society.

For example, if there is not some provision to ensure that in human relationships people can generally trust each other, the human condition may be gravely damaged.

Moreover, outside of tribal systems, which in a modern globalised world cannot provide an adequate basis for human existence, society needs to be organised in a way that provides for the needs of those who cannot fend for themselves. Again, the successful upbringing of the young is best achieved, at least in temperate climes, if this is undertaken by two parents living together in a fulfilled relationship.

Both law and morality, which of course have quite distinct roles in society, need to be built upon some common ground – and that ground has to be 'the common good' – a concept which Enda McDonagh remarks is 'in retreat before an aggressive individualism, coupled in Ireland with an antipathy to terms thought to be peculiarly Catholic in provenance'.

It is particularly unfortunate that the concepts of natural law and the common good should have been so damaged by what people have felt to be abuses designed to support positions specific to the Roman Catholic Church. For the loss of these concepts would, I believe, be gravely damaging to our, as indeed to any, society.

In a later chapter, Linda Hogan argues against what she described as the Irish hierarchy's 'majoritarian' view of the common good – asserting that the common good 'is not in essence related to numbers but is rather about the harmonisation of different values in the attainment of a just and cohesive society ... and about construing the relationship of the individual to society so that the limits and possibilities of both individual and communal well-being are preserved, and in which the appropriate responsibilities and obligations that exist among individuals are clarified and articulated.' That seems to me a good – if necessarily somewhat long! – definition of this important concept.

Behind much of this lies a particular Irish problem, deriving from the fact that the morality we have been taught in the past was based on authority alone, rather than on reason reinforced by authority. Someone who is told by authority, and certainly not by reason, that it is a sin to eat meat on Fridays or to miss Sunday Mass, and equally is told again by the same authority without reference to reason, that it is a serious sin to steal, may not easily recall in later life the fundamental distinction between these two sets of rules. (I know, of course, that technically the church always made a distinction between commandments of God and commandments of the church, but I doubt if in adult life many people remember this differentiation.)

It has always seemed to me that the Catholic Church in Ireland made a mistake by not stressing the extent to which its moral teaching is largely grounded on principles of ethics that exist independently of the church. In a sense Irish Catholics, many no longer practising, and others who are vague in adult life about what they had been taught in school years earlier, have as a result been left without an adequate sense of civic morality. This has greatly weakened the fabric of a society that is today much less strongly infused with Christian morality than used to be the case.

I note that, in discussing human rights in the context of the common good and natural law, Enda McDonagh favourably contrasts 'church leaders and spokespeople (who) tend to support the equal status and justiciability of social and economic rights' as well as fundamental civil and political human rights with 'politicians and civil lawyers (who) tend to deny this'. And he refers to 'the more individualist attitude to society of those who would deny the full legal impact of social and economic rights'.

There is, I feel, at least a partial misconception here. For although there are, no doubt, some politicians and civil lawyers whose attitude on this issue derives from 'an individualist attitude to society', there are many others who do not share that ideological stance and have strong commitments to society but who have a quite different, and in my view valid, reason for some reticence on this point. Justice needs to be done to their position on this matter.

Quite simply, social and economic rights potentially involve the allocation of finite resources to cope with economic needs that are almost infinite. The decision as to how best to handle this fundamental imbalance between needs and resources is of its essence a prudential one, and in a democracy it has to be taken by the elected representatives of the people, on the proposals of the executive that they have chosen to initiate legislation.

If these rights were to be made justiciable without qualification, then the final decision on the allocation of these resources would ultimately fall to judges – for example, how much in social welfare payments each unemployed person or widow should receive, what volume of social housing is to be provided, and so on. And that would ultimately involve judges deciding the whole balance between taxation and public spending – which would be neither democratic nor sensible.

Is there some middle way that would accord more weight than is given at present to social and economic rights without, however, undermining the democratic system? There is in fact one recent example of a democratic state that has moved some distance in this direction, viz. South Africa. Under that country's constitution, judges have been given a certain role in the enforcement of social and economic rights, subject, however, to a criterion of 'reasonableness'. Two cases relating to social or economic rights have already come before the South African courts.

One of these, the Grootbom case, related to housing provision. In this case the Constitutional Court decided that, whilst as far as it went the government's housing policy was outstanding, at the same time 'it wasn't reasonable to the extent that it made no provision for people in situations of desperation and crisis'. However, in the words of Mr Justice Sachs, 'responding on demand to all people in desperate circumstances would place an impossible burden on the court, requiring it to make decisions and determine priorities beyond its capacity', and 'possibly also giving advantages to those with the best lawyers ... leaving the poorest of the poor in worse situations'.

But, Mr Justice Sachs went on to say, 'the decision (sought) does not demand a response on a case by case basis to individuals, which would overwhelm the court, but a reasonable operational programme'. The plaintiff won her constitutional case, with the result that the government had to review its housing programme.

The second South African constitutional case on social and economic rights related to the availability of Nevirapine, a drug that helps prevent HIV passing from mother to child during pregnancy. The Constitutional Court, having re-affirmed its position on its role and powers in the enforcement of socio-economic rights – which it confirmed are justiciable – found that the state's policy of confining Nevirapine to research and training sites failed to address the needs of mothers and their new-born children who did not have access to these sites. And the court asserted its right not merely to make declaratory orders but also mandatory orders in relation to such matters, and to assume a supervisory jurisdiction.

However, this second case aroused controversy as it was argued that an 'unaccountable court' had appropriated the power of democratic government to determine social and economic policy.

A difficulty with extending the South African precedent to other countries is that the courts of different states are known to approach such matters in different ways. Thus Irish and German courts tend to take a relatively strong line *vis-à-vis* their government in relation to civil and political rights, whereas in some other European countries on such issues the courts seem more pliable in relation to their governments. So if, for example, citizens' social and economic rights were to be made justiciable throughout Europe, as was suggested at one stage in the European Convention in Brussels, these rights might turn out to be enforced in a quite different way in different states – and that could give rise to severe economic difficulties for states the courts of which tended to a rigid interpretation of rights.

In his chapter Dermot Lane looks back at the impact of Vatican II on the struggle for justice in the world. He points out that the pre-1960s neo-scholastic natural law approach to justice issues changed quite significantly at Vatican II, as can be seen from the contrast between the original schemata prepared for the council and the documents finally approved by it. This reflected a new openness to the world, and took the form of a move from anathema to dialogue, and from being a sub-culture within society to entering into a real dialogue with modernity, recognising the reality of pluralism.

Basing itself on the Bible, rather than on the traditional natural law approach, the Second Vatican Council grounded its teaching upon the dignity of every human being, the social character of human nature, and the right of every person to participate in society. Nevertheless, as Dermot Lane points out, forty years later, despite Vatican II, the top-down non-historical methodology espoused by the teachings of the church under Pope John Paul II on the one hand and the bottom-up historical methodology initiated by Vatican II on the other, still survive in parallel with and complementary to each other, but unhappily often work in stark opposition to one another, reflecting a deeper theological tension between theory and praxis within the life of the Catholic Church.

Dermot Lane suggests that the historical origins of Christianity in the liberating praxis of Jesus makes a strong case for privileging praxis over interpretation, at least as a point of departure. And in a world where wealth is distributed unjustly between rich and poor countries and peoples, recognition of praxis as a point of departure highlights the difference between what is and what ought to be. This has been reflected not alone in concern for the unjust distribution of wealth but also in a new found sense of responsibility for the future of the world which appears to me to be strongly felt in Europe – but much less so in the United States.

(It is perhaps worth commenting here that despite the fact the United States is a country in which there is a much higher proportion of practising Christians than in Europe, many European values seem more directly derived from Christian principles than is the case in America. This is true of the European commitment to human rights transcending national sovereignty and of Europe's commitment to the International Criminal Court; of prevailing European attitudes to violence and war, manifest in the creation of a zone of peace subject to the rule of law throughout most of Europe and the outlawing of capital punishment; of Europe's much stronger commitment to development co-operation in the Third World; and indeed of Europe's development of and active support for the concept of global ecology.)

Reviewing the wide range of bodies, and the voices of individuals in Ireland, which are alert to and seek to promote justice in our society, including particularly the CORI Justice Desk, Dermot Lane credits these with having created, even during a period when our society has become more individualistic and materialist, a deep awareness within our society of the need to bridge the gap between rich and poor as a matter of strict justice. Nevertheless he rightly notes a disturbing gap between generous

individual alms-giving and a relative neglect of social reform
and structural change. And he suggests that there may be a need
for a forum on justice that would bring together different justice-
oriented groupings as a unified voice within Christian communities.

Moving on to parts of the book which deal with specific aspects of our society, Kenneth Milne's chapter on Irish
Protestantism addresses a subject that has never received the
attention it deserves. For, whilst people of a Protestant background now represent less than 5% of the population of the
Republic, their role in our society is a good deal larger and more
significant than this might suggest. Moreover in the island as a
whole Protestants are, of course, a substantial 25% minority.

Kenneth Milne suggests that the claim made by some
Catholics in the past that Protestants are somehow less Irish
than others may derive from 'the well-attested fact that the great
majority of them traditionally saw their Irishness in an imperial
setting' – although we tend conveniently to forget that at least
up to 1918 this was true also of a significant element of the
Catholic community, especially amongst the middle class. But,
he goes on to say, with the passage of years the Protestant community 'has found itself in an increasingly congenial society.
Above all it has enjoyed (which is not perhaps too strong a term)
the increased opportunities for social integration and for sharing
religious experience ... A new generation of Protestants shares
in the general feeling of confidence that pervades society in the
Republic, and this, I would maintain, owes not a little to having,
perhaps unconsciously, come to terms with its past, or rather its
forebears' past.'

And Kenneth Milne remarks that most southern Protestants
'experience little sense of identity with the north' – although he
excepts Protestants in border areas from this comment.

In truth one of the most remarkable, although in general un-
remarked, features of the Irish state has been the disappearance
of Protestant unionism from most of the Republic. When the
state was founded almost all Protestants in its territory were
unionists: in other words they would have preferred to have remained in the United Kingdom. Today, south of the border area
one would be hard put to it to find any Protestants – for my part
I have come across only one – who would actually want to return to the jurisdiction of the UK government. What now differ-

entiates Protestants politically from Catholics is only the fact that they do not share the anglophobia that is still to be found in some sections of the Catholic population.

Kenneth Milne describes the process by which the Protestant minority in the Republic came gradually to shift their allegiance, moving from unionism to identification with the new state, as one of 'integration', which he defines as 'a reciprocal acceptance of belonging, inclusive of distinctiveness' rather than 'assimilation', defined as 'a dilution of distinctiveness to the point of disappearance'.

Nevertheless, despite efforts made by our first government – for example, half the members of the first, nominated, Senate were Protestants – our state at the outset was a rather cold place for Protestants. Some, especially in Munster, were victims of Catholic sectarian violence, and many prominent Protestants in rural Ireland had their houses burnt down. (My father's papers in the UCD Archive contain a letter from a prominent republican woman to the Chief of Staff of the IRA during the Civil War urging him not to burn down a particular house because its owner 'although a Protestant' was sympathetic to the republican cause.)

In the decades that followed, Protestants were also faced with specifically Catholic influences being brought to bear on the constitution and laws of the new state, as well as with the requirement that the Irish language, which was not part of the mainstream Protestant tradition, be taught in all schools and be an essential requirement for School Certificates, and also for entry into and promotion within the public service. All that was very off-putting for the Protestant community.

On the other hand, some of their worst fears were not realised. No one suggested that any Anglican churches be transferred to the Roman Catholic ownership – not even one of Dublin's two Church of Ireland cathedrals! And the major role of Protestants in business, banking and the professions was not challenged, although of course the Knights of St Columbanus sought to counter-balance the influence that the Masonic Order was believed to exert in defence of employment opportunities for Protestants.

In the last census in which questions about religion were asked, that of 1991, it emerged that in the sixty-five years since 1926 the proportion of Protestants engaged in better-paid non-agricultural employment (commerce, insurance, finance, management, administration and the professions), had actually risen from 32% to 39% – in other words by more than the increase in the proportion of the Catholic working population in these employment categories, which had risen only from 16% to 21%!

Moreover in 1991, in relation to their less-than-5% share of the population, non-Catholics (a category that, except perhaps in the case of medicine, in 1991 effectively meant Protestants), were over-represented three to four times amongst aircraft pilots, writers and journalists, actors, musicians, and lecturers and professors. They were twice to three times over-represented amongst government administrators, industrial designers, farm managers, ships' officers, insurance brokers, insurance, architects and technologists, as well as in films, broadcasting, and business and professional services. And in 1991 there was an also similar disproportion in ownership of farms over 50 acres, with 17.5% of the largest farms in Protestant ownership.

Against that background it is not too surprising that after the initial post-Treaty outflow and the higher rate of emigration of Protestants during the early decades of the new state, this process was reversed in the post-war period. From the end of the 1940s onwards the rate of Protestant emigration was consistently lower than the rate for Catholics, by margins which at different times ranged from almost 10% to nearly 30%.

What has been most striking about all this is that the continuing favourable social and economic situation of Protestants in the Irish state has never even been a subject for discussion, let alone criticism by the Catholic majority. Catholic bigotry and prejudice, which certainly existed at the time the state was founded, simply faded away and, after the time when the Republic was declared, our state, somewhat paradoxically, became gradually a warmer place for its minority Protestant community.

It is also worth remarking that the minority Protestant community did not have to risk unpopularity by agitating for a more pluralist society: that battle was initiated and fought by liberal Catholics, and thus did not risk creating inter-community tensions.

Finally a comment is called for on the decline in the Protestant population. Between 1926 and 1961 the number of people recorded as being of a religion other than Roman

Catholicism fell from 241,000 to about 134,000. (Later figures are distorted by the numbers refusing to state their religion at census time, or stating that they had no religion. By 1991 these two latter categories had attained a figure of 150,000 – which was in fact slightly more than the total number who were recorded as adhering to a religion other than Roman Catholicism.)

The decline of almost 45% between 1926 and 1961 in the number of Protestants reflected the operation of a multiplicity of unrelated factors: the fact that between 1926 and 1946 the emigration rate for Protestants had been one-quarter higher than in the case of Catholics (although by 1961 this must have been at least partly offset by the 15% lower Protestant emigration of the post-war period); a one-third lower Protestant fertility rate; a one-quarter higher Protestant death rate, amongst what was, of course, an older Protestant population; and finally the impact of the Catholic Church's approach to mixed marriages.

The proportion of Protestants marrying Catholics seems to have risen from not much more than 5% at the foundation of the state to a cumulative 39% by 1991, and although by the 1980s the proportion of children of such marriages recorded as Catholic had fallen from 95% to about 70% – and has probably declined to a much lower figure today – the rising rate of mixed marriages by Protestants must have involved a continuing drain on the Protestant community.

On the other hand, some proportion of younger Catholics as well as Protestants have in recent times been attracted to various new Christian sects, and this, together with the growth of the number of non-Christians as a result of immigration, had by 1991 increased the number of 'Other Stated Religions' to over 1% of the population – a percentage that must since then have risen sharply.

In her chapter, Geraldine Smith had the difficult task of discussing the situation of the churches in Northern Ireland, with specific reference to their role there during the thirty years of violence. At the outset, she notes that Eric Gallagher and Stanley Worrall[1] had asked in 1982 'might (the churches) not have adopted a more positive line of action to the process of secularisation'. And she goes on to remark on the irony of a situation 'in which some of the more positive results of the secularising process – for example the process of ignoring religious or political views in all contexts where they are irrelevant, such as employment, sport, social life – are just what Ireland needs to lessen its inter-community tensions'.

But, she says, the churches in the North had instead shown an obdurate face, by seeking to maintain their traditional rights and influence over all aspects of public life, drawing back from every issue where institutional sacrifice might be offered and might have made the necessary difference in a divided society.

Reading that, I could not but recall the interview I had with Pope Paul VI in March 1977. In his remarks to me in French, the pope's uncompromising theme was that Ireland was a Catholic country – perhaps the only one left – and that it should stay that way. Laws should not be changed in a way that would make our state less Catholic. When at the end of his brief address I started to say that an appallingly tragic situation existed in Northern Ireland to which we in our state were trying to respond in a Christian way, he immediately intervened to the effect that he knew how tragic the situation was there – but that this could not be a reason to change any of the laws that kept the Republic a Catholic state.

When later on that day I met Cardinal Casaroli, I raised with him again, as I had some years earlier, in 1973, the negative impact on community relations of the church's stance on mixed marriages. He responded by suggesting that I raise this with the Irish hierarchy. But when some years later this was done at my request by John Kelly TD at the New Ireland Forum, Bishop Cassidy of Clonfert responded by saying that if the hierarchy had felt that there was 'even a slight chance' that Rome would accede to an appeal for a derogation from the provisions in respect of mixed marriages, they would have made such an appeal: 'but we did not feel that'.

That kind of kicking the ball backwards and forwards between the Vatican and the Irish hierarchy seemed to me to smack more of bureaucracy than of religion.

Geraldine Smyth also comments that the North is still caught in what in conflict-analyis terms is apparently known as an 'accordion phenomenon', as a result of which the felt effect of antagonists coming into closer contact and exchange is to provoke a nervous reflex pull-back to familiar positions at a securer distance. This, she feels, may be true of the churches in Northern Ireland as well as the political parties there.

And she goes on to describe Christians and churches in Northern Ireland as 'maintaining the violent dynamic in segregated locations and clinging to those identity-forming symbol structures which sustain old rivalries and scape-goating – patterns that tend inexorably towards victimisation of "the other", with tribal notions of being a chosen people, or martyrdom as liberation and of selectively adapted doctrines of salvation by exclusion'. The churches in Northern Ireland, Geraldine Smyth sums up, have frequently operated less out of an ecclesial vision of service than as self-interested social entities.

I share deeply her sense of disillusionment at the absence in all this of anything that could be conceivably described as a Christian vision.

I think Linda Hogan is right when, at the outset of her chapter, she says that 'the unspoken assumptions that shape Catholic thinking on marriage have been embedded in the social fabric of Irish life so that recent attempts to untangle the theological from the political in relation to marriage have had to negotiate difficult territory.'

However, her statement that 'with the enactment of the 1937 Constitution of Ireland the boundaries between ecclesiastical and civil law in relation to marriage were blurred' does not seem to me to do full justice to the antiquity, and I have to say also the anomalous character, of Irish marriage law. From the time of the Reformation until the second quarter of the nineteenth century the only statutory form of marriage and annulment of marriage in Ireland was that of the Established Church of Ireland, but marriages of other churches had recognition as common law unions.

However, from the 1830s onwards a series of laws gave statutory recognition to marriage ceremonies of other Christian religions, with slightly different arrangements for each. In 1864 civil registration of births, deaths and marriage was introduced and, with the disestablishment of the Church of Ireland in 1871 the – very restrictive – annulment procedures of that church became part of Irish civil law.

From the outset the Roman Catholic Church in Ireland co-operated with the civil registration procedure, but it also applied canon law to marriage, annulment, and dissolution arrangements for its own members. This produced a somewhat uncomfortable conflict of jurisdictions, because the Catholic Church claimed and exercised the right to re-marry its members in some cases where the religious element of marriages had been an-nulled or dissolved by the church authorities, but where these marriages, recognised and registered by the state, had not been annulled under civil law.

Such re-marriages were, of course, bigamous in civil law terms, and in the absence of any divorce procedure in Ireland (even the earlier parliamentary divorce process that had earlier applied to Ireland as well as Britain was made to lapse in 1924), there was no way in which these re-marriages could avoid being bigamous where a civil annulment had not been sought, or had been sought but refused. (In Britain, where religious marriages were also given recognition as civil ceremonies, this problem was overcome by the Catholic Church requiring Catholics who sought to re-marry after a church annulment to secure a civil divorce before re-marrying in a church.)

This conflict of civil and canon law jurisdictions in Ireland seems to have been always ignored by the civil authorities; there appear to have been virtually no prosecutions for bigamy in such cases, a situation sometimes informally justified on the grounds of an alleged difficulty in securing evidence of the biga-mous religious ceremony, no record of which was furnished to the civil authorities.

In April 1986 this anomalous situation came up for discus-sion between Alan Dukes as Minister for Justice and myself and a delegation from the Catholic hierarchy.

I opened the relevant part of this discussion by saying that whilst this problem could, of course, be solved by separating the civil and religious ceremonies, as was done on the Continent, I was personally reluctant to contemplate such a separation if it could be avoided, in view of what I believed to be the attach-ment of most Irish people to the joint ceremony.

The member of the hierarchy deputed to deal with this issue then suggested a new arrangement under which a church re-marriage of someone who had benefited from a church annul-ment would constitute a purely religious event, which could make no claim to be, and give no appearance of being, a civil marriage.

I think that, in their concern to find a solution to their prob-lem that would not involve a civil divorce, the hierarchy must have failed to appreciate the implications of such a proposal for the government. For, what they were thus asking was that we connive at undermining the protection of marriage in the constitution, despite the fact that the government was, of course, bound to maintain this protection unless and until the constitutional provision on this matter was changed by the people in a referendum – which, of course, was precisely what the bishops were opposing.

The hierarchy representatives were, I think, taken aback by the strength of the reaction by Alan Dukes and myself, for we had been shocked by what appeared to us to be a proposal that we collaborate in undermining the c onstitution. It subsequently transpired that because of the strength of our reaction the hierarchy delegation failed to present some other proposals to deal with this matter, and also in our recollection failed to convey the fact that they would have had no objection to a complete separation of civil and religious marriage, aspects of which they would in fact have welcomed.

But none of that would have resolved the constitutional problem for, in our view, the constitutional reference to marriage could scarcely have been interpreted in such a way as to exclude religious marriages. The ways in which both sides recalled this discussion are set out in Appendix 1 to my autobiography.[2]

In the subsequent divorce referendum campaign it proved impossible to engage in rational debate. Most of those supporting the removal of the constitutional ban on divorce seemed content simply to claim that there was a 'civil right' to divorce, without explaining why this was so, or how there could be an actual 'right' by one party to terminate an indissoluble union – as distinct from there being a pragmatic case for making a provision for marriage breakdown that would permit partners to enter into a second union.

Those opposing divorce generated scare stories suggesting that it would bring a huge increase in family breakdown. Farmers were told that their wives would leave them and would demand and get half their farms, whilst farmers' wives were told that their husbands would throw them out without a penny.

In my view, however, the real issue was simply whether the destabilising effect on society of the increasing proliferation of unrecognised second unions, partners in which, and the children

of the partners in which, had no defined rights in civil law, out-
ran any possible negative effects of a fairly restrictive divorce
regime. But I found no one on either side willing even to discuss
the balance between these two considerations.

Instead we heard the hierarchy claiming a special sociological insight into what would be the impact of divorce on Irish
society. We now know that they greatly exaggerated the likely
scale of divorce under Irish conditions. On the basis of experience in Northern Ireland and in Catholic countries in southern
Europe, it always seemed to me unlikely that the introduction of
a quite restrictive divorce regime in Ireland would affect much
more than 15% of marriages, which has in fact turned out to be
the case.

After the defeat of the first divorce referendum, it was argued that my government should have prepared and published
details of the kind of divorce legislation that we would have introduced if the constitutional ban were to be removed. At the
time, I felt that such an action would have been presumptuous,
but in retrospect I may have been wrong to have dismissed the
idea.

Linda Hogan also refers to the anomalous Pauline and
Petrine privileges through which the Catholic Church claims the
right to dissolve marriages between 'pagans', or between a
Christian and a 'pagan' so as to enable converts to Christianity
to enter into new unions with fellow-Christians. These 'privileges' show that the church's teaching on divorce in Linda
Hogan's view 'is neither exceptionless nor unchanging'.

These two 'privileges', together with the claim that marriages
between Catholics that are not in accordance with canon law are
not merely illicit but also invalid, all seem to reflect some very
pragmatic reactions of the church at different moments in the
past to situations that appeared at a particular time to challenge
its interests as an institution. Since my teenage years at school I
have felt these to be theological aberrations that ought to be re-
viewed.

Elsewhere Linda Hogan remarks that the value of pluralism
does not seem to count amongst those moral convictions that the
Catholic Church feels obliged to impart. Indeed, she says,
'Throughout the divorce debates one might argue that pluralism
was only granted lip-service, and was not deemed to be constitutive of the church's moral convictions and moral teaching.'

Patrick Hannon's chapter tackles the contraception and abortion issues. He does not dwell on the merits and demerits of *Humanae Vitae*. But I would like to make the point that in that document Pope Paul VI was absolutely right to stress the profound impact that the ready availability of contraceptives could have on sexual morality in any society. Where the document's argument fails to convince, however, is in the jump from that wise sociological observation to the conclusion that the use of artificial contraceptives was intrinsically wrong.

Moreover, the attempt to make a major theological distinction between the morality of artificial and 'natural' contraception simply does not stand up. In terms of the effect of these two alternative methods on sexual morality, the issue is one of degree rather than of kind, and the distinction between placing a barrier in the way of conception as distinct from ingeniously avoiding a fertile time in the female cycle carries no theological conviction. For my own part the weakness of the argument in *Humanae Vitae* simply persuaded me that my own long-standing antipathy to artificial contraception had all along been aesthetic rather than moral.

The abortion issue is hugely complex, and I realise that my initial acceptance of the idea that there was a case for making some constitutional provision in relation to it was naïve. Because of my personal negative view on abortion I allowed myself to be persuaded that, in the light of the *Roe v Wade* decision of the US Supreme Court, there was a case for taking this issue out of the hands of the courts and leaving it to the Oireachtas. I did not realise that what the advocates of this amendment were actually trying to do was to take the whole issue out of the hands both of the courts and of our legislators – which to put it mildly was a tall order! I then compounded my initial error by accepting without legal advice the wording of a defective constitutional amendment proposed by Charles Haughey as Taoiseach.

However, in retrospect it is evident that it really did not matter what position I took up on this amendment, for the pressures placed on Dáil deputies, and the concern of many of them to be seen to be unambiguously anti-abortion, were such that, regardless of whether I accepted or rejected a particular amendment, and regardless of whether I was in opposition or in government, nothing was going to stop this defective wording being accepted by the Oireachtas, and being adopted by the electorate.

When I learnt of the potential dangers of this defective wording, which included both the possibility that it might either be interpreted as opening the way to the legalisation of abortion or, at the other extreme, as putting a stop to life-saving operations that had hitherto been accepted by both church and state, my party colleagues and I unhesitatingly decided that, regardless of the political consequences – which we knew would almost certainly involve the defeat of the government on this issue in the Oireachtas and in a subsequent referendum – we had no choice but to reject this wording and to seek another solution.

That decision, made in full knowledge of the likely political consequences, must surely have been one of the most exclusively morally-guided decisions ever taken by an Irish government. It was, therefore, both paradoxical and also very disturbing that, as I mentioned earlier, the Catholic hierarchy refused to meet the government to discuss this matter, deciding instead to send an agent to present their views to the Attorney General in an arms-length manner.

Of course, behind all this controversy lies the issue of when human life begins. The instinct of the church to protect human life from an early stage is clearly a sound one. But given the practical difficulties in legislating to protect life from the point of fertilisation onwards, it was inevitable that in devising a constitutional amendment on this issue the government should have employed implantation as the point from which life would be legally protected. In any event, the church's adoption of fertilisation as the key point comes up against the reality that fertilised eggs lost through natural processes have not been treated by it as if they were human life.

It is not surprising that the issue of the point of initiation of human life, and the separate issue of determining the point at which any intervention should be precluded by law, has proved such a controversial one in so many countries. For any attempt to define such a point later than implantation is inevitably going to be arbitrary, although humanly one is forced to recognise that a late abortion of a sentient being is more abhorrent than an abortion in the early weeks of pregnancy.

And that fact has some relevance to the Irish situation. For if, as has been suggested, the availability of abortion only outside the state contributes to an exceptional rate of late abortions to Irish women, this could raise a moral issue – albeit one that many of us would be reluctant to face.

At a more general level, Patrick Hannon points out that the debate about law and morality is misstated when it is presented in terms merely of a contest between Catholics and the rest – an approach that he sees as creating false polarities. The reconciliation of individual freedom with a common good is a task for every legal system, and not an eccentricity of the Irish people, Catholic or otherwise!

He also draws attention to the fact that since 1973 the Irish hierarchy has evolved a new way of seeing the role of the Catholic Church in Irish society – abandoning the old practice of simply telling people how to vote on certain issues. This, he points out, reveals a change in the self-understanding of the Catholic Church, as well as in the way in which its leadership understands its role *vis-à-vis* its membership and *vis-à-vis* the wider society. He sees this change in the church's approach as being on the whole for the better, yielding a potential for constructive participation in the future of our society. But he argues that even more change will be needed if the church, or perhaps the churches, are to be credible bearers of their own good news, and a source of spiritual and moral energy.

This new approach involves distinguishing first of all between morality and law and, second, going on to accept that determining the law is a matter for the consciences of the lawmaker and the voter. Third, however, the bishops assert the right to offer their own view of legislation, which they have done on matters such as contraception, by reference to what they see as certain malign consequences which they believe legislation to sanction the sale of contraceptives brings in its wake.

That is a perfectly fair approach and, as Patrick Hannon says, is a great improvement on the kind of dogmatism that we saw at the time of the Mother and Child controversy half a century ago.

There are three comments that can be made on all this, however. First of all, despite the adoption of this approach by the hierarchy, not all bishops have in fact restrained themselves from instructing people how to vote on certain issues. Second, the hierarchy and individual bishops have at times expressed themselves in terms that suggest that they had a particular expertise in social analysis that enabled them to forecast with authority the impact of a particular law on Irish social behaviour.

And, finally, in the case if the 1983 abortion referendum they also, astonishingly, took it on themselves to say dogmatically that the Attorney General was wrong in his advice that there was a danger that the Supreme Court might interpret the wording of the proposed constitutional amendment in a way that could have what they viewed to be perverse effects. There was no conceivable warrant for this attempt to claim superior expertise in constitutional law as well as in sociology. The Attorney General was proved right some years later, but there was no admission of error on the part of the bishops.

On a much wider front, Patrick Hannon asks a question that seems to me very relevant: 'How is it that "conservative" movements and initiatives are more likely to secure episcopal support than liberal ones? This is reminiscent of the question, how is it that liberal "dissent" is always silenced or dismissed, "conservative" hardly at all? ... A leadership which habitually fails to heed informed and conscientious questioning from whatever quarter is doomed to lose touch with the true *sensus fidelium*.'

Nevertheless Patrick Hannon concludes that the level of public discussion of religious and moral matters has greatly improved, although he, rightly, regrets the absence of theology from most of our universities.

Finally he can see in the debris of the present the prospect for the church not of death but of life – but only after a painful rebirth.

John Coolahan explains how the Irish Catholic educational system came into existence. The prime mover was Waterford Catholic unionist Sir Thomas Wyse, one of the first Catholics to be elected an MP after emancipation, who almost immediately persuaded the British parliament and government to create in Ireland an educational system at all three levels, that would be open to Catholics.

However, by 1850 the non-denominational national schools thus established had *de facto* become denominational schools, and in 1878 a system of second-level examinations was established which provided a technically non-discriminatory way of offering to the growing number of Catholic secondary schools state aid in the form of payments related to exam successes.

Thus by the 1880s a parallel state-supported structure of Catholic primary and secondary schools had emerged – which owed its existence to the fact that in previous centuries the only secondary education provision that existed had been that organised by the Established Church of Ireland for the 10% or so of the population who adhered to it. (As Ruth Barrington's account of the Catholic influences on the health services shows, this proved to be the case also with the hospital system.) Catholic denominationalism in both the education and health areas was thus primarily a response to what had previously been effective Anglican control of all such services. Critics of the Catholic Church's role in developing denominational education and health services should set this matter in its historical context.

John Coolahan describes how this system evolved over the next century. From 1930 onwards the secondary school system was complemented by a parallel system of local authority nondenominational vocational schools, which were tolerated by the Catholic Church on the basis that they would not provide 'general education' competing with Catholic secondary schools, but would be severely practical and vocational in their emphasis. Religious education was subsequently introduced in these schools, and soon the chairmen of the majority of Vocational Education Committees were priests. These vocational schools were designed to help children of less well off families, who could not aspire to secondary education, to be prepared for employment in a trade or applied occupation.

In the mid-1960s this whole structure of Irish education, as it had evolved since the 1830s, was examined by a team led by Professor Paddy Lynch, operating under the auspices of the OECD. In addition to exposing the extent of rural educational disadvantage deriving from the predominance of one-teacher and two-teacher national schools – a problem that despite some public resistance was tackled by mergers of many small schools, facilitated by the introduction of school transport services – it also established that in many parts of the country the availability of secondary education for boys was very limited, because of restrictions imposed by the bishops on the opening in their dioceses of schools for boys that would compete with their diocesan colleges, from which vocations to the priesthood in the diocese were drawn.

In dioceses in these regions neither laymen nor religious orders were encouraged to open Catholic schools and as a result, contrary to the situation elsewhere in the country and in the world at large, in no less than half of our twenty-six counties boys were at a considerable educational disadvantage, with the number of them receiving secondary education one-third lower than in the case of girls!

Faced with the exposure of this problem in the Investment in Education Report, the state was led to intervene from the late 1960s onwards to establish comprehensive or community schools in many rural areas, as well as in some less well served urban areas. The churches were accorded representation on the Boards of these new schools, several of which were in fact denominated as Protestant schools.

Together with the growth of Gaelscoileanna, the emergence of 'bottom-up' multi-denominational primary schools, referred to by John Coolahan, has recently started to modify the almost exclusively denominational character of the Irish school system. For the moment, the economic implications of this duplication process have been limited, because the primary sector has recently started to benefit from a recovery in the birth rate. Since 1994 this has brought the number of births almost half-way back to its 1980 peak, off-setting the effect of this duplication of primary school facilities, which in any event is largely confined to populated urban areas.

But it must be clear that in the longer run the country cannot afford an indefinite duplication of non-confessional and confessional schools. This, together with economic pressure to bring secondary and primary schools on to the same site, is liable in time to produce new tensions between church and state, and these tensions would be greatly aggravated if the recovery in the birth rate since 1994 were once again to be reversed. There has as yet been no sign of any willingness to recognise the likely emergence of this problem in the future.

In her chapter, Ruth Barrington addresses the role of the Catholic Church in the health sector. At the outset she explains that the process by which in the later nineteenth century the nursing orders gradually became involved in some of the workhouses was an informal one. Whilst some Boards of Guardians did not want to see publicly-funded institutions developing a Catholic ethos, others recognised that the free services of the religious orders improved the quality of care in their workhouses, within most of which the vast majority of inmates were Catholic.

She remarks that this trend quickened, at least in the southern part of the country, after local democracy was introduced in 1898, but she points out that this involvement of religious did not extend to publicly-funded mental hospitals, which were more centrally controlled.

The rationalisation of the poor law system which Ruth Barrington speaks of as taking place in the early years of the new state, had actually begun during the War of Independence. Ireland must surely be the only country in which an underground government – admittedly one that was under severe financial pressure because of shortfalls in the rates being collected by the 85% of county councils under its control – set about reorganising health and social services! These institutions were reorganised on a county basis despite considerable local resistance, county hospitals being substituted for what had previously been local workhouses.

Ruth Barrington also explains how in the 1930s, at a time when the financially strapped new Irish state lacked the necessary resources, the Hospitals Sweepstake helped to fund the Protestant and Catholic voluntary hospitals that had emerged in the nineteenth century.

(In this connection I should, I think, put into context her reference to the first government having in 1924 temporarily reduced by one shilling a week the Old Age Pension. Since the time when this payment had been doubled in 1920, the cost of living had fallen, and this cut was, of course, restored several years later, during a period of five years when the cost of living was in course of dropping by a further 20%.)

Ruth Barrington's brief account of the Mother and Child controversy of 1951 notes the extent to which on that occasion the church authorities acted under pressure from lobbying by medical interests. She comments that 'The hierarchy, under the influence of arguments refined by the medical profession, persuaded ... (the) government that it should not proceed with ... (these) proposals ... The implementation of the Health Act 1953 did mark the end of the commitment to establish a national health service on the British model in this part of the island ... Means tests ... were enshrined as a principle of access to many health services ... It is extremely difficult to determine where the public element ends and private practice begins.'

Just half a century later, the multi-level structure of our present medical services still bears the marks of that clash between the state on the one hand and the church and medical profession on the other.

In the concluding paragraphs of her chapter, Ruth Barrington looks ahead to the future, raising a number of questions about the possible future evolution of the state/church relationship in this sector. She asks rhetorically what is to be the role of Catholic and Protestant hospitals in the twenty-first century? Is the Catholic hospital to be defined only negatively, by reference to the services it does not provide? Is it simply the ownership that makes it Catholic? How compatible is religious involvement in private hospitals with the original commitment of the religious orders to the care of the poor? Is some vital interest of the church served by owning and operating modern hospitals?

These are all valid questions. But many Irish people, even ones who are not practising Catholics, have traditionally valued the particular kind of care that they feel they get in hospitals run by religious.

A rather different question also raised by Ruth Barrington is whether the prevalence of Catholic religious symbols in public hospitals staffed with religious sisters is compatible with the duty of publicly managed hospitals to respect all religions equally.

Reflecting on these two chapters one cannot help remarking on the extent to which the Catholic Church's building and part-financing of schools and hospitals, as well as churches, between the 1830s and 1960s is today taken for granted and even some-times, most unhistorically, denigrated. This was an immense achievement, financed by the willingly-given pennies of the poor – in the early decades by a people more impoverished than any others in Western Europe.

Of course, in retrospect we can make a judgement that it would have been better, as Bishop Doyle of Kildare urged at the time, to have accepted a non-denominational education system that would have brought together children of different branches of the Christian family. But that would have run against the cli-mate of the times, at the end of several centuries of exclusive control of the system of government by the Anglican Church, and at a time when evangelical Protestants were still engaged in an active, and at times less than scrupulous, campaign to recruit poor Catholics to their version of the Christian religion.

The fact is that not only our generation, but three or four gen-erations of our ancestors also, owe the Catholic Church a huge debt which, despite the exploitative behaviour of a very small minority of those involved, we are not entitled to forget or to denigrate.

The example of what generations of priests, nuns, and brothers achieved both here and overseas should be an inspiration to anyone looking to the church to play a prophetic role under the very different conditions of the decades ahead.

In her chapter, Maureen Junker-Kenny addresses weakness in the current Irish approach to questions of bio-ethics. She notes an extraordinary lack of debate in our society on issues such as techniques of assisted procreation, the permissibility of reproductive and therapeutic cloning, and embryonic versus adult stem research.

The surrounding culture, she remarks, shows a marked reluctance to accept these as themes for the agenda of politics and civil society, and she contrasts this with the space given in many newspapers to some of these issues.

As someone from outside our society, she speculates as to what might explain this apparent Irish opting out of what has become a global ethical debate. There may well be something in her suggestion that we are still so caught up in the battles of the recent past on contraception, divorce and abortion that we have simply failed to notice more recent threats arising from the commercialisation of the human body in bio-patenting, some techniques of assisted reproduction, and genetic testing.

But I would go further than she has done to suggest that public discussion of bio-ethical issues has been positively discouraged by the aggressive and sometimes personalised manner in which elements of the Catholic right in Ireland have in the recent past handled issues of this kind, especially the abortion issue at the time of the various referendums of the 1980s and 1990s. Accusations of being pro-abortion levelled at public figures who held no such view, but simply doubted the feasibility or appropriateness of seeking to deal with this complex issue by constitutional amendments, has led to a marked reluctance to participate in a debate on bio-ethics in which rational discussion of very complex issues might evoke a similar aggressive reaction from those circles. Our notable failure to address bio-ethical issues, some of which clearly require early legislative action, seems to me to have been an almost inevitable, if perverse, consequence of those past experiences.

Maureen Junker-Kenny suggests that yet another reason for the lack of debate in Ireland on bio-ethical issues may be what she describes as the 'dictates of questionable conclusions' arising from 'the deductive method of classical natural law as used by the Vatican' which led, for example, to the banning of *in vitro* fertilisation, even for married couples.

On the other side, the weakening of belief in moral standards in an increasingly materialist Irish society, combined with the almost absolute priority now given to attracting foreign investment of any kind, may also have contributed to the worrying situation in which, in Maureen Junker-Kenny's words, this is felt by some not to be 'the time for the moral proof-reading of biotechnical research projects and products'.

She is right in asserting that this complex of factors, leading to a public disinclination to engage in 'divisive issues', is not good for ethics, but is contributing to 'the privatisation of public matters'. And she suggests that Ireland should work out its own position between the different European bio-ethical camps, through a critical review of its own and other traditions.

I would hope that her detailed analysis of the issues at stake, drawing on the recent debate on genetic intervention between two schools of liberal social philosophy, those of John Rawls and Jürgen Habermas, will initiate just such a belated Irish discussion of these issues – drawing, as she suggests, on the resources of 'a philosophically oriented Christian anthropology'.

Sean Healy and Brigid Reynolds have made a major contribution to social equity in Ireland through the work of the CORI Justice Commission, including their well-researched budget submissions, and latterly also through their active participation, and indeed leadership role, in the negotiation of successive National Agreements.

A characteristic of their work has been their willingness and ability to translate Christian principles into a concrete vision of the action that could and should be taken to alleviate inequalities in our society. And because their proposals for action are generally both well-researched and quite specific, they have often been effective. So effective, indeed, that they have clearly got under the skin of the Minister for Finance, Charlie McCreevy!

Their chapter in this book sets out both the theological basis and the pragmatic approach they have adopted in tackling their task. Their work is deeply rooted in Catholic social thought, and they identify the essential components of their Christian critique of economic policy and practice as including a whole range of factors: social analysis, dialogue, realising that credibility comes through direct involvement, on-going action, vision building, resisting the temptation to become absorbed in the *status quo*, and instead being prophetic.

Their emphasis on conversation and dialogue is well-judged. For, it is through conversation in the first instance that a reformer learns what are the weaknesses of his case – or at any rate which parts of it can be resisted with some element of credibility. And it is through dialogue that the reformer with a good case forces a reluctant interlocutor to give ground. Nothing is more powerful than a case based solidly on unvarnished facts, and argued with incontestable logic. Of course you must first catch your interlocutor, and then get him or her to engage in dialogue – and with politicians that is sometimes difficult!

Healy and Reynolds say, with good reason, that planning our future is not a matter just for sociologists and economists: it is also very much a matter for philosophers and theologians – the best of whom can fashion a more profound vision and motivation.

But the wise philosopher or theologian grounds his or her vision on a good understanding of the sociological and economic realities that underlie the real world. CORI has always understood this, and whilst not everything they have proposed is based on these principles – enthusiasm can sometimes outrun the harsh realities of economics and politics! – their constant concern to ensure a measure of realism in their proposals has been a most important source of their effectiveness.

Finally, they are right in saying that whilst our governments have introduced a substantial range of anti-poverty measures that have targeted disadvantaged groups, they have not yet seriously addressed the structural causes of poverty in Ireland.

The chapter in which Joan Roddy, Jerome Connolly, and Maura Leen discuss immigration and also aspects of Irish development co-operation, is one of the most positive in this book, for the simple reason that they are writing about the witness that is currently being given by the Irish churches and Irish people to the Christian message, as it affects deprived people from or in other parts of the world.

Their account of how immigration of asylum seekers has become a major domestic issue in recent years is especially valuable; here we can see striking contrasts between the behaviour of church and state. The slowness and uncertainty with which the state reacted to the admittedly sudden emergence of a major inflow of asylum seekers contrasts with the flexibility of the churches' approach. The principal challenge to fumbling by the state came from the Catholic bishops, who early on got hold of the facts of what was happening and sought to face the state with its responsibilities.

Moreover, as the state began to move asylum-seekers out of Dublin in order to settle them throughout the countryside, the churches, acting together from September 1999 onwards, through the Churches Asylum Network, not only set their faces against racism but led in initiating positive measures to make the new arrivals welcome in the towns and villages to which they were sent. And to a remarkable degree they succeeded in these efforts – not everywhere, of course, but in very many places.

The authors of this chapter are not sparing in their criticisms of the way in which the state has handled its responsibilities, but they admit that it has not been stinting in its allocation of resources to the accommodation and welfare of asylum seekers. Indeed they remark that in many ways Ireland has done much better than many other EU states. But they note a drift towards increasingly restrictive policies and procedures, a key plank of Irish asylum policy now being 'pre-emptive exclusion', viz. the employment of administrative measures to prevent as many as possible asylum seekers getting here in the first place.

What should be the approach of the Irish authorities to this problem? The failure to allow asylum seekers to work is criticised by the authors – a criticism I would join in – and they also point to the negative impact of the provision of specific accommodation centres for asylum seekers which, they point out, severely reduces the possibilities of their integration into Irish society.

It is a pity that there has not been any attempt to secure a meeting of minds on this issue between the government and the social agencies and churches concerned with this problem. Clearly there is some limit to the scale of the inflow our small country can absorb. We should have been able to find some agreement, first on what that scale should be, and second, about how we could best arrive at such an outcome.

A most positive feature of Irish society has been the emergence of agencies dedicated to assisting the development of Third World countries, especially in Africa but also in Latin

America and in Asia – bodies such as Concern, Goal, and Trócaire, as well as the commitment of successive Irish governments to expanding both bilateral and multi-lateral aid. Developing out of past missionary efforts, and clearly inspired by Christian principles, the scale and effectiveness of these efforts represents one of the most positive features of modern Ireland.

In the final chapter, John Horgan addresses the question of church, state and media. He recalls the 1960s, when all three Dublin morning papers and RTÉ were subjecting the church to a new and informed critique, centred on the perceived slowness of Irish Catholicism to measure up to the norms established by Vatican II. But he points out that in the journalistic agenda of that time justice issues did not feature, largely, he suggests, because almost all journalists then were male and middle class. However, he has to admit that the subsequent emancipation of women in journalism from fashion and cookery to a wider agenda did not greatly change this pattern!

Another reason suggested by John Horgan for the failure of the media to tackle social issues was the irruption of Northern Ireland into political life in the Irish state which, he feels, diverted political, journalistic and social radicalism away from issues related to class into the maelstrom of nationalist conflict.

Nevertheless, he believes that if the Kennedy Report had been published at any time after 1984, the issues it raised would have been the subject of prolonged speculation and investigation of a kind that it failed to attract when it first appeared – because the later emergence of professional pressure groups would not have allowed a report of this kind to fizzle out.

'A number of events around that time combined to effect a distinct shift not only in power relationships but also in the perceived role of the key institutions involved.' The media became the 'moral policeman of the church', with the result that today 'the relationship between church, state, and media has come to resemble an eternal triangle of mutual recrimination'. A collective examination of conscience might be in order, he concludes.

What is perhaps a little surprising, from a journalist who forty years ago was involved in reporting on the Second Vatican Council, is that John Horgan does not comment on the failure of the media to discuss the church in its own right, as distinct from the failings of church people running institutions catering for social needs, or of the church leaders in their handling of various scandals.

In this connection it has to be said that, whilst what might be called the clerical press in Ireland is conservative and defensive, the lay press has remarkably little to say about religion, at home or abroad. The serious debate about religious issues in the lay press on the Continent, even in countries where the churches do not command the allegiance and participation of a majority of the population, has little or no Irish equivalent. It is as if we lack the capacity to take religious issues seriously. This may in part reflect what has always seemed to me to be a pre-occupation of Irish – as well as English – intellectuals with literary matters, to the virtual exclusion of philosophy and political ideas – let alone theology.

Churchmen sometimes complain about a media bias against the church. Of course, paranoia about the media is common to all walks of life, but I think it is fair to say that there does exist an anti-clerical, or at any rate non-religious, ethos in this sector. However, churchmen should be muted in their complaints on this score, as all too often it is they who have provided much of the ammunition being used by journalists who are not well-disposed to the church.

Another factor has been the striking unwillingness of lay people in Ireland to make explicit the Christian basis of their approach to life. In this we differ profoundly from a large part of the population of the United States – where, however, Christian fundamentalism has a considerable negative impact, counterbalancing the positive side of American religious commitment.

Some Irish people, of course, have lost their faith, and others are beset with doubts that make them unwilling to admit a Christian motivation that they no longer feel a clear right to avow. But even those whose faith remains strong rarely make it explicitly the basis of their words and actions, perhaps because of a wish not to embarrass others. And also, perhaps, because we have all suffered at one time or another from the rhetoric of native craw-thumpers, some of them self-evidently hypocritical.

The fact is that very many Irish people act as Christians most of the time, but they prefer not talk about why they behave the way they do. In government I can recall only one occasion when Christian principles were explicitly cited as a reason for action, viz. a government meeting just thirty years ago when in relation to my proposal to initiate a Development Aid Programme, the matter was settled by a minister exclaiming: 'If we're Christians at all we must agree to this!' But that does not mean that I have not seen very many matters decided conscientiously by ministers acting in a Christian manner but without any explicit reference to their motivation.

In a country where many people prefer to hide rather than announce what motivates them to do good things, we should perhaps not be too surprised at the almost exclusively secular tone of our media.

Conclusions

There is good and bad in our society. We must face the reality of the bad features, instead of sweeping the many defects in our society under the carpet, but we should also recognise, and be prepared to build upon, the good elements that are also present.

The speed at which Ireland has changed in recent times has been literally unprecedented. No European country has ever caught up on its neighbours as rapidly as Ireland has done in the period since the end of the 1980s. From having had a level of output per head almost 40% below that of the rest of the EU, Ireland is now at least as productive as the rest of the Union.

And, despite the fact that, wisely, a disproportionate share of what we produce is being ploughed back into investment in our future – we have a higher ratio of investment to output than anywhere else in Europe – our material living standards have nevertheless risen during this period by two-thirds – a quite astonishing increase in a period of only fourteen years. That recent rise in our living standards has been almost three times greater than that which has taken place in the rest of the EU during this period.

On what are we spending all this extra money? Not on food. Even when poor, Irish people always ate well: for decades past our average food consumption has been consistently higher than almost anywhere else in the world. So spending on food has scarcely increased during this recent period.

However, even after discounting the effects of inflation, the real level of spending per head on foreign travel, clothing, and communications (mobile phones!) is now between two-and-half and three times higher than in 1989, and on average we spend in real terms on recreation and entertainment and cars well over twice as much as was the case in 1989. So much for our material welfare.

Although this extraordinary spurt of economic growth has in substantial measure been due to wise economic policy decisions of past governments – no one should delude themselves that all this just happened of its own accord! – politicians receive none of the credit for it. On the contrary, politics and politicians are now held in much lower regard by the electorate than back in the miserable emigration-ridden late 1980s. This at least partly accounts for the drop of almost one-sixth in electoral participation in the intervening period.

Why, despite their remarkable economic achievements, are politicians held in such low esteem today? Partly because the exposure of financial malfeasance and, at least at local level, corruption amongst what is in fact a very small proportion of politicians has unfortunately seriously damaged public perception of all politicians. Perhaps also because politicians, infected perhaps by the general growth of materialism in our society, have recently appeared more concerned about their own remuneration and conditions of employment than ever seemed to be the case in the past.

But also, I think, because of a general unease with the downside of rapid economic growth. For this huge rise in material living standards has been accompanied by a sharp deterioration in the quality of life in our society, which has left many people unhappy about the way things have been going.

Thus, whilst there are no figures for spending on drugs, we know that far more of them are used now than in the late 1980s, and alcohol consumption per head has also risen by over one-third during this period. Moreover other measures of well-being, such as the suicide rate and the crime rate – especially crimes of violence – have also deteriorated sharply.

Again, more than half of all first pregnancies are now non-marital, and many of these are clearly unintended, as is evident from the fact that three out of every eight such pregnancies are aborted in Britain. And, whilst a majority of people in the country still attend church on Sundays, there are urban parishes where Mass attendance has fallen below 10%.

Finally, although this is more controversial, our society has become more materialistic, more selfish, less generous, than it used to be. For years past, much more emphasis has been placed on reducing taxes than on improving the lot of the less-well-off.

Of course it is true that excessively high taxation can discourage enterprise, and we certainly needed to bring it down from the excessive level to which it had to be raised temporarily in order to master the financial crisis of the early 1980s. But in the face of such deficiencies in our public services as high waiting lists for hospital treatment and for local authority housing, did taxation need to be reduced right down to the lowest level in the European Union? No, it did not.

This unhappy outcome has been the work of ideologists of the right who are a quite new, and in my view negative, element in the traditionally pragmatic Irish political scene. Their activities have helped to create what is now one of the most unequal societies in Europe – for ours is now a society in which a minority has become extraordinarily wealthy, whilst significant poverty still remains in our midst.

That is the less attractive face of Ireland – a post-Christian Ireland, one might almost say.

At least, that is part of that face. For there are some positive as well as negative features of our society, and we must not fail to recognise this fact.

Thus, marriages in Ireland remain more stable than in the rest of Northern Europe – the divorce rate seems to be settling at about one-third of the British level. And the marriage rate has risen by one-fifth since 1997, as more and more women who in the 1990s had been postponing marriage for career reasons have finally started to take the plunge. And, whilst there was a huge drop in the birth rate in the 1980s, since 1995 it has risen again by one-fifth – and not all of these additional are births to asylum-seeking women!

Moreover, by comparison with neighbouring Britain anecdotal evidence suggests that most Irish young people, who are much less prone than young people in Britain to seek higher education somewhere distant from their home, still maintain close links with their families and, despite the huge inter-generational change in mores, for example in relation to issues like pre-marital sex, there appears to be much less friction between the generations here than one might have expected in a society that has changed so very rapidly.

It is also of interest that, however negative most young people may be about the institutional church, they seem to retain a positive attitude to priests they know. And, outside deprived and neglected urban areas, educational motivation remains strong amongst the young, even if some of the manifestations of this, such as the points race, sometimes become a source of undue pressures and tensions.

In other words, Irish society has retained some at least of its traditional strengths.

But two things seem to me to be lacking: an overall vision, and, as mentioned earlier, a civic ethic. The absence of both of these reflects badly on the Christian churches – more particularly on the church to which the majority of our people adhere.

In the past the churches were, I fear, inhibited by the class basis of the Irish clergy from offering a vision of our society to which our people might have responded. Most clergy came mainly from middle class backgrounds, and predominantly from the property-owning part of the middle class, including particularly the farming community. In a society that in the past was marked by great deference to authority, this class factor may not have appeared to be a hindrance to moral leadership. But in reality it was bound to constrain, and certainly did so constrain, the moral vision of many who preached the gospel in our churches.

It is true that at that time absolute inequalities in our much poorer society were less marked than today, but in a poor society any inequality is likely to mean that a proportion of the population live in dire poverty. Yet our Christian churches were not merely slow to challenge this situation. Instead they went on the defensive, warning constantly against the dangers of socialism, and of threats to private property. And they were notably slow to challenge such evils as tax evasion, which was a prevalent feature of the society from which many of the clergy were drawn, and thus something few of them could have been unaware of.

Tax evasion is, of course, the only way in which a citizen can steal from all his neighbours, the poorest as well as the richest, for taxes not paid by some require a heavier impost on all in order to make up the consequent shortfall. And even the poorest people pay indirect taxes, from which, indeed, twice as much revenue is being raised as from progressive income tax.

Far from denouncing this evil – for I cannot recall ever having heard a sermon on the subject – children were instead taught in school all about 'unjust taxation' and 'penal taxes', so that when they grew up and started to earn their living, they all too often felt justified in deciding for themselves how much, or how little, they would pay. The fruits of this evil are to be seen today in the tens of thousands of well-off people who are now belatedly paying the price of their past evasion several times over.

In fairness it has to be said that in recent decades the churches in Ireland have become much more conscious of these issues and many clergy have come to play a leading role in advocating social justice, winning the respect of many of the laity for doing so – as well, of course, as the vocal hostility of some apostles of economic liberalism.

As for the related issue of encouraging the emergence of a civic ethic, as I remarked earlier, the Catholic Church's past insistence on grounding its moral teaching exclusively on authority, without explaining the rational basis for the main principles of this teaching, worked well enough so long as its authority remained undiminished. But as that authority began to fade in a new and less deferential world, many of our people have been left without an adequate sense of civic morality, and this has been major factor contributing to an increasingly amoral society.

How does an institutional church become a church of witness? How can it recover its prophetic role? I think this will involve a new concept of authority. Instead of the old top-down authority, 'Do what we tell you, because we know best', the authority of a church of witness will come from the evident authenticity of its message – uncomfortable but unchallengeable because founded on eternal truths and on a clear vision of how mankind can best find fulfilment, and presented by prophetic voices.

Notes

CHAPTER ONE

1. For a fuller and more scholarly treatment of these issues see Dunn, James D. G. and Mackey, James P., *New Testament Theology in Dialogue*, (London, 1987), esp. chapters 5 and 6.

2. See as an example of such textbook treatment of these matters Van Noort, G., *Tractatus de Gratia Christi*, (Holland, 1955), pp 135ff.

3. It would be amusing, were it not so tragic, to see conservative Roman Catholic leaders accuse so many modern theologians of capitulating to modern secularism to the point of allowing the substance of Christianity to be infected by its alien ideals, when it is so blatantly obvious that much of what these people are intent on conserving – in the examples of a cultic priesthood, a power- rather than a service-driven imperial-type government, and a crass example of gender discrimination – is all of it a very fine example indeed of just such capitulation to just such alien, albeit more ancient elements of secular structure and ethos, which are therefore named in this piece as intrusive falsifications in an otherwise sound Christian foundation myth.

4. On where 'God's plan for marriage' really came from, see Walters, D. B., 'Marriage and Christianity: Reflections on the Persistence of Secular Marriage Law in European Christianity,' *Studies in World Christianity* III.1 (1997), pp 22-37.

CHAPTER TWO

Select Bibliography

Whyte, J., *Church and State in Modern Ireland, 1923-1970*, (Dublin, 1970).

Bartlett, T., 'Church and State in Modern Ireland, 1923-1970: An appraisal reappraised' in Bradshaw, Keogh (eds), *Christianity in Ireland*, (Dublin, 2002), pp 249-258.

Keogh, D., *Ireland and the Vatican, The Politics and Diplomacy of Church-State Relations, 1922-1960*, (Cork, 1995).

Murray, P., *Oracles of God: The Roman Catholic Church and Irish Politics, 1922-1937*, (Dublin, 2000).

Inglis, T., *Moral Monopoly: The Rise and Fall of the Catholic Church in Modern Ireland*, (Dublin, 1998).

Fuller, L., *Irish Catholicism since 1950*, (Dublin, 2002).

Cooney J, *John Charles Mc Quaid*, (Dublin, 1999).

FitzGerald, G., *All in a Life*, (Dublin, 1991).
FitzGerald, G., *Reflections on the Irish State*, (Dublin, 2002).

CHAPTER THREE

1. D. H. Akenson, *The Church of Ireland: ecclesiastical reform and revolution 1800-1885* (New York and London, 1971), p 164.
2. Jacqueline Hill, *From patriots to unionists: Dublin civic politics and Irish Protestant patriotism 1660-1840* (Oxford,1997), p 6.
3. Senate Debates (11 June 1925), v, (1926).
4. For a more extended treatment of the question of the distinctiveness or otherwise of the Protestant, especially Church of Ireland, contribution to Irish literature, see the present writer's chapter in *The Laity and the Church of Ireland 1000-2000*, published by Four Courts Press in 2002.
5. *Journal of the Church of Ireland Special General Synod*, 16 April 1912, xlvii, l.
6. Finlay Holmes, *The Presbyterian Church in Ireland: a popular history* (Dublin, 2000), p 123.
7. D. L. Cooney, *The Methodists in Ireland: a short history* (Dublin, 2001), pp 97-8.
8. *Church of Ireland General Synod Journal*, 1922, p liii.
9. Holmes, *Presbyterian Church*, p 128.
10. *General Synod Journal*, 1949, lxxxiii-iv. Similar constitutional propriety was shown in the selection of hymns for inclusion in the fifth edition of the Church Hymnal (2000). What was to be done about 'God save our gracious Queen', included in the fourth edition (1960) in the section entitled 'Our country'? With scarcely any controversy, it was retained (no 534) with the rubric: 'For use in Northern Ireland'. To many church members resident in the Republic, such a compromise seemed in tune with the spirit of the recent Belfast Agreement, with its stress on respect for differing traditions. For the first time ever, the hymnal included, by specific direction of the General Synod, several hymns in the Irish language (with translations).
11. Recounted to the author by Dr E. C. Hodges, Bishop of Limerick 1943-60. Prior to that (from 1927), as principal of the Church of Ireland Training College, Hodges played a leading part in negotiations with the state on educational matters. Perhaps his major achievement was obtaining agreement on a state-supported scheme to transport Church of Ireland pupils (and other Protestant children) to the nearest national school under Protestant management.
12. George Seaver, *John Allen Fitzgerald Gregg: archbishop* (London and Dublin, 1963), pp 127-8.
13. D. F. Keogh, *The Vatican, the bishops and Irish politics 1919-39* (Cambridge, 1986), pp 213, 217, 220. This part of article 44, together with the recognition of other named religious denominations, was removed from the constitution by referendum in 1972.

14. J. J. Lee, *Ireland 1912-1985: politics and society* (Cambridge, 1989), pp 161-7.

15. F. S. L. Lyons, *Ireland since the famine* (revised ed., London, 1973), p 683n.

16. 'Political life in the south', by J. H. Whyte, in Michael Hurley (ed.), *Irish Anglicanism 1869-1969: essays on the role of Anglicanism in Irish life presented to the Church of Ireland on the occasion of the centenary of its Disestablishment by a group of Methodist, Presbyterian, Quaker and Roman Catholic scholars* (Dublin, 1970), pp 150-51.

17. 'The minority problem in the 26 counties' in Francis MacManus (ed), *The Years of the Great Test 1926-39* (Cork, 1967), p 99.

18. For a treatment of the situation in which some Protestants found themselves see Peter Hart, *The IRA and its enemies: violence and comunity in Cork 1916-23* (Oxford, 1998), chapter 12, 'Taking it out on the Protestants', and R. B. McDowell, *Crisis and decline: the fate of the southern unionists* (Dublin,1997).

19. Michael Hurley, 'The future', in *Irish Anglicanism*, p 215. See also, for the fate of the Mercier Society, John Cooney, *John Charles McQuaid: ruler of Catholic Ireland* (Dublin, 1999), pp 174 et seq. Ó Broin was a close friend of Frank Duff, founder of the Legion of Mary, who was likewise a member of the Mercier Society, as was Garret FitzGerald's father, Desmond (FitzGerald, *All in a life*, p 28.)

20. Garret FitzGerald, *All in a life: an autobiography* (Dublin, 1991), p 433.

21. I am indebted to Professor John Horgan of Dublin City University for this information. See John Horgan, 'Saving us from ourselves: contraception, censorship and the "evil literature" controversy of 1926' in *Irish Communications Review*, v (1995), pp 61-7. For a discussion of Protestant and 'ex-unionist' attitudes in the censorship debate see R. B. McDowell, *Crisis and decline*, pp 183- 5.

22. See D. H. Akenson, *A mirror to Kathleen's face: education in independent Ireland 1922-1960* (Montreal and London, 1975), pp 118-33, for a discussion of this issue, and the 'theological' aspect.

23. Stephen Rynne, *Father John Hayes: founder of Muintir na Tíre, people of the land* (Dublin, 1960), pp 179, 210.

24. See Kenneth Milne, *New approaches to the teaching of history* (The Historical Association, London, 1979), pp 7-10.

25. The General Synod Advisory Committee on Secondary Education (1962-5) that gave rise to the Secondary Education Committee (and on which many of the original Advisory Committee's members served) had warned that '... the present schools will not be able to provide our children with an education equal to that available to the rest of the nation, or up to European standards', (*General Synod Journal*, 1965, pp 142-3) and proposed a substantial reduction in the number of schools (which was largely achieved). Reporting to the General Synod in 1968, the newly formed Secondary Education Committee stated 'Every child should receive the education appropriate to his or her intellect, irre-

spective of means' (*Journal*, 1968, p 153). Similar thinking lay behind the strategy of amalgamating very small primary schools in the interests of children, particularly in rural areas, where the likelihood of such schools being provided with the amenities required by a new curriculum seemed remote.

26. *Careers in Ireland* (Church of Ireland Sparsely Populated Areas Commission, 1959) and *Careers in Ireland* (Church of Ireland Board of Education, 1969).

27. p vii.

28. Ronald Marshall, *Stranmillis College Belfast 1922-1972* (Belfast, [1972]), p 79. A speaker from the Rathcoole area of in Belfast said, in the course of a BBC Radio 4 broadcast on 1 August 1986, during Irish Arts Week, 'Our culture has been suppressed by religion.'

29. Alan Ford, '"Standing one's ground": religion, polemic and Irish history since the Reformation', in Alan Ford, James McGuire and Kenneth Milne (eds.), *As by law established: the Church of Ireland since the Reformation* (Dublin, 1995) p 14.

30. Perhaps we can capture something of the climate of those days by calling to mind our contemporary unease at the dangers attaching to some of the material made widely available by the internet ?

31. F. S. L. Lyons speculated that 'the historian of the future may well establish that the main credit for the ultimate reconciliation of the minority, not just to the Irish Free State, but to the Republic, will belong precisely to Mr deValera and his party.' See 'The minority problem in the 26 counties', p 102.

32. *General Synod Journal*, 1982, pp 123-4.

33. Ibid.

34. T. P. McCaughey, *Memory and redemption: church, politics and prophetic theology in Ireland* (Dublin, 1993), p 91.

35. Each decade seems to have produced its treatment of the subject: Michael Viney, *The five percent: a survey of Protestants in the Republic* (Dublin, 1965); Jack White, *Minority report: the Protestant community in the Irish Republic* (Dublin, 1975); Kurt Bowen, *Protestants in a Catholic state: Ireland's privileged minority* (Kingston and Dublin, 1983) and Kenneth Milne, 'Brave new world', in S. R. White (ed.), *A Time to Build: Essays for Tomorrow's Church* (Dublin, 1999). As yet there has been nothing on the scale of Marianne Elliott's *The Catholics of Ulster* (London, 2000).While the Church of Ireland (in particular) continues to engage the attention of authors, these have, in recent times, been more interested in analysing aspects the Church's theological and institutional past than in commenting on the present, which may say something about the extent to which today's Protestant minority is decreasingly perceived as a social phenomenon.

36. Peter Brooke, *Ulster Presbyterianism: the historical perspective 1610-1970* (Dublin and New York, 1987), p 202.

37. *General Synod Journal*, 1999. 'Sub-committee on sectarianism report 1999', p 181.
38. Which begs the question as to how comprehensive we intend the word 'religious' to be. For our purposes here I mean Christian.
39. McCaughey, *Memory and redemption*, pp 90-91.
40. Ibid., p 26.
41. H. R. McAdoo, *The Spirit of Anglicanism: A survey of Anglican theological method in the seventeenth century* (London, 1965), p v
42. *The final report* (London, 1982), p 3.
43. *New Ireland Forum: Report of proceedings 9 February 1984*, Irish *Episcopal Conference delegation* (Dublin, 1984),pp 48-9.
44. *Vatican Council II: the conciliar and post-conciliar doccuments* (ed. Austin Flannery, new revised edition, Dublin, 1973), i, 462. The decree refers to 'The churches and ecclesial communities which were separated from the Apostolic See of Rome during the grave crisis that began in the West at the end of the Middle Ages or in later times...' (Ibid, p 467).
45. Quoted in *Report of the working party on sectarianism: a discussion document for presentation to the Irish Inter-church Meeting* (Belfast, 1993), p 133.
46. Ibid, p 137.
47. Ibid, p 141.
48. Lyons, 'Minority problem', p 101.

CHAPTER FOUR

1. Eric Gallagher and Stanley Worrall, *Christians in Ulster – 1968-1980*, (Oxford, 1982).
2. Gallagher and Worrall, op. cit., p 205.
3. Vamik Volkan, *Bloodlines: From Ethnic Pride to Ethnic Terrorism*, Westview Press, Boulder, Colorado, 1997, p 101-102. Thus I would contend that the recurring demand of Belfast communities living on a violent interface for border-zones and 'peace-lines', should thus be construed, not as an out and out rejection of the changing social landscape. It rather reminds peace-makers and reconcilers – whether operating from a religious or political motivation – of the need to take feelings of insecurity seriously, and to keep testing the amount of 'closeness' to the erstwhile enemy that a community can sustain without forcing the degree of anxiety to intolerable levels.
4. Frank Wright, *Northern Ireland: a Comparative Analysis*, (Dublin, 1992), pp 20ff.
5. Cf. another Girardian analysis of violence in Northern Ireland, which proposes the Christian gospel as a contrast-culture and resource for transformation: Roel Kaptein with the co-operation of Duncan Morrow, *On the Way to Freedom* (Introduction by René Girard), (Dublin, 1993). See also, André Lascaris, *To Do the Unexpected: Reading Scripture in Northern Ireland*, (Belfast, 1993).
6. Martin E Marty, *The Public Church: Mainline-Evangelical-Catholic*, (New York, 1981), p 4.

7. See Grace Davie's seminal work in this area, *Religion in Modern Europe: A Memory Mutates*, (Oxford, 2000), which demonstrates the necessary distinction between religion in general, and those specific communitarian expressions which are fed by the collective memory and are capable of alternative patterns and mutations (both healthy and unhealthy). Davie adduces interesting evidence of this in European Christianity. In her *Europe: the Exceptional Case – Parameters of Faith in the Modern World*, (London, 2002), she casts a different light on the possible futures for European Christianity, and not just the predicted ones of secularisation, depending on whether the right choices are made.

8. Cf. two unpublished analyses of the International Social Survey Programme, 1998 – that of Professor John D Brewer (Queen's University Belfast), 'Patterns of Belief and Observance', and of Professor Conor Ward (University College Dublin), on 'Patterns of Religious Beliefs, Behaviour and Attitudes', delivered at a conference, in Dublin 2002, on *Church in the Contemporary World*, sponsored by Boston University and the Conference of Religious of Ireland Justice Commission. Addressing respectively Northern Ireland and Republic of Ireland, these papers clearly endorse the view that neither modernity nor secularisation have ushered religious belief and practice into the wings. So also, Desmond O'Donnell's more finely-tuned survey and analysis of young educated adults' religious and moral attitudes and practice, outlined in a special issue of *Doctrine and Life*, January 2002, demonstrates that despite their radically increasing latitude of belief and practice in the sphere of sexual morality and a diminishing religious knowledge base, the religious character of Ireland's young people has mutated, but is far from the convenient classification of 'post-religious'.

9. It must be noted, of course, that Christianity is not the only religion, present. Both North and South, churches should be to the fore in showing respect and concern to those who come with different belief systems, cultural practice, and different modes of relating to the secular world. Christians should remember that much of the totalitarianism of the past century, whether Christian, Islamic or Hindu in form – has grounded its truth claims in religious symbols, texts, or sectarian tradition. So too have churches chosen different ways of relating to other traditions, ranging from Crusade, to proselytism, to tolerant co-existence, to ethical co-operation, positioning themselves somewhere along an axis from hostility to hospitality.

10. Václav Havel, *Open Letters: Selected Prose*, (London, 1991), p 50ff.

11. On the transcending power of thoughtful communication, see Hannah Arendt, *The Human Condition*, pp 84-101, 168.

12. W. B. Yeats, 'Meditations in Time of Civil War', *W. B. Yeats: The Collected Poems*, (London, 1969), pp 225-232, p 230.

13. *A Citizen's Inquiry: The Opsahl Report on Northern Ireland*, ed., Andy Pollak, (Dublin, 1993), pp 120-122. There is a lamentable irony that less

than ten years later, the Congregation for the Doctrine of the Faith of the Roman Catholic Church (despite protest from the Pontifical Council for Christian Unity) sent a 'Note' to the Presidents of Conferences of Bishops, containing new reservations in regard to the recognition of Protestant churches as churches 'in the proper sense'. This was particularly hurtful to relationships with the Anglican Communion, whom Paul VI had addressed as 'ever beloved sister' in 1970. See 'Note on the Expression "Sister Churches"', Declaration *Dominus Iesus*, (Vatican City, June 30 2000). For a discussion of the crux issues, see Adrian Hastings, 'Sisters for all that', *The Tablet*, 21 October 2000, pp 1410-1411.

14. Alex Boraine, *A Country Unmasked: Inside South Africa's Truth and Reconciliation Commission*, (Oxford, 2000), pp 47-75.

15. See, for example, Denis Carroll, *Unusual Suspects: Twelve Radical Clergy*, (Dublin, 1998), for a narrative hermeneutics of retrieval of some such unremembered protagonists of the 1798 Rising and an analysis of the Republican and Reformed Christian vision which inspired their revolutionary, boundary-crossing spirit. Carroll is a Roman Catholic theologian and historian. Terence McCaughey, a Presbyterian minister, historian and Irish scholar of note, likewise retrieved and promoted the reconciling memory of Jemmy Hope, a Co Antrim Presbyterian weaver who played a significant role in the Republican cause, inspired by his own Reformed faith and the originating ideals of the revolutionary movements in France and North America. Terence McCaughey's lectures on the subject in Dublin, Belfast and Templepatrick (in collaboration with such bodies as the Irish School of Ecumenics and the Reformed Presbyterian Church in Templepatrick drew enthusiastic audiences. To their credit, the Department of Foreign Affairs, Dublin and the European Union (through the Community Relations Council in Belfast) supported the latter and other similar initiatives on the reconciling of history, during these bicentenary commemorations.

16. Paul Tillich, *The Protestant Era*, (Abridged Edition), (Chicago, 1957), pp 94, 109-110. For a critical extension of Tillich's insight, see also, Gabriel Daly, *One Church – Two Indispensable Values – Protestant Principle and Catholic Substance*, Irish School of Ecumenics Occasional Papers, (Dublin, 1998).

17. Geraldine Smyth, 'Panellist's Response', in Colum Kenny, ed, *Imprisoned Within Structures? The Role of Believing Communities in Building Peace in Ireland (The Believers' Enquiry 1997/'98)*, (Glencree, 1998), pp 185-186.

18. Zygmunt Bauman, *Modernity and Ambivalence*, (Cambridge, 1991), pp 232-233.

19. Bauman, op cit, p 234.

20. Bauman, op cit, p 234.

21. Walter Brueggemann, 'The Legitimacy of a Sectarian Hermeneutic', in his *Interpretation and Obedience: From Faithful Reading to Faithful Living*, (Minneapolis, 1991), pp 41-69.

22. See Cecelia Clegg and Joseph Liechty, *Moving Beyond Sectarianism*, (Dublin, 2001), pp 195-198; John W De Gruchy and Charles Villa-Vicencio, eds., *Apartheid is a Heresy*, (Grand Rapids, 1983), offer a range of critical and self-critical theological perspectives from South Africa.

23. Vamik Volkan, op cit, pp 108-109.

24. Cf. Seán Moran, 'Patrick Pearse and Patriotic Soteriology: The Irish Republican Tradition and the Sanctification of Political Self-Immolation', in *The Irish Terrorism Experience*, ed, Yonah Alexander and Alan O'Day, (Dartmouth and Vermont, 1991).

25. Although the Gaelic Athletic Association finally voted in 2001 to end the exclusion rule against police and army members, significantly only one of the nine Ulster Counties of the GAA had voted in favour of the abolition of the now notorious Rule 21. For an internal call for reform, see, Peter Quinn's keynote address at the Parnell Summer School, 2002, 'The Irish Revival – Cultural Inheritance or Cultural Baggage?' in which he seeks to recover the association's anti-establishment tradition of boundary-crossing as culturally necessary today. (Quinn, as well as being a member of the GAA Review Committee, is a member of the Parades Commission in NI.) See 'GAA Urged to Find its Cultural, Radical Past', a review by Tim O'Brien, *Irish Times*, 13 Aug 2002, p 10. There was, however, no mention of Rule 21 in the review.

26. Garrett FitzGerald TD, 'Christian Hope in Europe's Future', unpublished lecture, 2000, p 21.

27. *Too Young to Notice? the Cultural and Political Awareness of 3-6 Year Olds in Northern Ireland*, Paul Connolly, Alan Smith and Berni Kelly, A Research Project commissioned by the Community Relations Council, Belfast and Channel 4, published by CRC, Belfast, 2002. The research concludes that even taking into account the negative factor of ghetto-ised housing, educational segregation along religious lines must in some degree be held accountable for the entrenching of prejudice and sectarian attitudes among even the under sixes. One must also take into account the impact on young children of arson attacks on schools, and the kind of intimidation of children and parents as witnessed at the Holy Cross School protests 2001-2002, without losing sight of the courageous pastoral leadership of clerics like Rev Norman Hamilton and Fr Aidan Troy, nor of teachers who do educate children in mutual respect and understanding in the face of political apathy and paramilitary threat. The significance of Anglican Archbishop Desmond Tutu's walking alongside the Catholic children in June 2001 prompted some to reflect on the lack of an analogous ecclesial exercise of solidarity across the boundary of identity. Imaginative educational materials for adolescents deriving from the Clegg and Liechty research (see above) have been developed by the Irish School of Ecumenics _ Yvonne Naylor, *Moving Beyond Sectarianism: a Resource for Young Adults*, (Dublin and Belfast, 2001); for the 9-13 age group, Naylor has also developed an education pack, *Who We Are – Dealing with Difference*, (Belfast and Dublin,

2003); also Craig Sands, *Moving Beyond Sectarianism: a Resource for Adult Education*, (Belfast and Dublin, 2001). The recently established, 'Schools' Mediation Project' in North Belfast, aimed at educating young people in community transformation, is an area partnership model that others could follow. This is a joint initiative of the Presbyterian and Roman Catholic clergy and four local schools and youth organisations under their management. Churches must find fresh ways of developing further such initiatives, as well as extending and integrating the work of the now well-established interchurch Youthlink organisation as a way of taking responsibility for the deep structural impact on young psyches of a segregation copper-fastened by religious sanction.

28. Duncan Morrow, Derek Birrell, John Greer and Terry O'Keeffe, *Churches and Inter-Community Relationships*, (Coleraine, 1991).

29. See, Garrett FitzGerald, *All in a Life: an Autobiography*, for some observation (and exemplariness) on the painstaking commitment to such social reform, including the need for understanding of the other's position, and of generosity in the process of achieving a reconciliation of deeply entrenched contested views on such social reform, p 201. One can only rejoice in the quality of Christian leadership in this regard, of Desmond Rea, the Methodist Chair of the new Policing Authority of Northern Ireland and of his Deputy Chair, Roman Catholic, Denis Bradley, and also at the encouraging comments from the churches in respect of the new reforms and their aim at greater inclusivity and security and human rights for all.

30. Cecelia Clegg and Joseph Liechty, op cit, especially chap 7, 'Redeeming Identity and Belonging'.

31. The work of Niklas Luhmann is enlightening in respect of the challenge to churches and religion to creatively live in an in-between space, holding both to engagement in its primary call to religious 'performance' (relating the primary vocation of the churches to inspire faith, and witness to transcendence), and at the same time to be capable of exercising a religious 'function' (relating to the counter-balancing mission of reaching into other functional spheres of society, such as politics or economics or education which possess their own particular autonomy and rules). Living the tension of the call to specifically religious living and the imperative on (Christian) religion to be publicly influential has become a fraught and highly complex exercise in the contemporary world. For an insight into some relevant aspects of Luhmann's work (much of it available only in German), see Peter Beyer, *Religion and Globalization*, (London, 1994), especially pp 75-96.

32. Fortwilliam Park Presbyterian Church in North Belfast has given a cross-community lead in opening its doors to Kansas Community Group (Catholic and nationalist in background), whose Community Youth Club and Women's Group use the Church Hall for their weekly activities. Collaborative activities may yet emerge.

33. By enabling participants to tell their stories in some artistic medium, people found themselves able, sometimes after nearly thirty years, to

break the silence. In this way, through the support of artists, writers and others gifted with the skill of writing or listening, hundreds of unheard stories were shared, relations of mutual support and solidarity were celebrated in a ritual way that empowered the tellers to cross a threshold of freedom, and awakened the consciousness of the wider public to something of the hidden suffering and hope in the lives of forgotten victims and survivors.

CHAPTER FIVE

1. This essay will focus exclusively on the relationship between the Catholic church and the state. The divorce debates also give an interesting insight into the relationship between the state and other Christian denominations. Unfortunately this is beyond the scope of this essay.

2. This figure varys from 57% to 63% in the various analyses of the time. I have taken this one from O'Leary and Hesketh 'The Irish Abortion and Divorce Referendum Campaigns', *Irish Political Studies*, 3, 1988, p 56, quoting a poll in the *Irish Times* of 5 May 1986.

3. Sheila Rauch Kennedy, *Shattered Faith*, (Dublin 1997).

4. *The Canon Law, Letter and Spirit*, Canon Law Society of Great Britain and Ireland, (Dublin, 1995), #1137. Canon law makes a distinction between a valid and a putative marriage (which is the status that most marriages that are subsequently regarded as invalid have). A putative marriage is one that is entered into in good faith by at least one party. Its principal effect is to make legitimate such children as may be born of or conceived during it. Even if at a later date a putative marriage is declared to have been in fact invalid, the children are and remain legitimate. Canon 1061.4. Thus the children from marriages that were putative and subsequently declared invalid through annulment are considered legitimate regardless of the status of the marriage of the parents.

5. Cf. *The Divorce Act in Practice*, edited by Shannon, (Dublin, 1999), p 2.

6. See for example the statements of various Church of Ireland bishops on the issue of divorce during the divorce debates of 1986 and 1995.

7. See for example Dermot Keogh, *Ireland and the Vatican, The Politics and Diplomacy of Church-State Relations 1922-1960*, (Cork, 1995).

8. In fact this remedy was withdrawn in 1925 in the Dáil, but was only copper-fastened constitutionally in 1937.

9. Patrick Hannon's *Church, State, Morality and Law*, (Dublin, 1992), provides a substantial discussion of this aspect of theology and highlights its importance in the context of church-state relations.

10. The forum was but one step in Garret FitzGerald's programme to try to persuade the Irish public to remove any laws that might lead people to regard the Irish state as sectarian.

11. Submission of Dr Cahal Daly, Bishop of Down and Connor, to the New Ireland Forum.

12. Submission of Dr Joseph Cassidy, Bishop of Clonfert and Media Spokesman for the Bishops' Conference, to the New Ireland Forum, p

11.

13. James Donahue, *Religion, Ethics and the Common Good*, (Mystic, CT, 1996), p x.

14. Submission of Dr Cahal Daly, Bishop of Down and Connor, to the New Ireland Forum, p 13.

15. For an excellent discussion of the changes in church teaching on many moral issues over the centuries see John Noonan, 'Development in Moral Doctrine', *Theological Studies*, Vol 54, 1993, pp 663-677. The discussion on marriage occurs on pp 663-4.

16. Ibid., p 663.

17. Ibid., for a full explanation of the circumstances of the case.

18. Submission of Dr Dermot O' Mahoney, Auxiliary Bishop of Dublin, to the New Ireland Forum, p 24.

19. This is a summary of Kevin Kelly's discussion of the significance of scripture in arguments about the indissolubility of marriage in 'Divorce and Remarriage', *Christian Ethics An Introduction*, ed., Bernard Hoose, (London, 1998), pp 248-265.

20. Church of England General Synod Marriage Commission, *Marriage and the Church's Task* (London, 1978), n 100, quoted in Kelly's 'Divorce and Remarriage', op cit, p 255.

21. Ibid., p 255.

22. Herbert Doms, *The Meaning of Marriage*, (New York, 1939, published in German in 1935).

23. This issue figured prominently in the divorce debates and gives an insight into many issues including the significance of property, the economic dependence of some women, the representations of gender in the media etc. However it is not something that has been explored in this essay. This is because although central to understanding the divorce debates, it is slightly tangential to the relationship between church and state.

24. Tom Inglis, *Moral Monopoly: The Rise and Fall of the Catholic Church in Modern Ireland*, Second Edition, (Dublin, 1998), p 223, quoting *Irish Times*, 27 November 1995.

CHAPTER SIX

1. See Fitzgerald, Garret, *Towards a New Ireland*, (London 1972), chapter 5; Whyte, J. H., *Church and State in Modern Ireland, 1923-1979*, Second Edition, (Dublin 1980), esp. chapter 13. See also Lee, J. J., *Ireland 1912-1985: Politics and Society*, (Cambridge, 1989); Keogh, Dermot, *Twentieth-Century Ireland: Nation and State*, New Gill History of Ireland 6, (Dublin 1994).

2. *The Irish Reports*, 1974, p 322.

3. Whyte, *Church and State*, p 405.

4. In the Health (Family Planning) (Amendment) Act 1993.

5. An excellent summary, with statute and case references, of the law on abortion in Ireland, is available in the Government Green Paper on

Abortion, published by the Stationery Office and available from Government Publications Sale Office, Dublin.

6. Green Paper, p 29. A similar decision was given in 1997 in what became known as the C case; see Green Paper, p 32.

7. The relevant extract is in the Green Paper, Appendix 5.

8. *An Age of Innocence: Irish Culture 1930-1960,* (Dublin, 1998), p 189.

9. Fitzgerald, *Towards a New Ireland*, p 93.

10. Some account of Christian attitudes generally, and of their roots in Judaism, is found in Noonan, John T. Jr., *Contraception: A History of its Treatment by the Catholic Theologians and Canonists*, Enlarged Edition, (Cambridge, Mass. and London 1986).

11. See Whyte, *Church and State*, p 433.

12. Key documents are *Lumen Gentium* and *Gaudium et Spes* (Pastoral Constitution on the Church in the Modern World). See also the Declaration on Religious Freedom and the Declaration on the Relation of the Church to Non-Christian Religions, and the Decrees on Ecumenism and on the Apostolate of Lay People. English tr. in Flannery, A., ed., *Vatican Council II: Constitutions, Decrees, Declarations*, (Dublin, 1996).

13. The Conference's interventions are analysed more fully in Hannon, Patrick, *Church, State, Morality and Law*, (Dublin 1992); 'A Public Church', *The Furrow* 43 (1992), pp 10-14.

14. The reference to paragraph 73 arises because that paragraph says that 'In the case of an intrinsically unjust law, such as a law permitting abortion or euthanasia, it is therefore never licit to obey it, or to take part in a propaganda campaign in favour of such a law, or vote for it.' But it also says that an elected official (and in a referendum no doubt the voter) 'could licitly support proposals aimed at limiting the harm done by such a law and at lessening its negative consequences at the level of general opinion and public morality'.

CHAPTER SEVEN

1. Extract from the 14th Report of the Commissioners of the Board of Education Ireland, 1812, in Áine Hyland and Kenneth Milne, eds., *Irish Educational Documents*, Vol I, (Dublin, 1987), pp 64, 65.

2. Akenson, Donald H., *The Irish Education Experiment*, (London, 1970), p 223; see also John Coolahan, 'Primary Education as a Political Issue' in M. R. O'Connell, ed., *Education, Church and State*, (Dublin, 1992), pp 87-100.

3. Pastoral Quoted in *The Irish Teachers' Journal*, 6 October 1900, p 4.

4. Norman, E. R., *The Catholic Church and Ireland in the Age of Rebellion, 1859-73*, (London, 1965), p 59.

5. Quoted by O'Rahilly, Alfred, 'The Irish University Question VII – Secondary Education', *Studies*, LI, 1962, pp 147-155.

6. Coolahan, John, 'The Education Bill of 1919-20 – Problems of Educational Reform', *Proceedings of the Educational Studies Association of Ireland*, 1979, pp 11-31.

7. Reported in *The Times Educational Supplement*, 29 October 1921, p 323.

8. MacNeill, Eoin, 'Education – The Idea of the State', *Irish Review*, II, November, 1922, pp 28, 29.

9. Quoted in Mescal, John, *Religion in the Irish System of Education*, (Dublin, 1957), pp 56, 100.

10. *Report of the Department of Education for 1924-25*, (Dublin, 1926), p 7.

11. Letter from O'Sullivan, J. M., Minister for Education, to Most Rev Dr Keane, Bishop of Limerick, 31 October 1930.

12. *Divini Illius Magistri*, 31 December 1929, in *Papal Teachings: Education*, St Pauls Editions, 1960, pp 200-248.

13. Quoted by Akenson, D. H., *A Mirror to Kathleen's Face: Education in Independent Ireland, 1922-60*, p 137.

14. Corcoron, Rev T., *The Catholic Schools of Ireland*, (Louvain, 1931), p 6.

15. Council of Education, *Terms of Reference and Address of the Minister for Education and of the Chairman*, (Dublin, 1950), p 18.

16. Akenson, D. H., *A Mirror to Kathleen's Face*, op cit; Brian Titley, *Church, State and the Control of Schooling in Ireland, 1900-44*, (Dublin, 1983); Séamus Ó Buachalla, *Education Policy in Twentieth Century Ireland*, (Dublin, 1988); Tom A. O'Donoghue, *The Catholic Church and the Secondary School Curriculum in Ireland, 1922-62*, (New York, 1999).

17. Whyte, John H., *Church and State in Modern Education, 1923-1970*, (Dublin, 1970), p 21.

18. Ó Buachalla, Séamus, *Education Policy in Twentieth Century Ireland*, (Dublin, 1988), p 221.

19. Ibid., p 249.

20. CORI, *Religious Congregations in Irish Education: A Role for the Future?* (Dublin, 1997), p 15.

21. Randles, Eileen, *Post-Primary Education in Ireland, 1957-70*, (Dublin, 1975).

22. O'Connor, Seán, 'Post-Primary Education: Now and in the Future', *Studies*, Autumn 1968, Vol LVII, No 227, pp 233-249, p 249.

23. *Studies*, 1968, LVII, p 282.

24. Ó Buachalla, op cit, pp 233-234.

25. Akenson, *A Mirror to Kathleen's Face*, p 148, and Richard Breen *et al*, *Understanding Contemporary Ireland*, (Dublin, 1990), p 138.

26. Hyland, Áine, 'Irish Experiments in Sharing in Education: Educate Together', in *Pluralism in Education Conference Proceedings*, 1996, pp 237-244, p 243, and Jim Cooke, *Marley Grange Multi-denominational School Challenge, 1973-78*, (Dublin, 1997). See, for instance, Christian Brother Network of Schools, *Towards an Identity and a Contribution: Final Report*, (Dublin, 2001).

27. Coolahan, John, 'Regionalisation of Education: A Recurrent Concern', *John Marcus O'Sullivan Seminar Proceedings*, (Tralee, 1986).

28. Walshe, John, *A New Partnership in Education*, (Dublin, 1999), p 84.

29. Quoted in John Walshe, op cit, p 107.

30. The Christian Brothers Network of Schools, *Towards an Identity and a*

Contribution, (Dublin, 2001), p 5.

31. CORI Education Commission, *Religious Congregations in Irish Education: A Role for the Future?*, (Dublin, 1997 and 2001), p 28.

32. Ibid., p 27.

33. Ibid., p 48.

34. Coolahan, John, ed., *Report On The National Education Convention*, (Dublin, 1994), p 31.

35. Ibid., p 33.

36. Ibid., p 33

37. White Paper, *Charting Our Education Future*, (Dublin, 1995), p 24.

38. *The Irish Times*, 28 September 2002.

39. McCormack, Teresa, 'Future Directions for Trusteeship', in Catherine Furlong and Luke Monahan, eds., *School Culture: Cracking the Code*, (Dublin, 2000), pp 151-162, p 159.

40. Lane, Dermot A., 'The Expanding Horizons of Catholic Education', in Pádraig Hogan and Kevin Williams, eds., *The Future of Religion in Irish Education*, (Dublin, 1997), pp 128-137, p 137.

41. Ibid., p 130.

42. Ibid., p 137.

43. *The Irish Times*, 28 September 2002.

CHAPTER EIGHT

1. The rather rigid and hierarchical nurse training programmes developed in the nineteenth century survived with minimal changes until the present time. See the *Report of the Commission on Nursing: A Blueprint for the Future*, (Dublin, 1998).

2. Ruth Barrington, *Health, Medicine and Politics in Ireland 1900-1970*, (Dublin, 1987) pp 39-66.

3. Ibid., p 109.

4. Ibid., p 144.

5. See John Whyte, *Church and State in Modern Ireland*, second edition (Dublin, 1980) and John Cooney, *John Charles McQuaid: Ruler of Catholic Ireland*, (Dublin, 1999).

6. Ruth Barrington, op cit, pp 161-2.

7. See John Horgan, *Noel Browne: Passionate Outsider*, (Dublin, 2000).

8 See Alan Elliott, *Curing and Caring: Reflections on fifty years of health and personal social services in Northern Ireland*, (Belfast, 1998).

CHAPTER NINE

1. Cultural diagnoses speak of 'posthumanism' or of the 'crisis' or 'end of humanism'. There has rarely been less agreement on what it is to be human. The 'end of the great narratives' (Jean-François Lyotard) of Christianity, Marxism, Existentialism and other encompassing systems of orientation that provided resources of meaning by their hopes of salvation, emancipation, or authentic existence, has now reached the concept of the human itself. Both in postmodern philosophies and in

domain-specific ethics, it is controversial whether there can or should be any reference to the human person. Intellectually, it is an idea that can be historicised as an invention of the eighteenth century (Michel Foucault). Thus, the Enlightenment has joined the fate of Antiquity and the Middle Ages: its humanism now looks no less dated than the pre-modern essentialism and teleology from which it took over.

The post-humanistic convictions of the biosciences arise on a practical level. Their question is, 'Why should we be limited by former ideas of being human if we hold in our hands the power to change the genetic foundations of human life?' Thus, the concept of being human can be said to be eroded 'from the inside and from the outside' (Dietmar Mieth). I would like to show how the resources of a Christian view of the human person could help restore the contested notion of the human subject.

2. Cf. L. Siep, 'Zwei Formen der Ethik' (NRW Akademie der Wissenschaften Vorträge G 347) (Opladen, 1997), pp 19-20. All translations from German originals are my own.

3. D. Mieth, *Die Diktatur der Gene. Biotechnik zwischen Machbarkeit und Menschenwürde* (Freiburg, 2001), e.g. pp 17, 37.

4. D. Mieth, *Diktatur der Gene*, p 42.

5. Cf. K. Bayertz, 'Das Ethos der Wissenschaften und die Moral' and L. Siep, 'Wissenschaftsethos und philosophische Ethik', in L. Siep, ed., *Ethik als Anspruch an die Wissenschaft oder: Ethik in der Wissenschaft* (Freiburg, 1988), pp 9-20 and pp 21-33.

6. D. Mieth, *Diktatur der Gene*, p 42: 'A minimal consensus can be the starting point of international contracts. Yet this is too little for the process of reaching agreement on basic rights in the European Union. The law is not to confirm but to control the power of interests. Consensus formation should therefore orient itself by the maximum of basic rights that is necessary to allow all human beings to participate.' Cf. D. Mieth, *Was wollen wir können? Ethik im Zeitalter der Biotechnik* (Freiburg, 2002), pp 369-70. 'Then conflicts of values result in so-called minimal consensus, in pragmatic conventions and in the agreement on procedures of evaluation, since one cannot find agreement on the evaluation itself.'

7. A. Buchanan, D. W. Brock, N. Daniels, D. Wikler, *From Chance to Choice. Genetics and Justice* (Cambridge, 2000), p 25.

8. J. Rawls's two principles of justice in *A Theory of Justice* (Cambridge, Mass, 1971), pp 15, 302, are, '1. Each person is to have an equal right to the most extensive total system of equal basic liberties compatible with a similar system of liberty for all. 2. Social and economic inequalities, for example inequalities of wealth and authority, are just only if they result in compensating benefits for everyone, and in particular for the least advantaged members of society.' The final formulation of the second principle of justice is: 'Social and economic inequalities are to be arranged so that they are both: (a) to the greatest benefit of the least ad-

vantaged, consistent with the just savings principle, and (b) attached to offices and positions open to all under conditions of fair equality of opportunity.'

9. Cf L. Siep, 'Moral und Gattungsethik', *Deutsche Zeitschrift f. Philosophie* 50 (2002), pp 111-120, p 113, n 5.

10. Cf F. Schüssler Fiorenza, 'The Works of Mercy: Theological Perspectives,' *The Works of Mercy: New Perspectives on Ministry*, ed., F. A. Eigo (Philadelphia, 1992), pp 31–71.

11. Buchanan et al., *From Chance to Choice*, p 102: 'acknowledging that the domain of justice extends in principle to natural as well as social assets does not commit us to efforts to achieve "genetic equality" – at least not for the foreseeable future.' The reasons for this restriction are respect for pluralism in which different features are deemed desirable, and the danger that measures to achieve blanket genetic equality could reduce diversity, and flexibility.

12. A. Buchanan et al., *From Chance to Choice*, p 101.

13. A. Buchanan et al., *From Chance to Choice*, pp 101-02. The lack of clarity is not helped by the express requirement that 'competent individuals' should be able to consent to the measures suggested. Why is it necessary to state this, if the point was to provide equal access for those who wish to avail of such a state service? The authors do not seem to trust the institutions to respect the line between a free offer and a state-enforced eugenics programme:

'Due to value pluralism, in many cases there will be a lack of a rational consensus about what counts as a valuable genetically influenced trait, since in a liberal society there are and will continue to be deep differences among individuals and communities about the character of "the good life". Consequently, a reasonable public policy must proceed in a conservative manner, focusing on efforts to avoid what are clearly deprivations ... There is, of course, another extremely important qualification on our thesis that equality of opportunity will sometimes require genetic interventions and that the required interventions may not always be limited to the cure or prevention of disease. Interventions to remove barriers to an individual's opportunities should not be forced on that individual if he or she is competent and does not consent to the interventions.'

14. Cf S. Graumann, 'Experts on Philosophical Reflection in Public Discourse – the German Sloterdijk Debate' in *Biomedical Ethics* 5 (2000) pp 27-33.

15. A. Buchanan et al., *From Chance to Choice*, p 171.

16. Cf A. Buchanan et al., *From Chance to Choice*, pp 100-101.

17. L. Siep, 'Genomanalyse, menschliches Selbstverständnis und Ethik,' *Was wissen wir, wenn wir das menschliche Genom kennen?* eds. Honnefelder, L., Propping, P. (Köln, 2001), pp 196-205, 203: 'With regard to goals for the future, it should be the subject of public discussion how good it is for the human person to measure her natural "start conditions" solely by the scope of possible self-projects, and maybe try to

optimise them. Genetic and cultural fate, unless it predisposes to misery or severe illnesses, does not have to be a barrier (*Fessel*) for wishes and plans. This fate can also lead to meaningful tasks and experiences of value, which we could not have invented or dreamt of better ourselves.'

18. Cf A. Buchanan et al., *From Chance to Choice*, p 336.
19. L. Siep, 'Moral und Gattungsethik', p 112.
20. J. Habermas, *Zur Zukunft der menschlichen Natur. Auf dem Weg zu einer liberalen Eugenik?* (Frankfurt, 2001), pp 109-10. ET, *The Future of Human Nature* (Cambridge, 2003).
21. Cf D. Birnbacher, 'Habermas' ehrgeiziges Beweisziel – erreicht oder verfehlt?', *Deutsche Zeitschrift für Philosophie* 50 (2002), pp.121-126, 121-22.
22. Cf L. Siep, 'Moral und Gattungsethik', pp 112-13.
23. Cf D. Birnbacher, 'Habermas' ehrgeiziges Beweisziel', p 124.
24. Habermas observes that the authors only sense danger from 'communitarian' or state-led measures, but curiously enough, not from liberal eugenics (*Zukunft der menschlichen Natur*, p 106, n 64). One more curiosity is that 'communitarian' often seems to stand for extremist political and religious groups.
25. L. Siep, *Zwei Formen der Ethik*, p 13.
26. S. Benhabib, *Situating the Self: Gender, Community, and Postmodernism in Contemporary Ethics* (Cambridge, 1992), pp 74-5.
27. O. Höffe, *Ethik und Politik* (Frankfurt, 1979), p 221.
28. P. Ricoeur, 'On John Rawls' A Theory of Justice: Is a pure procedural theory of justice possible?' (1990), repr. in Henry S. Richardson, Paul Weithman, eds., *The Philosophy of Rawls*, Vol 1 (New York, 1999), pp 133-44.
29. O. Höffe, *Ethik und Politik*, pp 219, 225. See also O. O'Neill's critique: 'The entire device of the original position is instituted in order to baffle the unfortunate results of imputed rational self-interest.' *Towards Justice and Virtue* (Cambridge, 1996), p 47.
30. Cf O. Höffe, ed., *Über John Rawls' Theorie der Gerechtigkeit* (Frankfurt, 1977).
31. Cf S. Andersen, *Einführung in die Ethik* (Berlin, 2000), p 315.
32. Review 'Angewandte Ethik,' *Information Philosophie* 30 (2002), pp 84-88, 88.
33. J.P. Wils, '*Sensus communis* – ein 'Vermögen'? Quasi-anthropologische und hermeneutische Aspekte in John Rawls' Sozialethik', *Freiburger Zeitschrift f. Theologie und Philosophie* 48 (2001), pp 432-454.
34. Against, e.g. A. MacIntyre's claim of Aristotle for a particularist position, O. Höffe points him out as a universalist in his anthropology, ethics, and politics: 'Warum soll man heute (noch) Aristoteles lesen?' *Information Philosophie* 30 (2002), pp 7-21, 20-21.
35. The principle that 'every embryo is a future child of his or her parents' (Margot v. Renesse, SPD, Chairperson of the Genetics Enquete Commission of the German Parliament) has already been endangered

by the Irish units opting for embryonic instead of 'pronuclear' freezing. By allowing freezing only at the stage prior to the fusion of the genetic material from both sperm and egg that results in a genetically unique and sexually individualised embryo around hour 18 after fertilisation, Germany is respecting the status of the embryo as a person in keeping with its Constitution and the Embryo Protection Act of 1990. What are the implications of Irish hospitals having followed the British practice instead? Will Ireland also adopt the British five-year-deadline after which embryos are discarded or become 'spare' embryos on which one may experiment up to day 14? Will embryonic as opposed to adult stem cell research be concluded to be unproblematic as well? It will not be possible in the future to go on avoiding the debate about which practices in assisted reproduction and genetic research respect or violate the status of the embryo.

36. D. Mieth, *Diktatur der Gene*, p 58. In Rawls's list of 'primary goods' that features income and self-esteem besides rights and liberties as universal conditions of life plans, human dignity is conspicuously absent. Cf Höffe's critique of the mixing of empirical and rational preconditions in this list in *Ethik und Politik*, pp 216-18.

37. F. Schüssler Fiorenza, 'The Church as a Community of Interpretation: Political Theology between Discourse Ethics and Hermeneutical Reconstruction,' *Habermas, Modernity and Public Theology*, eds. D. Browning, F. Schüssler Fiorenza (New York, 1992), pp 66-91.

38. For a brief summary of this approach to Christian ethics, 'Autonomous morality in a Christian context', see D. Mieth, *Was wollen wir können*, p 464.

39. Both Beinert and Sullivan stress that the magisterium is subordinate to the Word of God, that it does not have a separate source of insight, and that it needs to go back to the faith of the entire church to formulate binding statements. Cf arts 'Ecclesial Magisterium' (pp 194-199), 'Reception' (pp 569-571), and 'Sensus fidelium' (pp 655-657), all by W. Beinert, in *Handbook of Catholic Theology*, eds. Beinert, W., Fiorenza, F.S. (New York, 1995): 'Vatican II integrates the doctrinal authority of the pope into the context of the self-realisation of the entire church. Infallible doctrinal authority is attributed to the totality of all the faithful (*Lumen Gentium* 12), to the council of bishops with the pope, as well as to the pope alone (*LG* 25); yet this doctrinal authority always remains subordinate to the word of God (*Dei Verbum* 10).' (p 195). 'To the extent that the magisterium does not establish the faith but preserves and communicates it as handed down by the community, it is subordinate to the *sensus fidelium*; to the extent, on the other hand, that the magisterium possesses its own apostolic commission to provide authentic interpretation and issue final decisions in matters of faith, it takes precendence over the *sensus fidelium* and ranks higher. Moreover, the presence of the truth and grace of Christ manifests itself not only in the *sen-*

sus fidelium and the magisterium but also in Sacred Scripture, tradition and theology; the *sensus fidelium* is therefore always related to these *loci'* (pp 656-7).
Francis A. Sullivan points out that even Vatican I's controversial declaration of papal infallibility 'did not, and could not, rule out a real dependence of papal definitions on the faith of the church. For the pope can define as a dogma of faith only what is contained in the deposit of revelation, which has been entrusted to the church' (*DV* 10) and is 'handed on in her teaching, life and worship' (*DV* 8). Since the pope has no independent source of revelation, he cannot define a dogma of faith without having in some real way consulted the faith of the church.' Art. 'Magisterium', *The New Dictionary of Theology*, ed. J. Komonchak, M. Collins, D. Lane (Wilmington, 1989), pp 617-623, 621.
40. Cf Vincent MacNamara, *Faith and Ethics. Recent Roman Catholicism* (Dublin, 1985).
41. D. Mieth, *Moral und Erfahrung. Beiträge zur theologisch-ethischen Hermeneutik* (Freiburg,1977), p 6.
42. *Faktizität und Geltung* (Frankfurt, 1992) is the original German title of *Between Facts and Norms* (trans. W. Rehg) (Cambridge, 1997).
43. J. Habermas, *Glauben und Wissen. Friedenspreis des Deutschen Buchhandels 2001* (Frankfurt, 2001), p 25.
44. Hans Joas, *The Genesis of Values* (Cambridge, 2000), pp 5. 1.
45. Cf with reference to F. Schleiermacher, D. Mieth, 'Bioethics, Biopolitics, Theology', in *Designing Life? Genetics, Procreation, and Ethics*, ed. M. Junker-Kenny (Ashgate, 1999) pp 6-22, 18.
46. Paul Ricoeur, 'The Difficulty to Forgive', *Memory, Narrativity, Self, and the Challenge to Think God*, ed. M. Junker-Kenny (Münster, 2003) (forthcoming).

CHAPTER TEN

References and some other relevant bibliography:
Agenda 21, *The Earth Summit's Agenda for Change*, Michael Keating, (Geneva, 1993).
Brueggemann, *The Prophetic Imagination*, Fortress Press, 1978.
Callan, T., B. Nolan, B. Whelan, C. Whelan and J. Williams, *Poverty in the 1990s*, (Dublin, 1996).
CARA Network, *Housing in Ireland: Village, Town and City*, (Dublin, 1992).
Clark, C. M. A. and C. Kavanagh, 'Basic Income and the Irish Worker' in Reynolds B. and S. Healy, *An Adequate Income Guarantee for All: Desirability, Viability, Impact*, (Dublin, 1995).
Clark, C. M. A. and J. Healy, *Pathways to a Basic Income*, (Dublin, 1997).
Collins, M. L. and C. Kavanagh, 'For Richer, For Poorer: The Changing Distribution of Household Income in Ireland, 1973–94', in Healy, S. and B. Reynolds, *Social Policy in Ireland: Principles, Practice and Problems*, (Dublin, 1998).

CORI Justice Commission, *Priorities for Progress: Towards a Fairer Future*, (Dublin: 1998).

CORI Justice Commission, *Prosperity and Exclusion: Towards a New Social Contract*, (Dublin: 2000).

Curran, E., 'Absolute Moral Norms in Christian Ethics' in *Christian Ethics: An Introduction*, Bernard Hoose, ed., (London, 1998).

Curtin, C., T. Haase and H. Tovey, *Poverty in Rural Ireland: A Political Economy Perspective*, (Dublin, 1996).

Eurostat, *Expenditure on Social Protection*, (Luxembourg, 2001)

Fahey, Tony, *Housing and Social Cohesion: Making Local Authority Housing Effective*, John Blackwell Memorial Lecture, Housing Institute of Ireland, 1998.

Focus Ireland, *Housing waiting list Survey 2001*, (Dublin, 2002).

Galbraith, J. K., *The Culture of Contentment*, Sinclair-Stevenson.

Gray, A. W., *International Perspectives on the Irish Economy*, (Dublin, 1997).

Healy S. and Reynolds B., 'Work for All: Why and How in a World of Rapid Change', Paper delivered at the Conference on *Work as Key to the Social Question*, New Synod Hall, Vatican City, September 13, 2001.

Healy, S. and Reynolds B., 'Towards a New Vision of Social Partnership: Values, Content, Process and Structure' in B. Reynolds and S. Healy, eds., *Social Partnership in a New Century*, (Dublin: 1999b).

Healy S. and Reynolds B., 'Progress, Paradigms and Policy', in Healy, S. and B. Reynolds, eds., *Social Policy in Ireland: Principles, Practice and Problems*, (Dublin, 1998).

Healy S. and Reynolds B., eds. *Social Policy in Ireland: Principles Practice and Problems*, (Dublin, 1998).

Healy S. and Reynolds B., *Irish Society and the Future of Education*, (Dublin, 1986).

Healy S. and Reynolds B., *Ireland Today: Reflecting in the Light of the Gospel*, (Dublin, 1985).

Healy S. and Reynolds B., *Social Analysis in the Light of the Gospel*, (Dublin, 1983).

Interaction Council, *In Search of Global Ethical Standards*, Vancouver, Interaction Council, 1996.

Layte, R., Maitre, B., Nolan, B., Watson, W., Whelan, C. T., Williams, J. and Casey, B., *Monitoring Poverty Trends and Exploring Poverty Dynamics in Ireland*, (Dublin, 2001).

Mkandawire, T and V Rodriguez, *Globalization and Social Development after Copenhagen: Premises, Promises and Policies*, Geneva 2000 Occasional Paper 10, (Geneva, 2000).

National Action Plan against Poverty and Social Exclusion, (Dublin, 2001).

National Anti-Poverty Strategy, *Sharing in Progress*, (Dublin, 1997).

National Economic and Social Council, *Opportunities, Challenges and Capacities for Choice*, (Dublin, 2000).

National Economic and Social Council, *Strategy into the 21st Century*,

(Dublin, 1996).

Nolan, B., *Child Poverty in Ireland*, (Dublin, 2000).

O'Connell, D., *Conversation: A Way to Justice*, Unpublished paper.

O'Donnell, R., *The Future of Social Partnership in Ireland: A discussion paper prepared for the National Competitiveness Council*, (Dublin, 2001).

O'Donnell, R., *Ireland's Economic Transformation*, University of Pittsburgh Centre for West European Studies, 1998.

O'Hara, P. and P. Commins, 'Rural Development: Towards the New Century', in S. Healy and B. Reynolds (1998), *Social Policy in Ireland: Principles, Practice and Problems*, (Dublin, 1998), pp 261-283.

Partnership 2000 for Inclusion, Employment and Competitiveness, (Dublin, 1996).

Powell, F. and D. K. L. Guerin, *Civil Society and Social Policy*, (Dublin: 1997).

Programme for Prosperity and Fairness, (Dublin, 2000).

Programme for Prosperity and Fairness (2001), *Final Report of the Social Welfare Benchmarking and Indexation Group*, (Dublin, 2001).

Report of the Expert Working Group on the Integration of the Tax and Social Welfare Systems, (Dublin, 1996).

Reynolds B. and Healy, S. eds., *Participation and Democracy: Opportunities and Challenges*, (Dublin, 2000a), (includes chapter by the editors)

Reynolds B. and Healy, S. eds., *Towards A Fuller Future: Developing Social, Economic and Cultural Rights*, (Dublin, 2000b).

Reynolds B. and Healy, S. eds., *Social Partnership in a New Century*, (Dublin, 1999a).

Reynolds B. and Healy, S. eds., *Progress, Values and Public Policy*, (Dublin, 1996), (includes chapter by the editors)

Reynolds B. and Healy, S. eds., *An Adequate Income Guarantee For All: Desireability, Viability, Impact*, (Dublin, 1995), (includes chapter by the editors)

Reynolds B. and Healy, S. eds., *Towards An Adequate Income For All*, (Dublin, 1994), (includes chapter by the editors)

Reynolds B. and Healy, S. eds., *New Frontiers for Full Citizenship*, (Dublin: 1993), (includes chapter by the editors)

Reynolds B. and Healy, S. eds., *Power, Participation and Exclusion*, (Dublin, 1992), (includes chapter by the editors)

Reynolds B. and Healy S. eds., *Development Policy: What Future for Rural Ireland?*, (Dublin, 1991), (includes chapter by the editors)

Reynolds B. and Healy S. eds., *Work, Unemployment and Job-Creation Policy*, (Dublin, 1990), (includes chapter by the editors)

Reynolds B. and Healy S. eds., *Poverty and Taxation Policy*, (Dublin, 1989), (includes chapter by the editors)

Reynolds B. and Healy S. eds., *Poverty and Family Income Policy*, (Dublin, 1988), (includes chapter by the editors)

Robertson, J., *The New Economics of Sustainable Development*, Report to the European Commission, (Brussels, 1997).

Robertson, J., *Benefits and Taxes: A Radical Strategy*, (London: 1994).

Robertson, J., *The Sane Alternative: A Choice of Futures*, (1983).

Task Force on the Travelling Community, *Final Report*, (Dublin, 1995).

United Nations Development Program, *Human Development Report – 2001*, (New York, 2001).

Vincentian Partnership for Social Justice, *One Long Struggle, a study of low income families*, (Dublin, 2001).

Waltzer, M, *Spheres of Justice. A Defense of Pluralism and Equality*, (Oxford, 1983).

Williams J. and O'Connor, M., *Counted In: The Report of the 1999 Assessment of Homelessness in Dublin, Kildare and Wicklow*, (Dublin, 1999).

Wogaman, J. P., *Economics and Ethics: A Christian Enquiry*, (London, 1986).

Wuthnow, R., *Communities of Discourse: Ideology and Social Structure in the Reformation, the Enlightenment, and European Socialism*, (Cambridge, Mass., 1989).

CHAPTER ELEVEN

1. *Research Project into Aspects of the religious life of Refugees, Asylum Seekers and Immigrants in the Republic of Ireland*, Irish Council of Churches, 2002 (unpublished).

2. *Refugees and Asylum Seekers – A Challenge to Solidarity, Trócaire and ICJP, 1997*. This paper was updated in March 2002 and was reprinted together with the text of five statements on Asylum and Refugee Issues published by the Irish Bishops' Committee on Asylum Seekers and Refugees, 1999-2001.

3. Among the first initiatives were the Vincentian Refugee Centre, SPI-RASI (established by the Spiritan community), and the Franciscan Justice Initiative, which focuses on immigrants and asylum seekers from Russia and other Eastern European countries.

4. *What The Bible Says About the Stranger: Biblical Perspectives on Racism, Immigrants, Asylum and Cross-Community Issues*, Fr Kieran O'Mahony OSA, Church's Peace Education Programme of the ICJP and the Irish Council of Churches, 1999.

5. *Refugees and Asylum Seekers – A Challenge to Solidarity*, ICJP/Trócaire, 2002, pp 51-101.

6. Core income covers money given by the Irish public to support the work of Trócaire but excludes special appeals, for instance for the crises in Afghanistan and Iraq.

7. For example, before the Salvadorean Peace Accords were signed in 1992 over 180 of Trócaire's partners had been murdered or had lost their lives in El Salvador

8. See *People, Power and Participation*, Trócaire Development Review (Dublin, 1998).

9. Interestingly, the Report of the Review Committee on Ireland Aid

(March 2002) notes, 'The historical roots of the Ireland Aid programme [*the Irish government's official aid programme*] lie in the remarkable work, which has been carried out over many years by Irish missionaries. In many respects, this work has provided a template for the development of Ireland Aid. It has also created a readiness on the part of the Irish public to show generosity to the poor and the disadvantaged and to accept the responsibilities which Ireland has as a state towards the developing world' (paragraph 9.1).

10. Excerpt from the joint Pastoral Letter entitled *Bishops of Ireland on Development* which marked the launch of Trócaire on 2 February, 1973.

11. *Trócaire 25 Declaration*, paragraph 1, Trócaire Development Review 1998, page 8.

12. *The Rough Guide to the Common Agricultural Policy (CAP)*, Catholic Agency for Overseas Development, www.cafod.org.

13. Ibid, *Bishops of Ireland*, 1973.

14. CIDSE (International Co-operation for Development and Solidarity) is a network of 15 Catholic development organisations in Europe and North America. Caritas Internationalis is a network of 154 national relief, development and social service organisations in 198 countries and territories. These networks co-operate on development and emergency programmes, and are increasingly undertaking joint national and international advocacy and lobbying work on key global policy issues.

15. See www.foreignaffairs.com

16. The overseas aid/GNP ratio was 0.41 per cent in 2002. Aid expenditure amounted to €422 million.

17. For an analysis of the role played by Ireland in the first year of its two year tenure on the UN Security Council (2001/2) in relation to the situation in Afghanistan see Karen Kenny, *Ireland, the Security Council and Afghanistan: Promoting or Undermining the International Rule of Law?* Trócaire Development Review, pp 101-128.

18. *The Fight for Tolerance*, Madeline Bunting, the Guardian newspaper, 20 January 2003.

19. *Integrating NGO Peace and Development Strategies – Lessons from the Philippines*, Sarah McCan, Trócaire Development Review 2000, pp 111-128.

20. *People, Power and Participation*, Keynote Address, *Human Rights beyond the Millennium*, Dr Barney Pityana, Trócaire Development Review 1998, pp 21-33.

21. Criteria for becoming a pro-poor advocacy institution taken from a recent study on rights and livelihoods by ODI/CAPE

22. See *Re-Righting the Constitution: the Case for New Economic and Social Rights – Health, Housing, Adequate Nutrition, an Adequate Standard of Living*, (Dublin, 1998).

CHAPTER TWELVE

1. Garret Fitzgerald, *All in a Life: An Autobiography*, (Dublin, 1991), p 66.

2. Published in *Liberation Theology: An Irish Dialogue*, edited by Dermot A. Lane, (Dublin, 1977), pp 67-86.

3. Ibid., pp 68, 74.

4. Austin Flannery, 'The Priest in Politics', *Questioning Ireland: Debates in Political Philosophy and Public Policy*, edited by Joseph Dunne, Attracta Ingram and Frank Litton, (Dublin, 2000), p 242.

5. *Pastoral Constitution on the Church in the Modern World* (1965), a. 1-5, *Vatican Council II: Constitutions, Decrees, Declarations*, ed. Austin Flannery, Revised Translation in Inclusive Language, (Dublin, 1996).

6. *Dogmatic Constitution on Divine Revelation* (1965), a. 8 and 14; *Pastoral Constitution on the Church in the Modern World*, a.33.

7. *Pastoral Constitution on the Church in the Modern World*, a. 4 and 5.

8. *Dogmatic Constitution on the Church* (1964), a. 23; *Declaration on Religious Liberty* (1965), a. 1 and 2.

9. *Dogmatic Constitution on Divine Revelation*, a.4 and 6.

10. *Decree on the Apostolate of Lay People* (1965), a. 5.

11. *Pastoral Constitution on the Church in the Modern World*, a. 4.

12. Ibid., a. 31.

13. *Social Problems (Octogesima adveniens)*, (London, 1971), a. 4.

14. For a fuller analysis of *Octogesimo adveniens* see Mary Elsbernd, 'Whatever Happened to *Octogesimo adveniens?*', *Theological Studies*, 56 (March 1995) 1, pp 39-60.

15. *Social Problems (Octogesima adveniens)*, a. 22.

16. 1971 Synod of Bishops, *Justice in the World*, (Vatican, 1971), p 6.

17. Ibid., p 14.

18. Ibid., p 17.

19. '32nd General Congregation' (1975), *Documents of the 31st and 32nd General Congregations of the Society of Jesus*, ed. By John W. Padberg, (St Louis, 1977), sections 4:47; 2:9.

20. *The Church in the Present-day Transformation of Latin America in the Light of the Council*, vol II, *Conclusions*, (1968) (Washington DC, 1973), no 10 section 2.

21. Gustavo Gutierrez, *A Theology of Liberation*, Revised version, with new Introduction, (London, 1974/1988), p 11.

22. Gustavo Gutierrez, *A Theology of Liberation*, p 11.

23. Ibid., p 12.

24. Walter Kasper, 'From the President of the Council for Promoting Christian Unity', *America*, 185 (26 November, 2001), p 29.

25. John Henry Newman, *Letters and Diaries of J. H. Newman*, ed. Charles Steven Dessian *et al*, vol 30 (1997), p 102.

26. Mt 9:17, taken from the New American Bible.

27. 'Why Sorrow', *Patrick Kavanagh: The Complete Poems*, (Newbridge, 1972/1984) p 176. I am indebted to Dr Una Agnew for this particular reference.

28. Lk 4:18-19.

CHAPTER THIRTEEN

1. *Irish Ecclesiastical Record*, July-December 1937, p 594.
2. McQuaid papers, Dublin Diocesan Archives, AB8/B/XXVI (a).
3. 'Should Christians Always Lose?', *Irish Broadcasting Review*, 12, Autumn-Winter 1981, pp 7-11.

CONCLUDING COMMENTARY

1. *Christians In Ulster , 1968-1980*, Eric Gallagher and Stanley Worrall, (Oxford, 1982).
2. *All In A Life*, Garret FitzGerald, (Dublin, 1991), pp 627-629 and Appendix 1, pp 648-652.

The Contributors

RUTH BARRINGTON is the Chief Executive of the Health Research Board. She is the author of *Health, Medicine and Politics in Ireland, 1900-1970* (1987) which analyses the forces that have shaped the Irish health services.

JEROME CONNOLLY was Director of the Irish Commission for Justice and Peace from its foundation until 2002.

JOHN COOLAHAN is Professor of Education at the National University of Ireland Maynooth.

PATRICK HANNON is Professor of Moral Theology and Director of Postgraduate Studies at Maynooth College. A member of the Irish Bar, he has written extensively on the relationships between religion, morality and law.

SEAN HEALY SMA has been co-director of the CORI Justice Commission for the past twenty years. Together with his co-director Brigid Reynolds SM he has written/edited sixteen books on social policy. He has played a significant role in achieving social partnership status for the voluntary and community sector. He is a member of the National Economic and Social Council.

LINDA HOGAN lectures at the Irish School of Ecumenics, Trinity College, Dublin. She is the author of *From Women's Experience to Feminist Theology* (Sheffield Academic Press) and *Confronting the Truth* (Paulist Press).

JOHN HORGAN is professor of Journalism at Dublin City University. He reported Vatican II and developments in Irish education for *The Irish Times*, and has served as a member of Seanad Éireann, Dáil Éireann, and the European Parliament.

MAUREEN JUNKER-KENNY teaches theology at Trinity College Dublin.

DERMOT A. LANE is President of Mater Dei Institute of Education and Parish Priest of Balally in Dublin. He is author of *Keeping Hope Alive: Stirrings in Christian Theology* (1996) and editor of *Catholic Theology Facing the Future: Historical Perspectives*, (2003).

MAURA LEEN is a college lecturer in the Centre for Development Studies in University College Dublin. From 1992 to 2002 she worked with Trócaire as Asia Project Officer and subsequently as co-ordinator of policy and research.

ENDA MCDONAGH is Emeritus Professor of Moral Theology at Maynooth College.

JAMES P. MACKEY was Thomas Chalmers Professor of Theology in the University of Edinburgh from 1979 until 1999. He is currently Visiting Professor at Trinity College Dublin.

KENNETH MILNE was Principal of the Church of Ireland College of Education, Dublin. He represents the Church of Ireland on the National Council for Curriculum and Assessment, and was chairman of the Irish Society for Archives. He is Keeper of the Archives of Christ Church Cathedral, Dublin.

BRIGID REYNOLDS SM has been co-director of the CORI Justice Commission for the past twenty years. Together with her co-director Sean Healy SMA she has written/edited sixteen books on social policy. She is a member of the National Economic and Social Council.

JOAN RODDY is a Sister in the community of the Daughters of Mary and Joseph. She has lived and worked in several African countries and is now involved with the Refugee Project of the Catholic Bishops' Conference where she has been Director since the Project's foundation in 1999.

GERALDINE SMYTH is a Dominican theologian from Belfast. Prior to being elected Prioress of her Dominican Congregation, she was Director of the Irish School of Ecumenics (1995-1999) where she is now a Senior Lecturer.